Gayl Jones

Gayl Jones
The Language of Voice and Freedom in Her Writings

CASEY CLABOUGH

Foreword by
DANIEL CROSS TURNER

McFarland & Company, Inc., Publishers
Jefferson, North Carolina, and London

Chapter 1 originally appeared in different form in *Callaloo* 29.2 (2006), 635–657.

Chapter 2 originally appeared in different form in *The Southern Literary Journal* 38.2 (Spring 2006).

Chapter 3 originally appeared in different form in *African American Review* 41.1 (Spring 2007).

Chapter 4 originally appeared in different form in *Contemporary Literature* 46.2 (Summer 2005), © 2005 by the Board of Regents of the University of Wisconsin System and reprinted by permission.

In the appendices:

Claudia C. Tate's "An Interview with Gayl Jones" originally appeared in *Black America Literature Forum* 23.4 (Winter 1979), 142–148, and is used by permission.

Charles H. Rowell's "An Interview with Gayl Jones" originally appeared in *Callaloo* 16 (1982), 32–53, © Charles H. Rowell and reprinted by permission of the Johns Hopkins University Press.

LIBRARY OF CONGRESS CATALOGUING-IN-PUBLICATION DATA

Clabough, Casey Howard, 1974–
    Gayl Jones : the language of voice and freedom in her writings / Casey Clabough ; foreword by Daniel Cross Turner.
        p.   cm.
    Includes bibliographical references and index.

    ISBN 978-0-7864-3379-7
    softcover : 50# alkaline paper ∞

    1. Jones, Gayl — Criticism and interpretation. I. Title.
PS3560.O483Z73   2008
813'.54 — dc22   2008020051

British Library cataloguing data are available

©2008 Casey Clabough. All rights reserved

No part of this book may be reproduced or transmitted in any form or by any means, electronic or mechanical, including photocopying or recording, or by any information storage and retrieval system, without permission in writing from the publisher.

Cover photograph ©2008 Shutterstock

Manufactured in the United States of America

McFarland & Company, Inc., Publishers
  Box 611, Jefferson, North Carolina 28640
    www.mcfarlandpub.com

For my coworkers, students,
and friends at Lynchburg College

*"If the world is wrong then
right/write your ownself."*
—*Brother Dave Gardner*

Acknowledgments

Extracted variations of the book's content have been published in scholarly journals. I am indebted to the following periodicals and their editors for allowing me to reintroduce my work in a larger and more complete context: *African American Review*, *Callaloo*, *Contemporary Literature*, and *Southern Literary Journal*. A number of individuals contributed to the researching, writing, and overall development of this project. Ariel Myers, as she has done for nearly all of my other books, skillfully acquired numerous documents by and about Jones. Joyce Pair, my unofficial editor on many occasions, promptly read and commented upon the manuscript. Patty Irwin helped me to negotiate electronic formatting issues and Amanda Linn generated the index. My Lynchburg College colleagues and students — especially those in the Gender Studies and English programs — and the institution's administrative leadership also indirectly contributed to the book by encouraging and supporting my research.

Contents

Acknowledgments vi
Abbreviations ix
Foreword by Daniel Cross Turner 1
Introduction: Liberating Voice 3

Chapter 1—"Toward an All-Inclusive Structure": Early Fiction 15
Chapter 2—Speaking the Grotesque: Short Fiction 47
Chapter 3—Toward Feminine Mythopoetic Visions: Poetry 73
Chapter 4—Afrocentric Recolonizations: 1990s Fiction 93
Chapter 5—A Quest for Wholeness: Criticism 121

Conclusion: Liberated Voice 133
Appendix I: An Interview with Gayl Jones, by Claudia C. Tate 139
Appendix II: An Interview with Gayl Jones, by Charles H. Rowell 157
Annotated Bibliography and List of General Works Cited 181
Index 203

Abbreviations

Frequently cited works by Jones are abbreviated in the following manner:

COR	Corregidora
EM	Eva's Man
HE	The Healing
HM	The Hermit-Woman
LV	Liberating Voices
MS	Mosquito
SA	Song for Anninho
WR	White Rat
XQ	Xarque and Other Poems

Foreword
by Daniel Cross Turner

In *Gayl Jones: The Language of Voice and Freedom in Her Writings* Casey Clabough dedicates himself to recovering the work of a heretofore underexamined, yet immensely skillful and important writer. Clabough's often visceral activist tendencies have here born intellectual fruit, as he explores aesthetic and political interchanges within Jones's fiction, drama, poetry, and criticism. He therefore helps to give voice to Gayl Jones's poetics of freedom. This critical study, the first single-author study of Jones's work, offers a thorough examination of her technical innovations as well as her willingness to explore controversial subject matter in order to represent a fuller range of African American experience. Moreover, Clabough skillfully interweaves components of Jones's biography — such as her interest in psychology and the tragic death of her husband — that shed significant light on the underpinnings of her work.

In the Introduction and Conclusion, Clabough outlines some of the crucial terms of analysis germane to the study of contemporary African American literature — such as questions of ethnicity, race, diaspora, and globalization — and describes how Jones's work both reflects and exceeds the limits of these concepts. In the five interceding chapters, he offers wonderfully nuanced and expansive close readings of Jones's texts that explain several of the core elements of her style, including her use of the grotesque, mythopoesis, and Afrocentricism. *Gayl Jones* is at once comprehensive and meticulous, offering an apt parallel for the "all-inclusive structure" of Jones's own literature. Clabough demonstrates how the oral tradition provides the foundation of Jones's search for a liberating voice. For Jones, orality presents a sometimes steadying, sometimes destabilizing force, offering an allegory for African American history and culture while also being open to the transculturations of an increasingly global age. Though Jones's work is always political, evolving to embrace an international Africanism in her 1990s fiction, she maintains a concern with universal issues of love and suffering. In the created worlds of her art, identity is not a given, but must be continuously reconstituted within and across multiple, even contradictory cultural registers. Despite the myriad obsessions and oppressions that disrupt the arduous process of agency, Clabough reveals that Jones never loses sight of the ultimate value of this journey toward a potentially liberating sense of identity, both personal and collective.

Casey Clabough is the author of three other scholarly monographs, the fascinating creative nonfiction book *The Warrior's Path*, and over two dozen articles in wide array of literary journals that cover an impressive range of literary figures and topics. This would be sufficient output for a full scholarly career, yet Clabough has accomplished all of this before the age of thirty-five. His output is striking not merely for its dazzlingly prolific nature, but equally for the excellence of the work. No matter the subject, Clabough writes with an intellectual intensity that refuses to bury itself in the jargon-riddled platitudes and obscurantism that mars too much current scholarship; in his critical analyses, complexity is interlaced with clarity. Through the quantity and quality of his critical endeavors, Clabough has already established himself as an eminent scholar of American, Appalachian, and Southern literatures, and in *Gayl Jones* he offers a highly perceptive and sharply balanced intervention into the study of contemporary African American literature and culture. Clabough has much to say about the multiplicity of meanings rendered by Gayl Jones's literary and critical outpouring, and he says it well. One has faith this excellent book will spark further critical exploration and scholarly debate that should be the just reward of Jones's life's work in literature.

Daniel Cross Turner
Siena College
Loudonville, NY

Introduction: Liberating Voice

> *"A dialogue of Plato's or a choral movement by Heinrich Isaac—in fact all the things we call a product of the mind or a work of art or objectified spirit—are the outcomes of a struggle for purification and liberation."*
> —Knecht in Hermann Hesse, *The Glass Bead Game* (*Magister Ludi*), 278–279

An introduction to what a given writer generally is attempting to achieve in her work sometimes is best initiated with the writer's own explanation of her agenda. In the first two sentences of her 1973 Brown University dissertation, "Toward an All-Inclusive Structure," Gayl Jones declares, "I believe that writing is essentially an evolutionary process, both in one's use of language and in one's way of looking at and using experience. I believe that verbal authenticity is crucial to the understanding of what people essentially are" (1). Remarkably, over the course of four novels, three books of poems, two plays, a collection of short stories, a book of literary criticism, and numerous uncollected pieces, Jones has stayed true to her initial prophetic assertion, consistently developing and evolving her themes and techniques while remaining wholly dedicated to portraying unique and legitimate voices. Although she has remained very much her own writer, shunning literary fashion in favor of her own sometimes eclectic aesthetic agendas, Jones conceptualizes her focus on "verbal authenticity" as a definitive byproduct of a collective African American heritage. In her scholarly book *Liberating Voices* she maintains, "Modern African American writers began to shape and modify their literature using models not only from European and European American traditions, but also from their own distinctive oral and aural forms" (1). Viewing the foundations of her own art as part of a collective literary practice, Jones conceptualizes an African American tradition stemming from a dialectic of European aesthetics and African orality. And it is from the latter quality — orality — that Jones perceives a new kind of aesthetic emerging. As she explains, "In order to infuse literature with new life and creativity, contemporary American writers turn to the oral procedures; this may not only produce linguistic and stylistic innovations but often modernize the text, sitting it in the writers' contemporary world" (*LV* 11). Perceiving oral aesthetic techniques as catalysts for new kinds of writing, Jones's criticism celebrates the significance of the African oral tradition amid a backdrop of undeniable, though not always debilitating, European cultural hegemony.

The tension inherent in this aesthetic struggle for cultural voice also has translated itself tragically into Jones's life. Amid widespread critical praise, as well as a few pointed attacks, for her controversial first two novels *Corregidora* (1975) and *Eva's Man* (1976), Jones took a teaching job at the University of Michigan, where in the late 1970s she met Bob Higgins, an intelligent and charismatic student with a history of conflict and mental illness. In 1983 Higgins was arrested after attending a gay rights rally during which he shouted offensive epithets at demonstrators and, after becoming involved in a brief scuffle, later returned wielding a shotgun. Higgins was arrested but fled with Jones to Paris before his trial, not however before Jones wrote a letter of resignation to the University, a copy of which also went to President Ronald Reagan. It included the statement, "I reject your lying, racist shit." Gayl and Bob Jones — he had taken her last name — returned to the United States in 1988, living near Gayl's ailing mother, Lucille, in Lexington, Kentucky, the city in which Gayl was born and raised. When Lucille passed away in March 1997, Bob became distraught, attributing her death to a local racist conspiracy and writing threatening letters to Lexington officials. When authorities finally discovered that Bob Jones had an outstanding warrant in Michigan, a standoff took place at the Jones home, culminating in Bob's violent suicide and Gayl's brief institutionalization at Eastern State Mental Hospital. That agency-related tropes from Jones's early work pertaining to gender, psychology, and violence had come to inform her literal existence surely must constitute one of contemporary literature's more haunting, unfortunate, and poignant biographical tragedies.

Introduction

Beyond yet intertwined with the crushing events of Jones's personal life, her critical positions regarding the importance of self-assertion and orality are meaningfully central to her work, and distinguish her among writers (African American and otherwise) of her time. As she confesses in an interview, "I have a tendency to trust a lot of my oral influences more than my literary ones, with some exceptions" (Harper 694). In *Liberating Voices* Jones defines oral literature and the value of its applications at great length, which indirectly traces its close proximity to her writing practices as well:

> Oral tradition, like written tradition, provides techniques and suggests new structures for the writer. In reinventing oral tradition for use in writing, it is often necessary, however, to combine the flexibility and fluidity of voice found in oral tradition with the extended character development, descriptive continuity and more elaborate dramatic scene-making necessary in written presentations. One must often balance and counterbalance techniques from oral tradition with those indispensable to writing in handling the dynamics of character, time and space, pacing and transition, and of making the words work visibly on the printed page. Such literature often reads better than it appears on the page; it must therefore oblige itself to visual as well as auditory magic. Even then, the most effective reading is the reading that "hears" it, rather than the strictly silent one. As in a dramatic text or music, such literature must be "played" to yield its fullest art [*LV* 13].

As Jones points out, written portrayals of orality make special demands of the reader, who must listen and hear what is being read, rather than silently attempting to generate meaning. Unlike most traditional western prose and bearing a closer affinity to poetry, oral literature functions as a kind of interactive performance for the reader, asking her to suspend temporarily traditional notions of narrative logic in favor of the linguistic play or "auditory magic" that is being rendered.

All oral narratives require special and varying conditions for interpretation. Textual study generally diverges from standard criticism because of the variety of forms in which the text exists, which Theresa Meléndez catalogues as "collected and published versions; irretrievable versions in the past; potential versions in the future; and versions to which analysts do not have access because they exist in the minds and performances of undocumented artisans" (80). When theories of a particular tradition do not meet the requirements of interpretive delineation, new culture-specific forms of analysis must come into play. Irrevocably bound to the complexities of history and culture, oral narratives require extensive knowledge of the cultural conventions that have generated them. This is especially true of African American language, the variations and evolution of which often function as allegories of African American history and culture. In fact, the voice of the African slave constitutes the root of the language employed by many contemporary African Americans. As Geneva Smitherman maintains, "Black English" is "an Africanized from of English reflecting Black America's linguistic-cultural African heritage and the conditions of servitude, oppression, and life in America. Black language is Euro-American speech with an Afro-American meaning, nuance, tone, and gesture" (2). More than a varied and nuanced form of English, African American or, as Smitherman labels it, "Black" language functions as a catalyst for transmitting the complexities of an oppressed heritage and culture — what, in *Liberating Voices*, Jones terms "the essential metaphor for ... the movement from the restrictive forms (inheritors of self-doubt, self-repudiation, and the minstrel tradition) to the liberation of voice and freer personalities in more intricate texts" (178).

Whereas African American English constantly transmits culture consciously and unconsciously, the act of oral telling functions as a cognizant act of interaction within and among cultural communities. Even at her earliest literary stage, while writing her dissertation, Jones discerned that oral literature, like written literature, at its most basic level constitutes a social allegory, the characters at hand shaping and shaped by their local communities and the larger state. Assertions of identity, individual and collective, lie at the core of this practice, a dynamic Jones observes in her own terms: "In most Third World writing there is a correlation between storytelling and the sense of being whole" (*LV* 179). More cultural legacy than calculation, the act of telling begins at the most basic communal level, the family, and moves outward, establishing and reworking identity. It has even been suggested that African American families establish their cultural continuity through a process resembling ritual behavior, the myriad varieties of which Gwendolyn Etter-Lewis recounts: "sitting on the porch in the summer after dinner, family reunions, modern-day Kwanzaa celebrations and so on" (171). With all family members on hand, an ideal and inclusive milieu arises for speaking a shared history. Transmitting narratives in a familial setting provides a positive environment for the merging of personal narratives with collective cultural heritage before the stories are disseminated into the larger community. Narratives may be edited, adopted and adapted by a new teller, discouraged, or kept within a family—all of these possibilities underscoring the fluid and constantly evolving nature of oral tales.

In specific written literary contexts, oral narratives tend to take on certain collective structural and thematic functions, most often involving individual or communal liberation from an oppressive narrative and/or larger social system. In her criticism Jones specifically celebrates freed communal voices, explaining, for example, that Pepita, in Gwendolyn Brooks's poem "In the Mecca," moves from invisibility and distortion toward having the ability to speak "for herself," becoming "perhaps the most vital voice of the community in speaking her own (to use Ellison's phrase) 'sense of possibility' in the world" ("Community and Voice" 203). Implicit in Jones's observation is the linking of individual and community in speaking oneself. In voicing herself Pepita also becomes the dominant spokesperson for her community. This meaningful interaction between personal and communal voice is a central and recurring theme in the African American experience. The recounting of a family's past forms a bond among young and old, portrayed in Jones's dissertation and elsewhere, which serves as a salve and defense against the pervasive psychology of racism. More literally, the experience produces a dynamic in which "structural features of the narratives and internal details (for instance, the role of women, identifying sources of authority, and so on) preserve cultural practices unique to African Americans" (Etter-Lewis 178). One of these particular examples, "the role of women," is especially applicable to Jones's observation concerning Brooks's poem. Of remarkable significance is the fact that Pepita, a young woman, is able to speak perceptively and successfully for her community. Implied here is the idea that Pepita's multiple levels of vulnerability and oppression (race, youth, gender) coupled with her courageous willingness to speak out, make her the most appropriate spokesperson for the problems and complexities of her surroundings. In her case study on women's storytelling

Mary-Jeanette Smythe remarks, "One of the more intriguing characteristics of the discourse shared by the women in this group was the high level of self-disclosure it contained. Deeply personal information and topics were shared as routinely as complaints about the vagaries of the weather" (278). Possessing an unimpeded gift for self-disclosure and having experienced her community from a humble perspective, Pepita serves as an ideal teller, weaving her narrative from the bottom up and inside out.

Beyond what is told, telling itself owes much of its success to how listeners hear, a factor often based on a rendered tale's degree of lyricism or musicality. In *Liberating Voices*, Jones admiringly refers to Ann Petry's success in "modifying the literary text through the use of musical strategies and procedures" (98). At the roots of this practice, West African music often makes use of the interplay between dual or multiple metrical frameworks as the central building materials for songs. The complexity of these musical structures becomes more abstract in contemporary African American narratives, many of which, either consciously or unconsciously, are informed by the more improvisational characteristics of jazz. Jones recognizes this dynamic when she praises Amiri Baraka's poem "The Screamers" "as a blending of aesthetic and moral function in a new mode, and it provides a breakthrough and a greater freeing of fictional boundaries through its use of jazz as subject, tonal structure, and aesthetic-ethical model" (*LV* 122). Maintaining the connection between music and narrative structure, Jones asserts that events in her own work should always unfold "*in process* [Jones's italics]" since they "strengthen my own feeling of connection with the oral storytelling and black music continuum. Modes of speech, character quality, all work themselves out in process" (Harper 697). Reconciling the natural flow of events with the musical structures used to render them, Jones employs a method of telling that allows the narrative to work itself out — an improvised form of composition meant to encompass the visceral realities of events and the natural rhythms with which they are related.

The interaction between literal events and narrative expression takes on a special complexity when considered specifically in terms of African American women's voices. Writing about the challenge of interpreting African American women's fiction, Houston Baker remarks:

> To discover the guiding spirit work of Afro-American women's expressivity through an examination of selected texts and culturally constitutive fields, is to transform a *garden* into an eternal and infinite image. Such a transformation tends dramatically, I believe, to reconfigure familiar and interested conceptions. It foregrounds a reverberant spirit worth that offers both an example of and hope for a perseverance and communality that have enabled a whole people to survive monstrously hard times in the past and to continue their forward movement in a weary land [155].

Although Baker's language here is highly euphemistic and metaphorical it underscores the aesthetic and cultural value and challenge of tracing African American women's voices in terms of spirit and community, an approach that yields valuable connections between art and contemporary African American life in the United States. Such an interpretive perspective is easily applicable to Jones. Toni Morrison, recalling her reading of an early version of *Corregidora*, explained, "What was uppermost in my mind while I read her manuscript was that no novel about any black woman could ever be the same after this. This girl had changed the terms, the definitions of the whole enterprise" (14). That Morrison — at the time a talented, though still-developing, African American woman novelist and critic — suggested Jones had fundamentally changed the African American female novel, points to the book's successful assimilation and reinterpretation of African American women's themes, the result of which, for Morrison and several others, marked an important reshaping of the genre.

Like Alice Walker, Jones is committed to exploring memorably what John O'Brien identifies as the "oppressions, the insanities, the loyalties, and the triumphs of black women" (192), yet — as evinced by the unique theories she espouses in her dissertation's introduction and, later, in the critical ruminations of *Liberating Voices*— she repeatedly does so in a manner that is wholly her own. Rich in its combination of communal dynamics with gendered and ethnic identity politics, Jones's voice is unique and easily discernible in what Baker calls the "guiding spirit" of African American voice.

As Susan Gubar points out in *Critical Conditions: Feminism at the Turn of the Century*, African American scholarship has impacted women's studies as much as it has been influenced by general feminist theory: "More than any other field, African-American and Postcolonial Studies have transformed the work of feminist critics in the past three decades" (21). Often catalogued beneath the more contemporary fields of ethnic and gender studies, traditional African American Studies and feminism still meaningfully come together to generate innovative readings of culture-rich texts. Speaking of African American ethnicity in her essay "Black Writing, White Reading: Race and the Politics of Feminist Interpretation," Elizabeth Abel argues that it "remains a salient source of the fantasies and allegiances that shape our way of reading" (497). As worn as the condition may seem, contemporary African American literature still teeters precariously between genuine development and the pressures of its readership, white and black. As Jones maintains, "African American literature seems essentially a literature 'of transition and experiment,' never fully establishing itself" (*LV* 187). However, if establishment and definition still seem far away, the literature is at least groping for it, and speaking all the while.

The fact that the destination of contemporary African American literature remains unclear has not kept scholars from advancing various interesting and intersecting theories and schools, some of which utilize and constitute innovative theories. For example, J. Lee Greene convincingly traces the evolving use of the "Eden trope" in African American literature: "African Americans' formation of a black discourse in the novel was in large part a direct response to Anglo-Americans' use of the Eden trope as a blueprint for American society" (5). Whereas Greene looks within African American cultural texts for defining patterns of meaning, other scholars call for a more universal conceptualization of African American literature and experience. Chief among these thinkers are those who study and chart the African Diaspora, a term initially derived from Jewish studies and coined in 1965 by George Shepperson for the purpose of identifying the collective and divergent experiences of Africans abroad. Adopted and manipulated under a number of different political and critical banners, the expression has come to embody multiple, frequently overlapping diasporas, complete with a comparative dimension that looks both within the African experience and beyond to other global diasporic communities. Giving a nod to theories of diaspora, Manning Marable says of the future of Black intellectualism, "The racial mountain offers only a partially privileged terrain from which we must interpret and engage with universal cultures and issues affecting the entire globe" (24). As Marable's forecast demonstrates, diaspora study is wed to totalizing frameworks of world culture, the conceptualization of which has come to be known as globalization. Like African Diaspora studies, globalization has been appropriated for a number of different purposes. However, its most basic core theory maintains that more nations are depending on worldwide conditions relating to communication, the international financial system, and trade. As a result, the world scenario progressively becomes more integrated through international economic and cultural transactions. Central to this discourse is the formative work of Paul Gilroy, who in *The Black Atlantic* identifies a general widespread neglect of slavery and African diaspora in modern and postmodern theory, which has hindered our understanding of twentieth-century European-derived thinking and disproportionately valued work by black intellectuals compatible with western modernity. The agenda of Gilroy's approach seeks to add significantly diverse experiences and histories to the eurocentric construct: a "promise to uncover both an ethics of freedom to set alongside modernity's ethics of law and the new conceptions of selfhood and individuation that are waiting to be constructed from the slaves' standpoint — forever dissociated from the psychological and epistemic correlates of racial subordination" (56).

Working usually against, but occasionally in concert with, Marable's and Gilroy's ideas of universalizing black identity is the somewhat beleaguered school of Afrocentrism, which focuses on the identification of tropes that reinforce the use of African culture as a reference point for examining data. Despite the relative openness inherent in its definition, Afrocentrism continues to come under attack for its sometimes aggressive shifting of the variables and interpretive structures of history. For example, in *We Can't Go Home Again: An Argument About Afrocentrism*, Clarence E. Walker maintains, "The scholars who call themselves Afrocentrists have not written history in the strictest sense of the term; what they have produced is a therapeutic mythology designed to restore the self-esteem of black Americans by creating a past that never was" (xvii). As Walker's argument demonstrates, part of the problem in the Afrocentric debate appears to stem from fundamental disagreements over who and what Afrocentrists collectively are and what constitutes responsible interpretive historical practices and identities. However, even if Walker's assertion is accurate, it is important to note that his position constitutes an indictment of Afrocentricism as a quantifiable social science rather than as a useful aesthetic and imaginative catalyst for poets, novelists, and other artists.

In *Conjuring the Folk: Forms of Modernity in African America* David Nicholls goes so far as to argue that since folk culture is a result of time and place, there can exist no definitive or collective "black folk culture":

> Findings unsettle the notion of a literary tradition centered on a solitary folk origin. They do so simply by noting that what exactly constituted the folk had not been consensually established during this period, if ever. This is so, to be sure, because metropolitan writers had different political and aesthetic investments in the idea of folk culture. It is also because these writers addressed quite different locations in their stories of African-American life [132].

Calling into question the very use of "African American culture" as a term, Nicholls further complicates the task of cultural generalizations. For Gayl Jones's part, she bluntly asserts, "I don't like direct political statements" (Rowell, "Interview" 42), framing cultural distinctions, at least in her early writings (dissertation included), in an indistinct area of background noise. Although this study addresses Jones's work mostly in formalistic literary terms, I strongly wish to avoid, or at least keep to a minimum, what influential Afrocentrist Molefi Kete Asante calls "blind alleys based in a monocultural reality" (Asante), underscoring instead what Jones labeled in *Liberating Voices* as episodes of "counterpoint to Western forms and voices" (179). Employing aesthetic variables to generate collective textual readings within the various and roughly chronological genres of Jones's *oeuvre* (early novels, plays, short stories, poems, late novels), the following chapters are concerned with illustrating how Jones's characters, and occasionally Jones herself, use voice (oral techniques) to liberate themselves from various debilitating, oppressive conditions.

The book begins chronologically with a consideration of Jones's earliest work—her seminal doctoral dissertation from Brown University ("Toward an All-Inclusive Structure" [1973]), two little known plays (*Chile Woman* [1974] and "Beyond Yourself (The Midnight Confession) for Brother Ahh" [1975]), and her first two novels (*Corregidora* [1975] and *Eva's Man* [1976])—examining her various applications of the specific components—psychology, eroticism, history, linguistic play, music—which collectively form the theoretical standard she established for herself in her dissertation. At the core of Jones's framework is a unique interest in the interplay of psychology and language, and Jones's background in psychology is delved into at great length — her estimation of what particular concepts from the discipline offer, the influence of specific theorists and texts, and her literary applications of them. Jones's special interests in abnormal psychology and mental illness often intersect with her references to the history of slavery in the Americas, a traumatic phenomenon which tortures many of Jones's characters in their contemporary settings. Psychology and slavery also come together to inform Jones's characterizations of problematic relationships between African American men and women, who often teeter precariously between overcoming or being consumed by their traumatic pasts (succumbing to the lies, denials, fantasies and horrors that plague characters like Eva Medina Canada).

In order to surmount their personal and cultural pasts, Jones's characters must recover their language and memory (bodies and memories) as a precursor to retelling and reinventing their histories — a process in turn that incorporates conventions of storytelling and oral history, occasional fantasy elements, and literary aesthetics. Despite its dark subject matter, Jones's early fiction collectively offers a tenuous form of hope drawn and expanded from the underlying aesthetic and philosophical tenants of her somewhat prophetic dissertation.

Building on these conclusions regarding Jones's formative early work, later chapters reconnoiter the divergent themes and directions Jones's art explores. Among these is her repeated use of the grotesque in her short fiction as a recurring condition from which African American protagonists are attempting to escape. Chapter 2 discusses how Jones's characters, existing in macabre surroundings or possessing abhorrent qualities themselves, attempt to overcome their personal and/or environmental circumstances, usually through physical migration or an attempted self-transformation which often involves a new oral assertion of self. The figures in Jones's short story collection *White Rat* often wander in nightmare worlds of madness and despair, often rendered by powerful and disturbing first-person narratives. Jones's shift to a third-person aesthetic in much of her uncollected 1980s short fiction would result in a more distanced perspective and less violent narratives, many of her protagonists establishing measured and varying degrees of freedom in hope, often in an artistic context.

INTRODUCTION

Of greater central importance to her work's overall gradual philosophical transition is Jones's poetry, the subject of Chapter 3, which across the decades of the 1970s and 1980s reflects a narrative aesthetic shift, from a concern with separate single voices involved usually in problematic personal relationships to viewpoints and utterances articulating cultural issues across time and place, most notably the abstraction of American slavery and race-based oppression to the historical milieu of Brazil. Jones's earliest poems were works of the African American blues tradition, meditating on the intersections between pain and love. However, in time Jones's verse became more politically informed, initially through the use of African American cultural concerns and later through the abstract medium of history: her trilogy of poetry collections invoking various periods of the Brazilian past. Though this trend would mark a shift toward an interest in the larger international workings of the African diaspora, most of Jones's later poems retain the peculiar mix of love and suffering that distinguish her earliest verse. Fundamentally then, Jones's poetry maintains its archetypal blues concerns while constantly searching for greater and more inclusive meaning in the African experience.

Jones's cross-cultural turn to South America and Brazil, inherently concerned with the transnational movements of Africans, becomes much more palpable in her 1990s novels, books that contain international characters of African descent as well as lengthy cultural ruminations on other ethnic groups and the imaginative contemporary role of Africa—tropes that suggest global, as well as diasporic, interests. Chapter 4 begins with a discussion of Jones's particular approach to international Africanism, a specialized Afrocentric form of postcolonialism rendered in Jones's distinctive style. This discursive foregrounding then proceeds to a tracing of Jones's special theory of the international African experience as it evolves over the course of her two 1990s novels, *The Healing* and *Mosquito*. Chapter 5 demonstrates the manner in which Jones's writing concerns reveal themselves in her criticism. As her aesthetic variations (old and new) and constantly-evolving cultural consciousness continually reveal, Jones remains a writer wholly committed to voicing the shifting variables of the world around her in a number of forms, the timber of her various utterances repeatedly striking the chord of hard-earned agency amid the dissonance of pain and oppression across time.

CHAPTER 1

"Toward an All-Inclusive Structure": Early Fiction

> "What was uppermost in my mind while I read her manuscript was that no novel about any black woman could ever be the same after this. This girl had changed the terms, the definitions of the whole enterprise."
> —Toni Morrison, "Toni Morrison on a Book She Loves: Gayl Jones' *Corregidora*," 14

When young Gayl Jones, having grown up in Lexington, Kentucky and gone on to receive her Ph.D. in English from Brown University in 1973, burst upon the literary scene in the mid–1970s with her two short novels *Corregidora* (1975) and *Eva's Man* (1976), she was met by a whole range of critical reactions—celebrations and condemnations of her portrayals of abusive patriarchal oppression, castigations and valorizations of her detailed, gender-conscious renderings of African American identity, praises and attacks for her frank and often violent portrayals of African American culture. The myriad, and often diametrically opposed, readings with which Jones' two novels were greeted pointed—among many other things—to their undeniable value as powerful, albeit controversial, contemporary commentaries on African American life in the United States. However, although the reviews constituted a diverse body of critical readings, most tended to focus on only one or two aspects of Jones's novels. For example, Raymond Sokolov concluded that *Corregidora* "is a book with virtually no other subject than sex" (22).[1] Other critics attacked and praised the two novels' unique sexual episodes and memorable gender characterizations through conscious and specialized political lenses. For instance, Carol Margaret Davison constructed Eva Medina Canada's act of oral castration on Davis Carter as an assertion of selfhood, which also constitutes "the most direct, shocking, and brutal attack on phallocentrism in African American literature" (396). By contrast, an anonymous reviewer condemned *Eva's Man* on political grounds for a perceived ugly, stereotypical portrayal "of black women seen purely as sexual beings" ("Review of *Eva's Man*," *Booklist* 1164).

Early reviewers were equally mindful of the books' acute vernacular and interesting narrative techniques, John Wideman asserting that *Corregidora*'s most important characteristic is its language.[2] Still others blended the novels' erotic, linguistic, and political themes to arrive at hybrid readings, such as Valerie Gray Lee's claim that *Corregidora*'s sexual and semantic concerns come together to comprise a gender-informed exercise in "folktalk"[3] Several critics who coupled the books' erotic and linguistic themes also discovered their cultural and historical implications. John Updike concluded that *Corregidora* "persuasively fuses black history, or the mythic consciousness that must do for black history, with the emotional nuances of contemporary black life" ("Selda" 81).

Connecting modern African American life and history in different terms, Charles R. Larson remarked, "Reading *Corregidora* one feels that this is not a novel at all, but oral history finally got down on paper" (17). Updike's and Larson's observations on the meeting of language, history, and consciousness would later receive support from Jones herself, who recounts, "Ursa in *Corregidora* tells her own story in her own language and so does Eva in *Eva's Man*. I was interested in having their language do everything that anybody's language used as a literary language can do" (Rowell, "Interview" 32). For Jones, the books' numerous themes, nearly all of them identified by various reviewers, ultimately remained subject to her protagonists' rich literary languages—filtered representations of her own aesthetic ambitions for the novels.

The multiple themes and sometimes controversial and hyperbolic readings—phenomena surrounding many meaningful works of art—arising from *Corregidora* in particular, led, perhaps inevitably, to blanketing declarations of its greatness. For example, Jones had achieved a masterpiece for reviewer Christopher Lehmann-Haupt who celebrated *Corregidora*'s unique and overarching artistic realism.[4] For a beginning novelist to impact powerfully the established genre in which she is laboring constitutes an exceptional achievement, requiring both adroit attention to the minutest details and sub-themes of the specialized area, and a simultaneously constant and unwavering gaze on the groundbreaking wholeness of her endeavor. Yet, remarkably, Jones had been preparing herself for this particular task throughout graduate school and, specifically, in her 1973 Brown University dissertation, "Toward an All-Inclusive Structure," a collection of experimental prose in which she applies a self-styled, conceptualized method of composition termed "an all-inclusive structure."[5] Jones articulates her theory as an encompassing aesthetic ideal:

> Which would theoretically include *everything*: experience and imagination, autobiography, history, legend, myth, ritual, metaphor, dream (essentially all forms both linguistic and experimental); it would make use of specifically black forms, both musical (blues, jazz, work songs, spirituals) and linguistic (the sermon, playing dozens, signifying, jive); it would see the erotic as an authentic method of expression ["Toward" 1].

While the young Jones's search for a comprehensive aesthetic initially may come across as a predictable and naive graduate student's pipe dream, her literal pursuit of it in her early fiction underscores the seriousness and success with which she sought to establish an original and ambitious artistic ideal.

This chapter attempts to measure the success of Jones's early extended fictional work—the dissertation, two published plays, and two novels she produced from the time of her dissertation in 1973 until the publication of *Eva's Man* in 1976—by examining her various applications of the specific components—psychology, eroticism, history, linguistic play, music—that collectively form the theoretical standard, the ambitious "all-inclusive structure," she established for herself. At the core of Jones's framework is a unique interest in the interplay of psychology and language, and I begin with a discussion of Jones's background in psychology—her estimation of what particular concepts from the discipline offer, the influence of specific theorists and texts, and her literary applications of them. Jones's special interests in abnormal psychology and mental illness often intersect with her references to the history of slavery in the Americas, a traumatic phenomenon that tortures many of Jones's characters in their contemporary settings. Psychology and slavery also come together to inform Jones's characterizations of problematic relationships between African American men and women, who often teeter precariously between overcoming or being consumed by their traumatic pasts. In order to surmount their personal and cultural pasts, Jones's characters must retell and reinvent their histories, a process that combines various conventions of storytelling and oral history, occasional fantasy elements, and literary aesthetics. The final portion of the chapter considers specific instances of productive and non-productive "telling," those that, as in *Eva's Man*, lure the protagonist into debilitating realms of fantasy and madness, and those that promise to liberate characters from the hegemonic and personal traumas of history and other discourses.

Psychological Models, Literary Applications

The first and most important component of Jones's extensive theoretical structure draws on a discipline that for years critics of her work have neglected to apply in any great detail: psychology.[6] Jones maintains she "first became aware of the *essential* relationship between language and experience in terms of the psychology of language [Jones's italics]" ("Toward" 2), citing the specific research of Emil Fröschels, Kurt Goldstein, and H. H. Goddard — psychologists from the first half of the twentieth century. Fascinated by the interplay of words and various mental conditions, Jones sought to utilize various psychological case studies for fictional characterizations as well as stylistic experiments:

> After my interest in the psychology of language as a means of getting to the psychological reality of patients, I was concerned with getting away from the extremes of psychological and linguistic deviation, and at the same time using the things I'd learned about language here (rhythmical flexibility, syntactical dislocation, forms of linguistic tensions) as a means of getting to the basic reality of people in general ["Toward" 4].

In identifying psychology as a primary aesthetic tool, Jones strayed from cultural thinkers who conceptualized the discipline as a possible affront to collective racial and cultural identity. However, she is not alone in treading this remote path. For example, in her study, *Psychoanalysis and Black Novels: Desire and the Protocols of Race* (1998), noted scholar Claudia Tate felt compelled to defend her application of psychological themes to African American fiction, which she defines as an attempt "to demonstrate how the racial protocol for African American canon formation has marginalized desire as a critical category of black textuality by demanding manifest stories about racial politics" (5). Jones herself believes psychology and conscious political representations generally are at odds, and that the greater literary value rests with the former. She asserts:

> I am interested principally in the psychology of characters — and the way(s) in which they order their stories — their myths, dreams, nightmares, secret worlds, ambiguities, contradictions, ambivalences, memories, imaginations, their "puzzles." For this reason I cannot claim "political compulsions" nor "moral compulsions" if by either of these one means maintaining a "literary decorum." I am interested in human relationships, but I do not make moral judgments or political judgments of my characters ["About My Work" 233].

Rejecting strategic polemical representations, Jones investigated psychology and language, hoping that her rigorous and clinically-informed narratives might yield more genuine and even unprecedented African American characters. As early as 1972 Jones appears to have felt intuitively what Claudia Tate articulated more than a quarter of a century later: that "a racially contextualized model of psychoanalysis [...] can help us analyze black textuality by identifying the discourses of desire [psychology] generating the text" (*Psychoanalysis* 17).

Delving into the work of Jones's chosen psychological authorities — Fröschels, Goldstein, and Goddard — reveals the specific types of scientific ideas she was interested in exploring in her art. Although the theories of these psychologists are now largely defunct from a clinical perspective, many of their general philosophical statements about psychology and language remain provocative, especially when considered as theoretically experimental blueprints for composing fiction. Providing the germ for Jones's interest in terms such as "rhythmical flexibility, syntactical dislocation, forms of linguistic tensions" ("Toward" 4), Fröschels, in *Psychological Elements in Speech* (1932), makes the general, yet important, observation that, "The formation of words is a continuous process taking place before us" (xi). Word formation and consciousness were especially interesting to Jones in terms of the ways they promised to establish and modify rhythms in a written work. She maintains, "In terms of the all-inclusive structure that I'm working toward, my work with the psychology of speech as a sounding board for creative experiments has helped to develop syntactical flexibility, which one can use both to compress and extend rhythm in a narrative structure" ("Toward" 4). Jones was also interested in the way powerful new stimuli to the mind might alter language and invent new terminologies. As Fröschels puts it, "New conditions and actions create new expressions, while the older words often have a modified meaning since the objects for which they stood have now disappeared or have been substantially changed" (xi). In the midst of creating and adopting more linguistic terms, patients or fictional characters begin to drift away from the dominant language and language-group. Fröschels emphasizes the importance of studying such phenomena from a linguistic perspective: "Grammatical investigation will be in a position to discover relationships among peoples as it establishes the similarities or differences between two or more language-groups" (xii). Of course, in Jones's work, Fröschels's psychological distinction of language difference is accompanied by variations in cultural language formation, as seen through her portrayals of different linguistic forms and dialects within and around the African American community. In fact, several of the narratives in "Toward an All-Inclusive Structure" constitute, on one level, extended literary experiments in psychologically-informed, cultural language differences.

Another central aspect of psychology and language Fröschels identifies is the importance of association. He maintains, "Speech is a function of the feeling for association (*Gemeinschaftsgefuhl*) which is hereditary to man, and the basis of all his relations with his environment" (239). Fröschels's assertion carries with it the implication that an inability to communicate is synonymous with alienation from one's culture. Jones applies this principle to several of her characters, most notably Eva Medina Canada, who often refuses to speak and is usually misunderstood — by listeners as culturally and intellectually disparate as Davis Carter and her psychologist — when she does. Without speech and association individuals like Eva do not function normally. Whereas such conditions may be debilitating to Jones's characters and confusing to critics, Jones enjoys employing them for the representational and interpretive freedom they afford both her and her characters: "I think that abnormal psychological conditions affect sensitivity to certain things, change proportions, affect 'significant events/relationships, etc.' There are some critics who can't separate or don't want to separate the 'persona,' the character's neurosis/psychosis, from the author's psychological autonomy" (Tate, "Interview" 146). Arguing that her characters' abnormal psychological behaviors are a result of her psychological reading and serve as effective catalysts for her aesthetic aims, Jones dismisses readers who interpret her characters autobiographically.

Whereas Fröschels afforded much of the theoretical basis for Jones's fictional psychological applications, the work of Goldstein and Goddard provided her with concrete case studies from which she could draw character details and specific behavior patterns. In *Language and Language Disturbances* (1948) Goldstein asserts that the purpose of his work is to "present those speech disturbances observed in lesions of the brain cortex in a form useful both for practical and theoretic purpose in the clinic" (ix). Recounting and analyzing specific instances of head trauma, Goldstein notes the accompanying disruptions in speech and language, often identifying highly unconventional patterns of meaning amid the semantic gibberish of his test subjects. Bleak, ominous, and less scientifically-informed than Goldstein's work, Goddard's *Feeblemindedness: Its Causes and Consequences* (1932) is composed "in the form of a report on work done at the Vineland Research Laboratory during the past five years in an attempt to discover the causes of the feeble-mindedness of the children in the institution" (vii). More a series of didactic and pejorative character sketches than a scientific study, *Feeblemindedness* recounts the genealogy, physical characteristics, habits, and personalities of institutionalized young people. The impact of *Feeblemindedness* on Jones's work is less apparent than the books of Fröschels and Goldstein, yet once again, the influence is best glimpsed in the figure of Eva Medina Canada, whom one reviewer described as "a character with the mentality of a child ('I tell them I'm not getting things straight') in the body and the social complex of an abused adult woman" (Cooke 150). *Feeblemindedness* also corresponds with Jones's work in the way its test subjects often are evaluated in terms of their ability to express themselves through language, both oral and written. Indeed, the various fascinations Fröschels, Goldstein, and Goddard held for language most likely account for Jones's powerful interest in their work; for she certainly might have turned to and benefited from the research of more contemporary, clinically-sound, and scientifically-rigorous psychologists. Yet, the focus on language in the research of her unlikely trio of scientists apparently led Jones to believe that she had discovered innovative, applicable theories for constructing new and important characters and narrative strategies in her work.

Articulating Slavery

Feeblemindedness's subjective and derogatory descriptions of its test subjects as undesirable and expendable betray its unfortunate philosophical alliance with an early twentieth century eugenics ideology espousing the extraction and sterilization of the mentally infirm from the general population — a philosophy that later would be seized upon in Germany for even more sinister purposes. Just as certain early areas of psychology demonized and demeaned specific groups of people, so slavery in the Americas used questionable and often circuitous racial, cultural, and economic theories to justify the bondage of African and African-descended populations. In Jones's fiction psychological injuries and the inherited wounds of slavery are closely knit, plaguing her protagonists as they attempt, through language, to assuage the traumas of the present and banish the ghosts of the past.[7] Links between slavery, racism, and mental illness are most palpable in Jones's unpublished story "Take Refuge in Madness," the play *Chile Woman*, and the novel *Eva's Man*, which offer different reactions to the problems of bondage and racial and gender exploitation. Not surprisingly, the works' separate responses are determined by the linguistic styles and terminologies of various types of characters. For example, the protagonists of "Take Refuge in Madness" and *Eva's Man* decide — as the title of the former work implies — to choose fantastic, linguistically-creative, alternative realities over the debilitating horrors of their own. By contrast, *Chile Woman* offers a whole spectrum of characters and voices, responses that reflect madness and reconciliation, as well as bitter, reactionary hatred.

Regardless of their various responses, Jones's characters function beneath the guiding principle that their histories, their linguistic ability to tell about themselves, must be reclaimed. As Ishmael Reed says of Jones, "I guess she's right that our destinies are still being decided by the slave master. We use the language that he invented and we have certain attitudes that he left with us" (Martin). In seeking to overcome such a condition, many of Jones's characters attempt to establish a personal authority that comes with "speaking" the slave experience. As Dickson D. Bruce Jr. argues in *The Origins of African American Literature*, this is "an authority growing out of the lived experiences of those who could tell about slavery's brutal core" (21). Jones enriches the struggle between her characters' anguished linguistic accounts and the historical master narrative by offering convincing portrayals of the unsympathetic slave owners' perspectives. In *Corregidora* Ursa recounts the obligatory inhuman objectification of slaves when she asserts that Simon Corregidora and other slave owners considered their slaves primarily as valuable economic investments. This remotely abstract historical observation is confirmed on a personal level when Simon Corregidora labels Ursa's great grandmother "*A good little piece. My best. Dorita. Little gold piece* [Jones's italics]" (*COR* 10). Supporting general historical assertions with emotionally-charged narrative sequences, Jones constructs a framework of rhetorical authority that is as vivid as it is convincing.

One of the best remarks on the value of literature that investigates and portrays slavery comes from George Handley in *Postslavery Literatures in the Americas*:

> Because stories have the power to remember the past, to shape the present, and move us toward the future, the stories we tell about slavery — in tales, poems, and narratives — more directly engage and combat the forces of historiography and official memory. They have the capacity of prophecy, since the way the past is remembered shapes how we live and identify ourselves now [187].

Of Jones's works, the play *Chile Woman* is perhaps the most effective in portraying what Handley might call "conflicting prophecies" — characters who remember and react to their oppressive pasts differently, thereby shaping their disparate participations in the present. In *Chile Woman* Jones presents two debilitating reactions to the historical legacy of subjugation: "Crazy Woman"'s mental illness and almost helpless victimization and Fanny's unfettered hatred of white people and general bitterness toward the world. "Crazy Woman" alternates between saying, "Have to get something" and "Have to get out" (8), but — having ostensibly been assaulted by the police and beaten down psychologically — she lacks the agency required either to escape her conditions or reclaim the things she has lost. By contrast, Fanny flaunts her agency to a hyperbolic degree, defining herself against white people and their culture with linguistic violence. After a white bus driver accuses her of drinking on the bus, she recounts, "I said, Shit, white-ass motherfuckin bastard, I said, And tha's your mammy too. I said tha's your cunt face mammy too. At cracker told me to get off the bus. I said I done paid my fare and I'ma ride. I said I fuck him up his ass if he don't quit messin with me" (26). Feeling ridiculed and violated by the bus driver's accusation, Fanny linguistically assaults him in turn, insulting his heritage ("tha's your cunt face mammy too") and threatening him with rape — a violent physical subordination of his agency — if he does not desist ("I said I fuck him up his ass if he don't quit messin with me"). A third and more constructive reaction to the racial oppression portrayed in *Chile Woman* belongs to the conjure woman and prophetess Ella, who claims, "There's no poetry in oppression. They think it is though. People in nese books tryin to make poetry outta oppression. What we got to have is our whole souls ringin — even the flesh of our souls, stretched over drums like steel, hammer hands and spirits" (31). For Ella, the most productive future for African American culture and language rests in being able to forsake the legacy of bondage in favor of celebrating the spirit. While slavery will always constitute an important undeniable aspect of African American identity, Ella does not feel it should constitute the defining quality of the poetry and songs of African Americans. For her, the endeavor of the future is to transcend oppression through the essence of the spirit ("the flesh of our souls"), singing the songs of her people in their rich entirety.

Relationships Between African American Men and Women

In order for Jones's protagonists to, as Ella says, get their "whole souls ringin," they must succeed where "Crazy Woman" and Fanny fail, overcoming present and personal, as well as past and abstract, oppressions.

Chapter 1—"Toward an All-Inclusive Structure": Early Fiction

Resembling several notable literary meditations on slavery outside the United States — the work of writers such as Edouard Glissant, Juan Bosch, Jorge Romado, and Patrick Chamoiseau — which often go beyond conventional polemical, historical commentary, Jones's early work emphasizes the interplay of slavery across the Americas with debilitating psychological conditions and contemporary cultural forces.[8] Thus, the roadblocks to Ella's idealistic theory of freedom remain substantial and numerous, visceral and psychological, and often linked together across time. For example, in *Corregidora* Ursa says of her slave ancestors, "Their survival depended on suppressed hysteria" (*COR* 59); while in the contemporary milieu of *Eva's Man*, Eva is told that hysteria is one of Elvira's problems (*EM* 45). "Womb" is derived from the Greek word for hysteria and originally the term designated a link between certain nervous disorders and diseases of the female sexual and reproductive organs. It was thought that there was a direct connection between these physical pathologies localized in the female organs and certain nervous symptoms. Furthermore, Freud believed that every hysteria is based on a sexual seduction at the time of early childhood, to which the child reacted with something resembling presexual sexual fright (Freud 152). Linked with slavery then is the pervasive fear among several of Jones's female characters of enduring sexual illness and trauma. Perhaps the most extreme example of slavery-infused hysteria in Jones's work appears in the character of "Crazy Woman," whom another character claims has been assaulted by the police (*Chile* 8). Infusing "Crazy Woman"'s gender-conscious abuse with historical forces, Jones later relates her contemporary victimization at the hands of white male authority figures to the general mistreatment of African Americans under slavery (*Chile* 17).

Whereas "Crazy Woman"'s hysteria is a result of her exploitation at the hands of white male police officers, many of Jones's female characters suffer from equally violent and destructive events involving black men — a distinction that has not gone unnoticed by critics. For example, Faith Pullin reads *Corregidora* as "a convincing analysis of the punitive relationships between black men and black women and proof of the validity of Lynne's statement in *Meridian*, 'black men and women *are* scared to death of each other'" (Pullin 201). During an interview, Jones had partially anticipated Pullin's observation on African American gender friction when she remarked, "My earlier writings have been concerned with the relationship between men and women" (Harper 283). In attempting to examine the causes and discover solutions for a perceived African American gender crisis, Jones employed numerous characters, female and male, who agonize over and — in some cases — are destroyed by their relationships with the sexual other. As Amy Gottfried argues in her consideration of *Corregidora*, "Reclaiming desire means first recognizing the potential for mutual abuse between men and women" (567), and Jones does not shrink from this task, venturing deep into the abyss of physical and psychological destruction between the sexes. As she remarks in an interview, "Perhaps brutality enables one to recognize what tenderness is" (Tate, "Interview" 147). Jones's fictional renderings of this philosophy — troubling to many readers — take on a number of different forms. In *Corregidora* Ursa's mother ponders, "How much was hate for Corregidora and how much was love" (131), as if the trauma and complexity accompanying his memory confuse all emotional signifiers, leaving Ursa's mother with a powerful and unavoidable, yet ambiguous, feeling. The same enigmatic distinction appears in *Chile Woman* through "Crazy Woman"'s paradoxical language in statements such as, "They kiss you with teeth" (28), which confuse and overlap the otherwise separate expressions of physical love and abuse. As powerful and disquieting as these examples may be, clearly the most striking manifestation of Jones's meditations on brutality and love takes place in her play "Beyond Yourself (The Midnight Confession) for Brother Ahh" when Clell severely beats Letha while a voice offstage repeatedly whispers "I love you." Mingling fists and loving whispers, kisses and teeth, Jones presses and confuses the boundaries of love and violence, all the while searching for a groundbreaking, genuine means of profound communication between the sexes.

Although Jones's investigation of the ambiguities of love and abuse in African American relationships appears to have been altogether genuine, she found herself treading upon dangerous representational ground as critics of her first two novels struggled to grasp the philosophical purposes of her violent, erotic narratives. While some readings merely identified Jones's enigmatic gender renderings — interpretations that insist Ursa's inheritance in *Corregidora* "involves an ambiguous and ambivalent relationship with black men" (Kent 107) — and moved on, others interpreted her characterizations literally and attacked her negative portrayals of African American relationships. For example, Ishmael Reed criticized *Corregidora* for its demeaning physical renderings of African American males, claiming they appear "as brutes, apes" (Martin). Darryl Pinckney proceeded a step further with the blanketing assertion, "Gayl Jones' novels are, finally, indictments against black men" (27). Ironically (given the outcry against Jones's portrayals of black males), a number of critics also saw Jones as either attacking black women or unnecessarily subjecting them to negative representations. In his review of *Corregidora* John Updike remarked, "The men in this novel do not live except in the wonderful transcriptions of 'sweet talk,' of seduction's musical mumble, and the women retain a certain occluding severity" ("Selda" 82). Damning Jones to a greater extent, albeit from a female critic's perspective, June Jordan — building upon Reed's sensitivity to the brutish qualities of Jones's male characters — attacked Jones's collective portrayal of African Americans in *Eva's Man*, rhetorically inquiring, "What does it mean when a young black woman sits down to compose a universe of black people limited to animal dynamics?" (37). Even Loyle Hairston, who had stomached the violence of *Corregidora* and reviewed it favorably,[9] backed away from *Eva's Man*, condemning it as "repelling in its panting fixation on male genitalia as the consummate despoiler of the female soul, in its squalid appraisal of the souls of Black folks" (133). Perhaps inevitably, many of these readings bear the polemical fingerprints of the Black Arts Movement of the 1970s, which spurred the association of African American characters with traditional stereotypes, regardless of the overall aesthetic or political intention. Offended by Jones's blunt, visceral characterizations of men, women, and African Americans in general, several critics sought to condemn her work while either subordinating or altogether ignoring its considerable philosophical themes and implications.

Jones was captivated by the adverse responses to her portrayals of eroticism and violence, and even expressed sympathy for such readings: "I can understand the negative reactions to the use of sex in the books. It's something I'm interested in as a dilemma of subject matter in Afro-American literature" (Rowell, "Interview" 46). However, rather than abandoning the controversial theme she later resolved to make it the central philosophical cog for her German novel, *Die Vogelfängerin* or *The Birdcatcher*,[10] which recounts the artistic, racial, and sexual dilemmas of a struggling black female sculptor. Whereas negative reviews of Jones's first two novels had failed to dissuade her from continuing to investigate sexuality and abuse, she found herself altering the book's events for fear of political repercussions, choosing, for example, a white woman to perform an important violent act, "because of what I consider the too easy dismissal of any black characters who act in certain ways as stereotypes or supporting stereotypes" (Rowell, "Interview" 47)—a provision that never seems to have entered into the compositions of her first two novels. The white woman, who is also an artist, produces successful erotic and violent paintings, which the black protagonist envies and is afraid to attempt because of her ethnicity and the negative stereotypes her pursuit of such themes may arouse. Thinly buried here then is Jones's own artistic dilemma: whether or not to delve into vivid sexuality and abuse among African Americans for fear of appearing to embrace negative stereotypes and earning political censure. In the novel, the black female artist abandons her sculpture, called *Die Vogelfängerin,* for this very reason, scuttling her promising aesthetic instincts in exchange for political solace. Jones draws upon autobiography again in her characterization of the protagonist's friend, a black writer who—like the white painter and Jones—portrays highly sexualized, violent themes, which invite the contempt and embarrassment of her friend. In the end *Die Vogelfängerin* offers two rigidly distinct aesthetic paths for African American artists: the route of uninhibited creative freedom without reference to cultural identity or the road of positive polemical and cultural harmony at art's expense. Although Jones presents both troubling routes convincingly, her favoritism of the former road remains clear enough. After all, the novel's white painter and black writer are serious and successful artists, while her protagonist's aesthetic potential remains unrealized, inhibited, and ultimately stunted by her pervasive paranoid fear of the relationship between violent sexual themes, cultural stereotypes, and racial politics.

Regardless of how readers, critics, and Jones herself interpret them, episodes of sexual violence—usually involving the abuse of African American women by African American men—in Jones's work are numerous and often function as memorable epiphanic moments, carrying with them philosophical implications for the non-physical, abstract dimensions of relationships between men and women. For example, in "Beyond Yourself (The Midnight Confession) for Brother Ahh" Letha critiques Clell's objectifying physical desires as a roadblock in their ability to communicate with each other: "Blood mixed with my laughter. Holding blood in my fists. Fear in my groin again. Again and again. Your fingers. And I'm supposed to tell you how good it is and you. You want only that part of me. I came to you with everything and you want only that part of me" (80). Similarly, in *Eva's Man* Elvira says of men in general, "All they think about is where they going to get their next piece" (151). Letha's and Elvira's observations on the male propensity to reduce female identity to a manifestation of carnal lust is developed further in *Eva's Man* when young Freddy Smoot's sexual harassment of Eva is overlooked and even subtly encouraged by an adult male. When Eva tells Freddy to leave her alone, Mr. Logan, a man standing nearby, "just looked at me grinning, and walked on by" (14). In addition to being confronted with specific and isolated episodes of potential sexual exploitation, Jones's protagonists face an unspoken and often unconscious philosophical bond of abusive desire in the males around them. Intentionally or not, Jones employs subtle linguistic echoing to underscore this relationship across her first two novels. In *Corregidora*, while talking to Max Monroe, another club owner who initially tries to exploit her, Ursa recounts how when she was a little girl a strange vulgar man reached for her genitals while repeating, "Gimme what you got. What you gonna gimme? Gimme what you got" (95). In *Eva's Man* Eva's psychiatrist, an educated professional, uses almost identical language after he coaxes her into speaking, boasting, "I got *something* out of you [Jones's italics]" (81). Transcending race, education, and social standing, the male impulse to exploit, to "get something" out of women, constitutes an important defining visceral and philosophical dimension among Jones's male characters. Even more troubling, though, is the unconscious adoption of the male victimizing philosophy by women in the community, as if they, too, conceive it to be the natural order of things. In a scenario strikingly similar to that involving Freddy Smoot, Mr. Logan, and Eva, Gayl Jones's mother, Lucille, recalls an authentic incident from her life in which a boy named Franklin kept telling her he loved her when she was nine years old: "I ran in the house to Mama and said. 'Make that black boy stop saying he loves me.' I kept telling her to make that black boy stop. She didn't though. She didn't do anything" (Jones, "Interview with Lucille Jones" 32). Whereas Lucille Jones's experience is autobiographical and does not appear in Jones's fiction, it serves to suggest that the potential for masculine sexual intimidation and violence, though originating among males, is not restrictive to them; which makes it significantly more dangerous, having influenced and pervaded even the female spheres of the community.

Just as many of Jones's male characters are subtly linked by their conscious and/or unconscious desires to exploit women physically and psychologically, several of Jones's female protagonists form bonds with other women based predominantly on their shared experiences of victimization. When Davis's wife comes to look at her in prison, Eva feels their abuse at the hands of the same man brings them together: "She just stood there outside the cell and stared at me, and I stared back. The only thing I kept wondering is how did he treat *her* [Jones's italics]" (*EM* 4). Drawn by an impulse more powerful than any emotion of sympathy or guilt, Eva is able to identify with Davis's wife by pondering their shared abuse. The fear of and experience with predatory male sexuality also brings Ursa and Eva together across their respective narratives, thematically uniting Jones' first two novels. As one reviewer summarizes, Eva has "been grabbed at, molested and propositioned for as long as she can remember" ("Review of *Eva's Man*," *Kirkus Reviews* 90), and just as Ursa is penetrated by a dirty popsicle stick when she is only a child, so young Eva fears Mr. Logan because she "kept expecting something white to come out of him" (*EM* 19). Focusing on powerful traumas suffered by prepubescent girls, these episodes recall Freud's conception of hysteria, which connects such debilitating childhood events to the nervous disorders of adults. Not surprisingly, as an adult Ursa is unable to overcome her feelings of emptiness or consistently enjoy sex, conditions that are exacerbated after Mutt Thomas sends her tumbling down a flight of stairs. Later, when she catches Tadpole McCormick in bed with Vivian, he denigrates her sexuality and womanhood, asserting that the teenage singer has "got more woman in her asshole than you got in your whole goddamn cunt" (*COR* 89). Eva is subjected to a similar form of psychological abuse—ironically, for a sexual predisposition precisely the reverse of Ursa's—when Davis criticizes her vigorous sexual appetite ("You made me tired" [*EM* 118]). Shaped by earlier sexual traumas, Ursa's sexual inhibitions and Eva's ravenous desires are both denigrated by their male partners, uniting the women in their victimization.

The physical and psychological abuse suffered at the hands of their intimate partners and members of their communities threatens to destabilize further the mental health of several of Jones's protagonists, a theme Jones reinforces through Elvira, who claims she once knew a man who "drove every woman he had crazy" (*EM* 17). In addition to her sexual traumas and challenges, Ursa must also contend with psychological, racial hostility from women who refer to her as a "red-headed heifer" (*COR* 72). Claudia Tate asserts that Ursa's light skin and straight hair "constitute the tangible evidence of evil which she says was transmitted to her by an incestuous white ancestor" ("*Corregidora*" 140), which means, in addition to the hatred of other women, Ursa also must contend with self-loathing for her unwanted, invasive Caucasian features. By contrast, Eva's erratic self-image is attached to her distorted notions of sexuality. For example, her first husband, James Hunn, is surprised but then amused when she laughs at his military stories concerning unabashed prostitution and bestiality (*EM* 108). Of course, in retrospect such incidents, when considered together, lead quite logically to Eva's culminating sexual dismemberment of Davis. In fact, Jones had explored this process and the accompanying themes in a dissertation story called "Pross," which recounts the relationship between Kate, a prostitute, and Floyd, the possessive man she genuinely loves. Like several of Jones's female characters in other works, Kate hates and fears her man, yet is still obsessed with him ("Toward" 87). Floyd's eyes, "Hurt worse than anything. Or bring the most joy" ("Toward" 93), confusing in Kate the pain and delight she feels. Having established a framework of love, abuse, and strained consciousness, the work's conclusion confuses the terms further: "Floy, I. You called me your sweat mama. My tongue between your teeth. You bite down hard. Bite down" ("Toward" 106). Anticipating both *Corregidora* and *Eva's Man* in its construction of a concluding scene involving painful, yet tender, sexual biting (albeit involving a tongue rather than a penis and a male, rather than female, perpetrator), "Pross" serves as a small-scale model of how ambiguous emotions and repeated victimization may lead to unbalanced psyches and accompanying violent acts.

A final symptom of the psychological paradox — the overlapping love, torture, sexual fulfillment, and perversion — that haunts many of Jones's female protagonists in their relationships with men is their accompanying lack of will — reducible, once again, to their exploitation at the hands of intimate male partners. As one of Jones's influential psychologists, Kurt Goldstein, maintains:

> Patients with impairment of abstract attitude may not appear to deviate grossly from normals in everyday behavior, because many routine tasks do not require the abstract attitude once these tasks have been learned. However, on observation of the patients in a variety of situations it becomes evident that they do not react even then like normal individuals. They appear more stereotyped and reserved. They lack initiative and spontaneity. Tasks which demand choice or shifting particularly reveal the defect [6–7].

Carrying out Goldstein's formula, Eva is able to hold jobs and function in society at the beginning of the novel despite the multiple abusive relationships and accompanying resignation to which she subjects herself. However, she is wholly incapable of resisting Davis's increasingly unreasonable demands and — once he strips society from her, keeping her locked in his room — she is also unable to ward off the seductive and persistent overtures of madness. As Jerry Ward, Jr. summarizes, "From the university to the streets, Eva learns that sex is fucking and women are bitches and men are eternally on the watch for a good lay. She has the will to resist sexual abuse, but the will is stunted" (101). Like "Crazy Woman" in *Chile Woman*, Eva is beaten down and exploited to the point that she surrenders her agency to the fantasies of the mind. Embodying the title of one of Jones's dissertation stories, Eva "takes refuge in madness," a development that holds destructive consequences both for Davis and herself.

Precursor to Reconciliation: Recovering Language and Memory, Body and Spirit

Looking beyond the dynamics of personal relationships between Jones's male and female characters, a host of critics have described Jones's first two novels as Faulknerian in their focus on multi-generational legacies of psychological torment which must be recovered.[11] Although Jones never acknowledges any conscious debt to Faulkner, her early work reflects her powerful interest in the intersections of personal and cultural traumas.[12] For example, in the *Chile Woman* Prelude from her dissertation Jones claims she attempted to reconcile "private and collective experience" through a "flexibility of consciousness (an all-inclusive yet at the same time private consciousness)" ("Toward" 6). As we have seen, *Chile Woman* is important for its conflicting personal reactions — those of the characters "Crazy Woman," Fanny, and Ella — to a legacy of collective racial and gender oppression. In the Prelude, the unnamed female speaker anticipates the play's various interpretations by linguistically fusing personal and cultural imagery. For example, she claims, "I am chile woman. History began between my thighs" ("Toward" 110), labeling both her personal identity and her matriarchal creation of a cultural legacy. Later, she asserts, "I'm Sojourner stripped naked to prove what I am" ("Toward" 110), relating her own identity to that of Sojourner Truth, an important African American female cultural figure who in 1858 refuted claims that she was a man by exposing her chest to a Silver Lake, Indiana audience.[13] Jones's aims for *Chile Woman*, stated in her dissertation, became even more explicit with its publication, at the beginning of which she included as an epigraph the final lines of "Four Part Poem."

In the poem, by combining notions of personal identity with collective cultural constructions such as "we" and "our," Jones sets the tone for *Chile Woman*'s meditations on African American identity and history. Furthermore, when Jones concludes the poem with the term "Yester-/tomorrow," she adds a temporal dimension to her endeavor, underscoring the importance that any meaningful construction of a contemporary self depends on reconciling the memories and language of the past. As Wolfgang Iser notes, "[C]ulture rests on and arises out of memory, which makes what has passed loop into culture's continual emergence" (25).

One of the main themes of *Corregidora* centers around Ursa's attempts to come to terms with her family's distant troubled past, as well as her own traumatic personal history. Ursa speaks of her mother's and grandmother's insistence on passing down the story of Simon Corregidora's abuse "from generation to generation so we'd never forget" (*COR* 9). Despite the fact that learning of Corregidora's crimes is a difficult experience for Ursa,

Ursa's mother recounts that her grandmother's stories of Corregidora's abuse seemed to be therapeutic for her, "*As if the words were helping her, as if the words repeated again and again could be a substitute for memory* [Jones's italics]" (*COR* 11). Ursa's mother believes that linguistic repetition of the family's history, along with the survival of the family line, may serve as salves for the wounds of the past. Thus, when Ursa, one month pregnant, is sent rolling down a flight of stairs, the possibility of her developing a reconciliation with the past is brought into jeopardy. In fact, Ursa informs Tadpole McCormick the event is linked with her personal destiny, "As if part of my life's already marked out for me — the barren part" (*COR* 6). Unfortunately, Ursa's accident serves as a kind of double-edged temporal sword: it jeopardizes her future by forecasting a possible inability to produce generations and an incapacity for making peace with the traumas of the distant past. Ursa realizes this intuitively during her recovery, feeling, "As if something more than the womb had been taken out" (*COR* 6). Having forfeited the Corregidora hope for past and future reconciliation, Ursa remains listless and depressed, unsure of how to go about her existence.

Corregidora translates into English as "female judge" and part of Ursa's challenge is to determine how she will move forward after the dominant self-defining characteristic of the Corregidora women, the womb, has been stripped from her. Judging involves language and Ursa's solution formulates itself through the judicial terminology of her grandmother, who tells her, "*They can burn the papers but they can't burn conscious, Ursa. And that what makes the evidence. And that's what makes the verdict* [Jones's italics]" (*COR* 22). The "conscious" of which Ursa's grandmother speaks — necessary she says for both evidence and judgment — is also shared by Ursa, who muses, "It was as if their memory, the memory of all the Corregidora women, was her memory too, as strong with her as her own private memory, or almost as strong" (*COR* 129). While the physical ability to make generations has been taken from Ursa, she still possesses the psychological means by which to judge the past, speaking both its evils and her repudiations of them — a process which holds the promise of a harmonious future.

Although Ursa entertains the possibility of a personal and historical harmony despite the loss of her womb, physical expression and sexuality remain important components of what Jones conceptualizes to be a fully realized identity. In "Beyond Yourself (The Midnight Confession) for Brother Ahh" the visceral protagonists Letha and Clell are mirrored and complemented by two spiritual figures, Root woman and Root Man, who counter and balance their doubles' sex and violence with wisdom. For example, Root Man relates that Clell, "Knows that his manhood is not in the muscles of his groin, but that he must go deeper, that he must go into his own memory and blood for it. History, memory, metaphor, and blood. It is not a knowing that has words" ("Beyond Yourself" 79). However, Root Man includes among his prescriptive intellectual abstractions — history, memory, and metaphor — the visceral essence of blood, underscoring the undeniable importance of literal, physical identity. Blood also plays an important role in *Corregidora* when Ursa is told:

> ... *They burned all the documents, Ursa, but they didn't burn what they put in their minds. We got to burn out what they put in our minds, like you burn out a wound. Except we got to keep what we need to bear witness. That scar that's left to bear witness. We got to keep it as visible as our blood* [Jones's italics] [72].

Implicit in Ursa's instruction is the mingling of physical and mental abuse, which Ursa experiences in the contexts of both personal and family history. In making mental wounds as visible as blood, the sufferer ostensibly transcends the rigid and debilitating traditional categories of physical and psychological suffering. Correspondingly, in "Beyond Yourself," Root Woman maintains that Letha and Clell must, "be able to see the body and the soul together, To stare beyond. To go beyond themselves. To get beyond themselves, and each other, and return home" (79). Mixing blood and psychology, form and spirit, Jones dramatizes a transcendent condition which contains the possibility of reconciliation between men and women and their personal and cultural memories.

Non-solutions and Failures: Lies, Denial, Fantasy, and Horror

Echoing her ambitions for several other works, in "The Trial of a Man and a Woman," an early version of *Eva's Man*, Jones claimed she hoped to use "dialogue and instances of metaphor to show both emotional and psychological tension in the direct rendering of human relationships" ("Toward" 4). Whereas *Eva's Man* is more ambitious than *Corregidora* in its explorations of both dialogue and metaphor, at least one reviewer believed that Jones had "managed to become monotonous. The sameness of the telling has already diluted the impact of the tale" (McMurtry C5). Yet, Eva, the weaver of much of the speech and symbolism in Jones's second novel, is a decidedly different speaker than *Corregidora*'s Ursa. In fact, the fragmented and often seemingly random musings of Eva caused Melvin Dixon to conclude that she "never gains control over her voice" (245). However, as Francois Lionnet summarizes, it is equally possible that Eva, having been exploited repeatedly by men and placed in jail, purposefully disrupts her language for subversive purposes: "The narrative fragments do not add up to a coherent picture of the past, and the novel thematizes its structural discontinuities by stressing the gaps and the fissures in Eva's memory, by suggesting that she can manage to slip out of the symbolic domain, and disrupt the culture's master narrative" (145). For Lionnet Eva's unusual linguistic allusions serve as means for claiming her own voice and story against the hegemonic presence of science and the legal system. Janelle Wilcox adds a gender-conscious, political dimension to this interpretation when she suggests that readers should not label Eva insane since it "denaturalizes both the dominant male discourse that relegates her to dual roles of whore and castrator and the logic that designates her made for performing these roles" (89). For more than one critic then, Eva's unconventional language and behavior serve as consciously liberating, rather than debilitatingly insane, forces, which promise to free her narrative from society's censure, even if they cannot free her.

Although Eva's language is vivid and convincing, it often lacks the genuine, heart-felt poignancy of Ursa's accounts. In fact, Jones claims that with Eva she "wanted the reader to have a sense of not even knowing whether the things that she recalled were, in fact, true, that she might have been, perhaps, playing a game with the listener" (Tate, "Interview" 143). Eva's "play" is perhaps most noticeable in the silence-game she repeatedly employs against the legal system, prison psychologist, and Elvira. As Biman Basu observes with regard to *Eva's Man*, "[S]ilence itself may be empowering" (199), and although it does not refute the readings of other characters, Eva's muteness does strengthen her position since her enigmatic story and motive(s) for murder remain all her own. However, accompanying Eva's playful methods of expression — such as utter silence and temporal juxtaposition — is the strong possibility that many of the expressions themselves may be lies altogether, which threatens to erode the trust and empathy of both fellow characters and readers.

Like the perceptions of Pecola Breedlove in Toni Morrison's *The Bluest Eye*,[14] Eva's interpretations of reality become increasingly fantastic and unreliable over the course of the book, which is commiserate with Jones's interconnected uses of dialogue, lying, and psychology in the novel. As she explains, "I'm sort of dealing with memory and fantasy as well as storytelling but I want everything to be on the same plane of reality" (Harper 701). In Eva's language these factors eventually reach the point where they are in fact functioning on the same level, which causes certain characters and readers to label her speech ambiguous, insane, and fraudulent. Her jumbling of fantasy and memory appears in statements such as, "Sometimes they think I'm lying to them, though. I tell them it ain't me lying, it's memory lying" (*EM* 5). Ostensibly unable to differentiate memory from fantasy, Eva claims that her recollections betray her even as she attempts to tell the truth. Anxious to label Eva's condition, the prison psychologist readily accepts this interpretation: "I tell the psychiatrist what I remember. He tells me I do not know how to separate the imagined memories from the real ones" (*EM* 10). Yet, it is very possible that Eva, who is educated and intelligent, is merely playing a game with the psychologist, consciously presenting her mind in a manner that is easy for science to package, possibly for some indeterminate future purpose of her own. Correspondingly, in Jones's dissertation story "Take Refuge in Madness," Freddie Jones — an institutionalized character who anticipates Eva in a number of respects — provides a string of fragmented, docile commentary before suddenly and unexpectedly killing his doctor, the doctor's wife, and an attendant because "they would not let him alone" ("Toward" 16). Not unlike Eva, Freddie Jones had been told that he must "either develop habits of meeting the problems of life or take refuge in madness" ("Toward" 18). Despite the fact that his doctor apparently thought otherwise, Jones's actions suggest he has chosen the latter course. Furthermore, as is the case with Eva, Freddie Jones's fantastic musings are partially contingent on being alone, his murder of the doctor and his companions serving as retribution for their repeated intrusions upon his coveted seclusion. Significantly, Eva's most dramatic plunges into fantasy and irrationality occur after Davis isolates her from the outside world for a few days and when she is placed alone in a jail cell. Earlier, Jones had tellingly articulated this theme in her dissertation story, "The Judgment," in which Jake, a young boy with mental problems, consciously chooses solitude and dreams over human interaction and reality. When Jake is institutionalized for the second time, Dr. Hun believes he should be brought out of solitary confinement so he can, as Jake expresses it, "develop wit peple and funchion in a worl with oter peeple" ("Toward" 27), which Jake vehemently resists, preferring instead — like Eva and Freddie Jones — to be left alone amid the strange, violent dreams of his private fantastic reality.

In addition to silence and solitude, Jones also explored the fantastic qualities of Eva's mind through temporal juxtapositions, which often serve to underscore her denial of "real" events. Jones explains, "The handling of time in the novel is most improvisational; what I mean by that is that the ordering of the events is primarily improvisational. I wanted to get the sense of different times and different personalities coexisting in memory" (Tate, "Interview" 143). Once again, the seeds for this theoretical approach appear in Jones's dissertation. For example, Jones relates that the story "Pross" "uses a linear temporal pattern that draws upon the caprices of memory to get in and out of time" ("Toward" 5). Although, unlike *Eva's Man*, it follows a conventional narrative chronology, "Pross," like Jones's second novel, plays with representations of time through the rendering of its speaker's/protagonist's impressions and memories. In *Eva's Man*, rather than conforming to any consistent linear temporal pattern, events appear to be categorized by Eva based more on the similarities of specific personalities and situations. For instance, Eva pairs the temperaments and language of the thumbless man who eventually tries to molest her ("I could go places if I had you" [*EM* 79]) and her manipulative cousin Alfonso ("Yeah, I been places" [*EM* 79]), consolidating their respective desires to have sex with her across time. As in "Pross," in Jones's dissertation story "Take Refuge in Madness" Freddie Jones's ideas and sentences are incomplete and his use of time and grammatical tense jumbled. However, a significant difference exists between these two experimental narratives and

Eva's Man in the sense that Eva is educated, clever, and occasionally poetic, making her descent into fantasy more complex and difficult to trace. When Elvira tells Eva about the photographs of Davis and herself in the newspaper, she relates, "I wanted to see it at first, but then when she sneaked it in with her down in her underwear, I wouldn't look at it. I made her tear it up and flush it down the toilet" (*EM* 3). Initially gripped by the desire to literally confirm her violent murder of Davis, which she conceptualizes in a highly-personalized, abstract, fantastic realm, Eva panics when she actually is presented with the newspaper, realizing—consciously or unconsciously—that the very evidence she seeks constitutes a serious threat to the fantasies in which she indulges.

Reviewing *Eva's Man*, John Updike, though ignoring the book's fantastic properties, detected a purposeful intent by Jones to manipulate and stunt traditional humanistic qualities in her characters, observing, "[T]he characters are dehumanized as much by her [Jones's] artistic vision as by their circumstances" ("Eva and Eleanor" 75). Confirming both Updike's point and the importance of the book's fantastic characteristics, Jones confesses that she thinks of *Eva's Man* "as a kind of dream or a kind of nightmare" (Tate, "Interview" 146). Jones's comment is supported quite literally by Eva's own dream sequences, which are anything but peaceful and benevolent. For example, in Eva's dream in which she kisses a one-thumbed man, "her memory turns to blood" (*EM* 143) after he departs. Such vivid passages threaten to propel the book from the confines of fantasy into the grotesque shadows of horror, a transition that becomes all too evident when Eva literally conceptualizes herself as an archetypal female monster. After she poisons Davis and bites off his penis, she confesses, "I'm Medusa[...]. Men look at me and get hard-ons. I turn their dicks to stone" (*EM* 130), an identification which accompanies the symbolic implications of mythological witchcraft and destruction in her middle name: Medina. Sally Robinson argues that Jones's two novels reference powerful archetypal female figures such as Medusa, Medina, and the Queen Bee "in order to conceptualize a black female subjectivity in the interstices of hegemonic representations" (25). Like Eva, these strong female figures speak themselves through their notable critiques of hegemonic discourses, or as June Jordan summarizes more simply, "You gather from the name that she, this woman, embodies bad news for men" (36).

Whatever symbolic and archetypal connotations Eva's name and actions may carry, it is difficult to establish much hope or beauty from the book's literal narrative, which one reviewer described as a "sad, dark chant ridden with sex and blood" (Major 834). Summoning the dynamics of horror fiction, Keith Byerman sees Eva's relationship with men in terms of a gothic paradox: "She finds both sexuality and men simultaneously enthralling and repulsive; she is inexplicably drawn to them even though her encounters are consistently painful and unattractive. This aspect of her character lends an air of inevitability to her experiences" ("Black Vortex" 95). In addition to identifying herself as a monster, Eva's relationships contain elements of monstrous gothic perversity, her ambivalent coupling of attraction and revulsion suggesting the relationships between stereotypical gothic heroines and their attractive yet dangerous and diabolical male counterparts, who appear in the guises of sexually aggressive vampires, demons, and incubi. Yet, reviewers either ignored or condemned this dynamic and at least one critic argued that the book's gender-conscious gothic qualities obscure the importance of its racial implications, Gloria Wade-Gayles interpreting the novel as a vision of "horror" which "emphasizes sexual victimization almost to the exclusion of any concern with racial oppression" (156–157).[15] Just as Eva indulges in grotesque fantasy, so Jones seems to have fragmented and abstracted Eva's voice and the novel's themes to the point that she could not reconcile them in the end. Articulating her frustration with the book, Jones recounts:

> In many ways, *Eva's Man* is a horror story. It really is. And I'm sure people will ask me if that's the way I see the essential relationship between men and women. But that man and woman don't stand for men and women — they stand for themselves, really. But I don't have any definition for the kind of man-woman relationship that *Eva's Man* describes. Their ritual isn't a blues ritual. I don't know what it is [Harper 701].

Evoking the blues tradition, the repetitious healing formula Ursa employs to reconcile her identity in *Corregidora*, Jones emphasizes the harmonizing dynamic *Eva's Man* lacks. Having constructed a compelling and entertaining exploration of time, fantasy, and horror, Jones found it difficult to cut a viable path out of the tangled forest of metaphor, dialogue, and temporality she had created. Like Eva, the book itself remains overcome by the very elements of fantasy and horror it provocatively generates.

All-Inclusive Conclusions

If *Eva's Man* constitutes an admittedly dark, failed attempt to define the self in a way that is liberating and meaningful, it functions as a distinct and nonetheless important anomaly amid the rich body of Jones's early work, which — as we have seen — is full of serious, though often brutally frank and violent, attempts to reconcile African American relationships and identity. Yet, little has been mentioned thus far in terms of how Jones's specific fictional reconciliations function and come together to form a collective humanizing vision. At the center of Jones's unique searching narratives rests a familiar and basic desire to achieve gender equality through linguistic communication. As Susan Sellers says of two other women's novels, Fay Weldon's *The Life and Loves of a She Devil*[16] and Carter's *Nights at the Circus*,[17] "The touchstone for the future is an equality in which individuals can relate to one another freely and in which the needs and complexities of each are fully recognised" (Sellers 131). Jones's fiction treads a dangerous path upon which such thematically unlikely bedfellows as honesty and fantasy attempt to address and overcome the psychological traumas of domineering sexual relationships. In suggesting a cultural solution for a perceived lack of sexual assertiveness in women — displayed at different points in Jones's fiction, most notably through Ursa's and Eva's compromised wills — feminist psychologist Patricia J. Morokoff urges women and men "to work toward sexual fantasies that are not based on dominance and submission. If arousal means images of dominance and submission, the resulting sexuality is an exploitive one regardless of whether men are dominant over women, women are dominant over men, or same sex partners play the roles" (316). Each of Jones's early novels appears to achieve a measure of positive, or at least non-abusive, sexuality in their respective conclusions, Ursa exploring a more balanced, though still very physical, relationship with Mutt Thomas and Eva relieving her sexual tensions through Elvira. Whereas both relationships still present potential serious problems, the closing scenes through which they are rendered suggest their respective capacities for healing.

In addition to dramatizing the potential sexual reconciliations of her protagonists, Jones also explores ways in which characters may accept and confront their past traumas through storytelling and song. However, her idea of orality is more nuanced and complex than that of a writer such as Toni Cade Bambara, who in narratives like "My Man Bovanne" flirts with packaging spoken cultural transmission in a sentimental wrapping. Noting *Corregidora*'s narratives of self-assertion, Katherine Boutry asserts that the novel "explores the power of composition in liberating the female performer from her objectified body and song" (106). However, in addition to the protagonist's "composition" or narrative, Jones is also interested in the concomitant reactions of the listener or reader. She explains:

> At the time I was writing *Corregidora* and *Eva's Man* I was particularly interested, and continue to be interested, in oral traditions of storytelling — Afro-American and others — where there is always that consciousness and importance of the hearer, even in the interior monologue where the storyteller becomes the hearer. That consciousness or self-consciousness is important in terms of the selection of significant events [Tate, "Interview" 143].

Jones believes the input of the hearer, even if the listener is also the speaker, serves as a kind of reaffirming agent for the rendered narrative, making it more genuine and beneficial for the speaker. As Ashraf Rushdy observes, "Jones's characters listen to others' stories so attentively as to feel that they are living out the experiences they describe, hearing them with such intensity that they assume an intersubjective communion with the narrators" (273). Often the bond achieved between speaker and hearer is expressed, literally or symbolically, in musical terms. As Jones asserts, "The relationships between men and women I'm dealing with are blues relationships" (Harper 700), comparing the dynamics of her characters' intimate interactions to the themes and organization of blues music. Recognizing that "critics have frequently overlooked her use of form" (257), Donia Elizabeth Allen analyzes Jones's use of call and response, repetition, and blues break in *Corregidora*, perceptively cataloging her literary interpretations of blues themes. Tracing the implications of blues music beyond its multiple aesthetic forms, Patrick Johnson notes, "Blues performances resist final or stable meaning — the blues singer's rhythms suggest change, movement, action, continuance, unlimited and unending possibilities" (27). Echoing the hope of blues music while avoiding sentimentality, Jones concludes many of her narratives by emphasizing the open possibilities of relationships that, like the blues, contain coexisting elements of chaos and violence and harmony and love.

Inherent in the blues techniques employed by Jones's characters is the creative impulse — the attempt to interpret experience in new terms, thereby more fully making experience one's own. *Chile Woman* opens with a blues singer lamenting a broken relationship, which symbolically asserts the fragmented psyches of the play's women, who attempt to make peace with their identities and create new ones by recounting their traumas. Not unlike Ursa, in "Beyond Yourself," Clell tells Letha that he is attempting to become a whole being through the performance of music: "Sometimes I felt that by creating *it* I could…" (83). Ursa's own transition in identity through the blues is noticed by Cat, who says of Ursa's singing: "Your voice sounds a little strained, that's all. But if I hadn't heard you before, I wouldn't notice anything. I'd still be moved. Maybe even moved more, because it sounds like you been through something. Before it was beautiful too, but you sound like you been through more now" (*COR* 44). Ursa's negative experiences and her performance of the blues come together to form a richer and more beautiful new voice; as one critic summarizes, Ursa "constructs her own story which finally puts an end to this sadomasochistic cycle" (Horvitz 250). Ursa herself underscores the importance of the blues as an outlet and healing force against the dark legacy of Simon Corregidora, asserting, "*They squeezed Corregidora into me, and I sung back in return* [Jones's italics]" (*COR* 103). For Ursa and several other Jones characters, the blues functions as an innovative linguistic salve for the personal and cultural violence of the past. In *Chile Woman* "Crazy Woman" asks, "What will be the new language?" and answers herself by repeating "I love you" and "Won't hurt" (22). Adding a temporal dimension to the importance of language, "Crazy Woman" uses the negativity of her victimized history to envision a future without pain and full of love.

Just as Jones symbolically emphasizes the dual importance of spirituality and physicality, so her comments on linguistic blues healing are balanced by realistic considerations, which come together to articulate the all-inclusive structure she established for herself as a graduate student. In *Chile Woman*, Ella maintains, "You don't need a new language of love or anything. We need a new habit of tenderness. A whole way of being with somebody. Y'all mens treat a woman like she ain't nuthin but a piece a shit. You ain't spose to treat a woman like no piece a shit" (49). Although Jones demonstrates language to be a powerful tool in reconciling traumas of the past, it cannot completely guard against the possible debilitating events of the future. Just as individuals individually accept their histories through language, several of Jones's characters must recall together their shared destructive actions in order to prescribe their policies in relation to each other for the present and future. When Letha and her man make up in *Chile Woman*, Letha says, "I guess we took each other through hell, didn't we? ... Yeah, I'm still your woman" (55), emphasizing their shared abusive past and her decision to stay with him both in spite of and even because of it. As Root Woman says in "Beyond Yourself," "There is hardness and tenderness. We must tear the fear and anger apart to make these dreams" (79). For Root Woman, the adversity and tenderness of relationships help to banish the negative emotions of the past, from which new imaginary narratives become possible. Letha vows that she and Clell "will survive the pain and the anger and fear and after we survive it, the love, the great love!" ("Beyond Yourself" 92), coupling love with Root Woman's concept of dreams as positive byproducts of rage, trauma, and pain. In the play's final passages then, Jones demonstrates the importance of past traumas in providing a foundation for the dreams, love (physical and spiritual), and happiness of the future. Using artistic terminology, Letha tells Clell that he paints "the dreams everywhere, on my body and soul too, because they have come together, they have returned, laughing and holding you" ("Beyond Yourself" 92). Not surprisingly, "Crazy Woman"—perhaps the most abused figure in all of Jones's fiction — echoes this condition while adding to it the fundamental healing powers of singing and making generations: "We are the songs of our children. Our children are our songs. A black man and woman are the bone and marrow of each other. This is the reality that is still in us" (*Chile Woman* 21). Across the reconciliations of these narratives Jones offers a conclusion to her ambitious, multi-faceted, all-inclusive structure. Experience, imagination, autobiography, history, legend, myth, ritual, metaphor, psychology, dream, black forms (musical and linguistic), and the erotic as an authentic method of expression come together to form the essence of hope for the future. Though many of these elements appear ugly and troubling when considered alone, Jones's remarkable ability to interweave and reconcile them, to impressively meet the demands of her own demanding theoretical structure — generating beauty and art from the isolating but omnipresent baseness of violence, madness, and slavery — constitutes a unique and powerful literary achievement.

Notes

1. Other reviews that notably conceptualize sex as the defining dynamic of Jones's first two novels include "Review of *Corregidora*," *Playboy* 22.6 (June 1975) 33–34; Ivan Webster, "Really the Blues," *Time* 105 (16 June 1975) 79; John Avant, "Review of *Corregidora*," *New Republic* 172 (28 June 1975) 27–28; Ann Goode, "Review of *Corregidora*," *Black Books Bulletin* 3 (Fall 1975) 46–47; Horvitz (238); Margo Jefferson, "A Woman Alone," *Newsweek* 87 (12 April 1976) 102–106; Charles R. Larson, "The Violent and Poetic Puzzle of *Eva's Man*," *National Observer* (17 April 1976) 19; and John Leonard, "Violence Born in a Woman's Hate," *New York Times* (30 April 1976) C17.

2. "Frame and Dialect: The Evolution of the Black Voice in American Literature," *American Poetry Review* 5 (September/October 1976) 34–37.

3. "The Use of Folktale in Novels By Black Women Writers," *CLA Journal* 23 (1980) 266–272.

4. "Women in Pain ... or Giggling," *New York Times* (21 April 1975) 27.

5. Two selections from "Toward an All-Inclusive Structure," "The Trial of a Man and a Woman" and "Chile Woman (Prelude)" constitute early versions of the published works *Eva's Man* and *Chile Woman* (1974) respectively. Other prose pieces contain themes that would later appear in print. For example, in "Take Refuge in Madness" and "Pross" Jones explores mental illness and tumultuous African American gender relationships using methods and devices that also function in *Corregidora* and *Eva's Man*.

6. Notable recent essays that employ general psychological theories to various degrees include Ann DuCille's essay, "Phallus(ies) of Interpretation: Toward Engendering the Black Critical 'I,'" which uses political and psychological readings to bring "the penis under scrutiny, at once acknowledging and problematizing its power" (566), Carol Margaret Davison's "Love 'em and Lynch 'em: The Castration Motif in Gayl Jones's *Eva's Man*," Deborah Horvitz's "'Sadism Demands a Story': Oedipus, Feminism, and Sexuality in Gayl Jones's *Corregidora* and Dorothy Allison's *Bastard Out of Carolina*," Nickesia S. Gordon's "On the Couch with Dr. Fraud: Insidious Trauma and Distorted Female Community in Gayl Jones's *Eva's Man*," and Keith B. Mitchell's "'Trouble in Mind': (Re)visioning Myth, Sexuality, and Race in Gayl Jones's *Corregidora*" (all listed in bibliography). A specific dialogue concerning pain, sexuality, and traumatic anxiety in *Corregidora* exists across the following essays: Naomi Morgenstern, "Mother's Milk and Sister's Blood: Trauma and the Neoslave Narrative," *Differences: A Journal of Feminist Cultural Studies* 8.2 (1996) 101–126; Bruce Simon, "Traumatic Repetition: Gayl Jones's *Corregidora*," *Race Consciousness: African-American Studies for the New Century*, eds. Judith Jackson Fossett and Jeffrey A. Tucker (New York: New York UP, 1997) 93–112; Elizabeth Yukins, "Bastard Daughters and the Possession of History in *Corregidora* and *Paradise*," *Signs* 28.1 (Autumn 2002) 221–249; Elizabeth Swanson Goldberg, "Living the Legacy: Pain, Desire, and Narrative Time in Gayl Jones's *Corregidora*," *Callaloo* 26.2 (2003) 446–472; Jennifer Griffiths "Uncanny Spaces: Trauma, Cultural Memory, and the Female Body in Gayl Jones's *Corregidora* and Maxine Hong Kingston's *Woman Warrior*," *Studies in the Novel* 38.3 (Fall 2006) 353–371; and Stephanie Li, "Love and the Trauma of Resistance in Gayl Jones's *Corregidora*," *Callaloo* 29.1 (Winter 2006) 131–151.

7. Numerous reviews and essays have interpreted *Corregidora* predominantly as a dramatic, personalized, traumatic history of black women's brutal, oppressive suffering from slavery to the present. See "Review of *Corregidora*," *Kirkus Reviews* 43 (15 February 1975) 195; Larry McMurtry, "A Bold, Strong First Novel from Gayl Jones," *Washington Post* (28 April 1975) B6; "Review of *Corregidora*" *Booklist* 71.18 (15 May 1975) 941; Margo Jefferson, "Making Generations," *Newsweek* 85 (19 May 1975) 84–85; Karla Kuskin, "Cycle of Sex and Slavery," *Village Voice* 20.21 (26 May 1975) 42; Ivan Webster, "Really the Blues," *Time* 105 (16 June 1975) 79; Updike (79); Bernette Golden, "Review of *Corregidora*, " *Black World* 25 (February 1976) 82; Melvin Dixon, "Review: *Corregidora*," *Obsidian* 3 (Spring 1977) 72–74; Gloria Wade-Gayles (156); Richard Jackson, "Remembering the 'Disremembered': Modern Black Writers and Slavery in Latin America," *Callaloo* 13.1 (Winter 1990) 131–144; Gottfried (559); Angelyn Mitchell, *The Freedom to Remember* (New Bunswick: Rutgers UP, 2002) 149–169; Elizabeth Yukins, "Bastard Daughters and the Possession of History in *Corregidora* and *Paradise*," *Signs* 28.1 (Autumn 2002) 221–249; Gil Zehava Hochberg, "Mother, Memory, History: Maternal Genealogies in Gayl Jones's *Corregidora* and Simone Schwartz-Bart's *Pluie et vent sur Télumée Miracle*," *Research in African Literatures* 34.2 (Summer 2003) 1–12; and Hershini Bhana Young, "Inheriting the Criminalized Black Body: Race, Gender, and Slavery in *Eva's Man*," *African American Review* 39.3 (Fall 2005) 377–394.

8. In *Bridging the Americas: The Literature of Toni Morrison, Paule Marshall, and Gayl Jones*, Stelmaris Coser summarizes "the influence of Latin American writers on the scope and style of [Jones's] storytelling" (122).

9. "No Feminist Tract," *Freedomways* 15.4 (1975) 291.

10. Hamburg: Rowohlt, 1986. The novel has not been translated into English.

11. Reviews that perceive a Faulknerian influence on Jones's work include Larry McMurtry, "A Bold, Strong First Novel from Gayl Jones," *Washington Post* (28 April 1975) B6; John Avant, "Review of *Corregidora*," *New Republic* 172 (28 June 1975) 27–28; Charles R. Larson, "Master and Slave Became Fused; Past Lives in the Present," *National Observer* (9 August 1975) 17; Elizabeth Pochoda, "Shades of a Black Female Faulkner—*Corregidora*," *Glamour* 73.9 (September 1975) 97; Kent (107); Charles R. Larson, "The Violent and Poetic Puzzle of *Eva's Man*," *National Observer* (17 April 1976) 19; and "Review of *Eva's Man*," *Choice* 13.7 (September 1976) 823.

12. Although Jones does not mention Faulkner, she answers questions about her wide-ranging literary influences in Michael S. Harper's "Gayl Jones: An Interview" (705–710) and comments on characteristics of southern literature in Charles H. Rowell's "An Interview with Gayl Jones" (38–39). Not surprisingly, her literary interests include writers, such as Ernest Gaines, clearly influenced by Faulkner.

13. Truth occasionally was accused of being male on account of her large physique and deep speaking voice.

14. New York: Holt, Rinehart and Winston, 1970.

15. Bernard Bell classifies *Eva's Man* and *Corregidora* as black feminist works with grisly gothic elements (267). Other accounts of Jones's work that explicitly note its gothic qualities include Ivan Webster, "Really the Blues," *Time* 105 (16 June 1975) 79; Jessica Harris, "Review of *Eva's Man*," *Essence* 7.2 (June 1976) 87; and Byerman, "Black Vortex" (93).

16. (New York: Pantheon, 1983).

17. (New York: Viking, 1985).

CHAPTER 2

Speaking the Grotesque: Short Fiction

> "Most [of the stories in White Rat] are written in first person and most deal with tensions in relationships, dynamics of psychology—psychic landscape—and [...] the 'inward.'"
>
> —Gayl Jones in Rowell, "Interview," 49

Several reviewers of Gayl Jones's first two novels, *Corregidora* (1975) and *Eva's Man* (1976), sought to interpret the books primarily in terms of their dark, violent, and even gothic qualities, muffling the formidable aesthetic dynamics of those works beneath the sensational, problematic vividness of their respective brutal episodes.[1] Critics of *Eva's Man* in particular used the novel's literal and psychological violence to accuse the text of social and aesthetic irresponsibility, Loyle Hairston attacking the book for its "squalid appraisal of the souls of Black folks" (133). Summing up the majority of critical reactions to the book, Clarence Major characterized Jones's second novel as a "sad, dark chant ridden with sex and blood" (834). Amid this stormy climate of reviewer condemnation—only a year after the publication of *Eva's Man*—appeared Jones's first collection of short stories, *White Rat* (1977). Not surprisingly, at least one reviewer was quick to equate the slender volume of short fiction with the perceived philosophical despondency of *Eva's Man*, Carol Pearson arguing that the stories "suggest no alternative to solipsism and despair" (1678). Yet, this assessment did not herald a chorus of critical censure. Noting the book's narrative power, one anonymous reviewer labeled the collection an impressive demonstration of "forcefulness" ("Review of *White Rat*,"

Booklist 140). Weighing the selection's unflinching and potentially disturbing subject matter with Jones's aesthetic craftsmanship, Barbara Bannon adroitly extended the "forcefulness" reading, concluding, "The excellence of her [Jones's] creations increases their impact and the result is literature, no matter how the stories affect the sensibilities" (63). Subordinating the connotations of potentially problematic subject matter to the dynamic "impact" of Jones's telling, Bannon dubbed the collection a literary success.

In her condemnatory review of *White Rat* Carol Pearson makes an important observation about the general tenor of Jones's imagery, arguing that, rather than attempting to establish any kind of humanistic vision, the stories "are characterized instead by unrelieved distaste for the body, for sexuality, and for human life" (1678). Although it likely was not her intention, Pearson here suggests elements of the grotesque and, in fact, her comment might even serve as a partial definition of that important and evasive aesthetic form. Other critics generally have ignored the explicit grotesque qualities of Jones's work. However, Keith E. Byerman evaluated the gothic qualities of *Eva's Man*[2] before identifying its grotesque characteristics as seen predominantly through Eva Medina Canada's crime: "a symbolic liberation from the particular grotesqueness of her society" ("Intense" 452). For Byerman, *Eva's Man* is a work of the grotesque in terms of the way it renders and interrogates the ugliness of racist, patriarchal American mores: "The supposed normalities of American life are shown to be absurd and ominous distortions" (447). Byerman's important observation serves as a foundation for other avenues by which the value of Jones's work — and her short stories in particular — may be illuminated through an investigation of its grotesque qualities.

Wolfgang Kayser, in *The Grotesque in Art and Literature*, details the etymology of the grotesque, relating how the Italian word literally translated as "from the cave or grotto" (hence grotto-esque) and became the accepted moniker for an entire genre of art (19–20). As early as 1502, church officials were commenting on the cave drawings, which were characterized as "an unreasonable fashion" and "monstrous forms" that "never existed, do not now exist, and shall never come into being" (20). By 1515, this art form, which the Renaissance conceptualized as "not only something playfully gay and utterly fantastic, but also something ominous and sinister in the face of a world totally different from the familiar one" (20–21), was firmly established. Soon thereafter, the Italian term passed into the French language as "crotesque," the English borrowing not far behind. In popular language the grotesque is defined by figures or designs characterized by comic distortion or exaggeration. The comic element, however, if indeed there is always a humorous element inherent the grotesque, is of a decidedly nervous sort. Dieter Meindl suggests in *American Fiction and the Metaphysics of the Grotesque* that:

> [N]otwithstanding the multiplicity of scholarly treatments of the grotesque, there exists a certain amount of agreement as regards its essential nature. The grotesque emerges as a tense combination of attractive and repulsive elements, of comic and tragic aspects, of ludicrous and horrifying features[...]. Without a certain collision of complicity between playfulness and seriousness, the grotesque does not appear to exist [14].

Mikhail Bakhtin anticipated Meindl's concept in *Rabelais and His World* and expends a great deal of effort to extend and clarify how the grotesque differs from mainstream or "normal" art. Furthermore, Bakhtin's examination of the term focuses especially on unnatural changes in the body through eating, defecation, and sex. He holds that the grotesque highlights the body where it:

> [O]utgrows its own self, transgresses its own limits[...]. Next to the bowels and the genital organs is the mouth through which enters the world to be swallowed up [...] the grotesque image ignores the closed, smooth, and impenetrable surface of the body and retains only its exrescences (sprouts, buds) and orifices, only that which leads beyond the body's limited space or into the body's depths [317–318].

Uniting the visceral excesses and penetrable cavities of the human body with abstract concepts of comedy and horror, the grotesque functions as a harbinger of uncertainty and ambiguity, disrupting and sometimes overwhelming the essence of normality with the decentering potency of its otherness.

In her short fiction Jones appears to employ the grotesque as a condition from which her African American protagonists are attempting to escape. Existing in macabre surroundings or possessing abhorrent qualities themselves, her characters attempt to overcome their personal and/or environmental circumstances, usually through either physical migration or attempted self-transformation. As Jones herself has demonstrated, this theme is not restricted to her art. During her discussion of Zora Neale Hurston's *Their Eyes Were Watching God*, in her book of literary criticism, *Liberating Voices*, she observes:

> Often, as here, fiction in the African American tradition contains models not of what one might be or become but the reverse: examples of what one must escape, nets to avoid in order to achieve wholeness. While some works contain examples of autonomous, self-realized characters who provide moral revelations or possibilities for the unrealized ones, central characters are often like Janie [*Their Eyes were Watching God*], emerging to recreate or create themselves without guideposts or blueprints except their own, or signs telling them where not to go [*LV* 133].

As much warnings of "where not to go" as "moral revelations," Jones's short fiction investigates the debilitating and grotesque aspects of the African American and general human experience while often offering possible avenues by which a marginalized character might gain some degree of agency: a dialectic that uses the grotesque in order to dramatize dynamics of both oppression and liberation. Often the protagonist's path toward reconciliation and greater freedom involves the practice of storytelling — of speaking an experience in a way that allows her, and sometimes even her community, to accept or reconcile herself to a set of circumstances previously perceived as deviant or grotesque. Praising Jones's compelling use of voice, George Garrett asserts that her stories in *White Rat* "are linked not only by their concentration on race and racism and their lean, spare mannerisms, but also by the fact that they are all intended to be echoes of and variations on the ways of oral history and telling" (468–469). In addition to serving as thematic means of escape and acquiring agency, Jones's narrative voices also function as aesthetic exercises, practicing different and often unconventional forms of telling while attempting to push the boundaries of literary language.

As reviewer Gay Wilentz summarizes, "Jones's attention in her work to oral voicing, and to those who have been rendered voiceless, is the basis of *White Rat*" (143), and in the stories' collective investigation of oral oppression and expression Jones achieves a kind of communal chorus. In "The Storyteller," Walter Benjamin makes an important distinction between the communal storyteller, a participant in cultural customs and practitioner of an oral tradition, from the novelist, the objective and alienated recorder of details (86). Embodying Benjamin's idea of the communal storyteller, Jones emphasizes the importance of communication and personal interaction in her stories: "I start with story — people — speech — relationships — situation. Story for me isn't 'action' or 'plot sequence' or theories about how things should be/are. It's people doing/being certain things *in relationship* to other people — mainly men and women" (Harper 696). Significantly, Jones often includes her own voice or at least the voice of her fictional speaker/narrator in the communities she portrays, especially when she employs first-person narration, tracing her technique to the influence of Ernest Gaines: "For me, Ernest Gaines solved the problem of perspective and narrative/dialogue relationship: the storyteller being a part of the same speech community, the same essential world view, and telling the story to those people who also identify with that language and world view and with those human values" (Harper 702). Attempting to establish a communal connection between the authorial telling voice, fictional characters, and the hearer of the tale, Jones seeks to follow Gaines in presenting an authentic representational experience — one in which all of the participants share the same moral, cultural, and dialogic signifiers. As Jones summarizes, "Actually, in oral storytelling there are three kinds of identification — the identification of the storyteller with the story, the identification of the storyteller with the hearer, and the identification of the hearer with the story" (Harper 699). When each of these identifications is successful the music and cultural references of oral telling come together to produce an intimate community of artist, story, and hearer, even as the tale itself conveys its fictional community. More than an aesthetic form or polemical stance, Jones's use of communal storytelling serves as a method for coupling the implications of artistic telling with problematic and often grotesque social dynamics. In its *modus operandi* then, Jones's theory resembles Amiri Baraka's artistic and thematic utilization of jazz, which she outlines in *Liberating Voices* as creating:

> a form that shows the integration of the artistic and social imagination. The story doesn't entirely resolve social dilemmas and paradoxes of consciousness, but it is successful as a blending of aesthetic and moral function in a new mode, and it provides a breakthrough and a greater feeling of fictional boundaries through its use of jazz as subject, tonal structure, and aesthetical model [*LV* 122].

Combining aesthetic and social qualities "in a new mode"—that of communal storytelling—Jones, like Baraka in his use of jazz, achieves a potential means by which to liberate the teller, story, and hearer from the limiting and usually grotesque hegemony of other discourses.

In his negative assessment of *White Rat*, Mel Watkins concluded, "[I]t is the lack of character development that finally makes this assemblage of misfits and neurotics unbelievable or, worse, uninteresting" (C17). Watkins' observation is important not only for its unknowing evocation of the grotesque (Jones's "assemblage of misfits and neurotics"), but also for its recognition of Jones's seemingly purposeful minimalist and unsympathetic sketches of her characters. Another initial reviewer, Jessica Harris, perhaps was more accurate than she realized when she made the analogy, "Reading these stories is like reading case histories, each one opening the door to a new malaise" (55). Carried a small step further, Harris's statement suggests that Jones may have been more interested in creating and investigating grotesque psychological and social environments than inventing character-driven narratives and bulky interior monologues. There is significant support for this reading. In 1976, only a year before the publication of *White Rat*, African American psychologist Robert V. Guthrie published a groundbreaking and controversial history of African American psychology in the United States entitled *Even the Rat Was White*. Expounding upon a perceived inherent racism in his discipline, Guthrie remarked, "Some of the dubious research of the 1920s has lingered nearly fifty years as a phantomlike apparition of pseudointellectualism. Present-day proclamations purporting to present evidence of limited intellectual capacities in black Americans resemble the claims of biased 1920 educational psychologists" (193). Correspondingly, some of the stories in *White Rat* interrogate psychologically-based cultural assumptions about African Americans, the problematic function of psychological paradigms created by whites, and the psychological conditions of various African Americans as perceived by themselves or from within their own culture. Whether or not there is a literal connection between *White Rat* and *Even the Rat Was White* (a remarkable cultural coincidence if there is not), both texts display an interest in analyzing the problematic relationship between African Americans (usually female individuals in Jones's fiction) and psychology (a discipline created and initially practiced almost exclusively by white, male Europeans). Jones herself has identified psychology as the dominant concern of the stories in *White Rat*, relating, "Most are written in first person and most deal with tensions in relationships, dynamics of psychology—psychic landscape—and [...] the "inward" (Rowell, "Interview" 49). Drawing on the research of early psychologists such as Emil Fröschels, Kurt Goldstein, and H. H. Goddard,[3] Jones sought—from the writing of her Brown University dissertation up through the compositions of her early plays and first two novels—to utilize various psychological case studies for fictional characterizations as well as stylistic experiments, the result being an often grotesque landscape in which the dilemmas of African American culture, concepts of psychology, and pressures of the dominant society conspire to overwhelm her characters with violence, despair, and madness.

A Macabre Collection

Confronted with a plethora of societal, philosophical, and general identity problems, many of Jones's characters end up—either literally or figuratively—taking refuge in madness, which—though debilitating and grotesque in several respects—at least offers them a certain measure of freedom. Jones's earliest published investigation of this theme appears in "The Return: A Fantasy" (1971), which follows the intellectual and spiritual odyssey of Joseph Corey, a brilliant African American college student who suffers from schizophrenia. His mind and development hemmed in by the didactic social structure of the university, Corey's mental condition serves as a symbolic and literal catalyst for liberation. As the narrator and Corey's bride-to-be, Dora, explains, during his fits of depression Corey would "take off whenever he wanted" (*WR* 107). Unfortunately, Corey's schizophrenic desire for freedom is accompanied by destructive delusions of grandeur in which he conceptualizes himself as a messiah: "I am not come into the world to be understood. I am come to save. I am come to be believed upon" (*WR* 109). Dora, who falls in love with Corey, does believe in him and wants to marry him in spite of his condition, which sets the stage for the story's remaining painful episodes. In fact, after Corey tells Dora of his disorder, he asks her if he can, "Hurt you into marrying me?" (*WR* 111), foreshadowing the grotesque, paradoxical elements their relationship will come to display.

Although Corey's condition affords him a certain measure of imaginative spiritual and intellectual freedom, it is also debilitating, producing wild images of the very bondage he wishes to escape. At one point, he awakes screaming and tells Dora that the angel "Gabriel had chained his right hand to his neck and his left hand behind his back" (*WR* 115). Furthermore, Corey's condition is aggravated by the fact that he and Dora move to Corey's childhood home, the haunted site of domestic discord and his mother's mental breakdown. This familial dynamic is further complicated when Joseph's father, Avrahm Corey, appears in the story and informs Dora that Joseph's mother was "lewd," and that he "tried to save him from this memory" (*WR* 125). Yet, rather than having protected his son, the elder Corey functions only as an agent of turbulence, fueling Joseph's psychosis. Joseph also is pushed toward madness by Dora's brother, Steven, who supposedly also is his best friend. A frustrated intellectual himself, Steven appears resentful and jealous of the imaginative freedom Corey's schizophrenia affords him. Steven cultivates a romantic, idealistic image of the thinker which borders on the grotesque, at one point comparing himself to a Chinese artist "who locked himself in his studio and hung the sign 'Dumb' on the door outside, and made weird noises and pulled his hair out" (119). In addition to entertaining a grotesque, narcissistic image of himself as artist, Steven becomes a kind of grotesque in his literal relationship with Joseph, taking over his apartment (*WR* 110)—a sign of his buried desire to resemble and perhaps even become Corey—and giving irrational and ill-advised advice (*WR* 123) which further distances Joseph from Dora and reality. More interested in the intellectual dynamics of Corey's condition than the literal health of his friend and sister, Steven often recalls Corey's schizophrenic episodes, as if he constantly is attempting to trigger another onset. As he explains to Dora, "He wanted to break away from everything, everyone. I only helped him along" (*WR* 129).

If Steven has "helped [Corey] along," it has been toward a grotesque, rather than purely liberated, state of existence. As Steven notes, Corey becomes a kind of living grotesque paradox, which, to a degree, constitutes the very nature of schizophrenia: "He's made himself both the doctor and the patient, the curer and the ill" (*WR* 132). This diagnosis is confirmed in Jones's other adaptation of Corey's story, entitled "Version 2," which relates several of the events of "The Return: A Fantasy" from Joseph's perspective. As Jones notes, "Version 2" constitutes a meditation on the relationship between psychological and linguistic fragmentation: "I was working on experimental stories — only a couple of pieces have been published in post-modernist journals — which dealt with how psychological states influenced speech and language patterns and the making of stories, the kinds of fragmentations that would occur in such storytelling" (Rowell, "Interview" 50). The narrative's concern with fragmentations of identity and language is evident through Joseph's abrupt shifts in perspective, vocabulary, and subject matter, perhaps best epitomized by his comment that he has the ability to turn into Jesus or an ant (*WR* 173). Yet, the prospect of such transformations, accompanied by a distorted sensual focus on food (*WR* 173–174), is grotesque rather than truly liberating. Although Corey's brain is free of society's grotesque strictures, it generates unproductive contradictions rather than useful meanings; turning in upon itself it immobilizes rather than liberates Corey, making him a prisoner in his own mind.

Whereas Corey's grotesque relationship with madness is a personal affair, marked by contemplations of his own mind and spirit, the perverse psychosis which concludes the story "Jevata" (1973) is at least partially a result of societal forces. From the narrative's very beginning it is apparent that Jevata's neighborhood/community has taken on grotesque aspects through its repeated gossiping and theorizing about the fifty-year-old Jevata's sexual relationship with Freddy, an eighteen-year-old man from another area. As the story's narrator, Jevata's devoted friend Floyd, remarks, "[Jevata] used to say I was the only one that she could trust, because the others always talked about her too much" (*WR* 56). The mouthpiece for the gossiping community is Miss Johnny Cake, a physically repulsive elderly woman who sits on her front porch with her legs wide open, contemplating the shape of Jevata's breasts, Freddy's sexual habits, and the physical aspects of his relationship with Jevata. Whereas Miss Johnny Cake constitutes a grotesque in terms of her physical appearance and squalid concerns, Freddy's and Jevata's relationship is far from idyllic and even possesses elements of the grotesque itself. For example, when Jevata initially picks Freddy up she takes him to a carnival (*WR* 71–72). As Bakhtin explains in *Rabelais and His World*, carnivals traditionally function as distinctive phenomena in which appearances and social norms often are bent and disfigured to the point of becoming grotesque (32). The almost archetypal foundation of their relationship takes on an additional dimension later when Freddy has sex with one of Jevata's young sons, thus giving credence to Miss Johnny Cake's vulgar theories regarding Freddy's possible homosexuality. This revelation drives Jevata into a mad fury and then a permanent state of dementia which causes her to believe that Freddy — still the pedestaled object of her affection, despite having left Jevata and fled town — has been reincarnated for her in the form of the baby he leaves with her. In the end, "Jevata" is a story of individuals with unrequited desires — Miss Johnny Cake's lust for sex, Jevata's love for Freddy, and Freddy's attraction to males — who become grotesques in the process of pining for the things they cannot have. The exception to this interpretive arrangement is the narrator, Floyd, who, though he has loved and desired Jevata for decades, never displays resentment at her firm resolve not to marry him. As one anonymous initial reviewer maintained, "[Jones's] put-on, ironical, middle-aged men are best" ("Review of *White Rat*," *Kirkus* 872), and Floyd is an ideal and sympathetic narrator in his long-suffering and unwavering dedication to Jevata and her children. In an environment of grotesques, Floyd functions as an agent of love and stability, holding together both the narrative and Jevata's family to the very end.

No such reliability or endearing loyalty informs the "The Coke Factory" (1977), the short tale of Ricky Bean, a presumably retarded teenager who is made into a grotesque by his guardian, medical science, his school, and society in general. Told from Ricky's perspective in his own voice, the story demonstrates how preconceptions about retardation and mental illness can serve to construct and even demonize the behaviors of ostensibly challenged individuals. Believing he is an imbecile, Rickey's guardian, Ali, complains about him openly, even though he appears to grasp all that she says. For example, Ricky knows that Ali has tried to get rid of him, both through institutionalization and by returning him to his biological family. He also is aware that she is looking forward to his eighteenth birthday, when she can, "sent me out to eastern state that the mental hospital" (*WR* 97). Fueled mostly by Ali's complaints of his behavior, the community has come to regard Ricky much as his guardian does. In the local drugstore a woman named Fany laments, "Hes a bad boy. Oh, hes bad" (*WR* 100). Likewise, the mental hospital that evaluates Ricky comments on his uncouth behavior rather than his medical condition. As Ricky recounts, they tell Ali he is "too bad to learn. But they didn't want to do with me" (*WR* 97). Ironically, much of Ricky's unorthodox conduct, such as violently knocking over his own collection of coke cans (*WR* 99), are premeditated and suggest a frustrated and disgruntled, rather than retarded, teenager. In fact, it seems probable that, to a significant degree, Ricky is signifying on the retardation narrative of his community because it affords him a generous measure of latitude and agency. Kept out of school and excused in his violations of etiquette on account of his "feeblemindedness," Ricky is happy to play the role of the community "retard" so long as he can pursue his guiding passion of collecting empty bottles, for which he receives free sodas and a smug sense of satisfaction.

A similarly subtle application of signifying appears in "Asylum" (1977), another very brief story in which grotesque behavior serves as an agent of freedom for an institutionalized protagonist. Wolfgang Karrer has characterized the tale as "another exercise at a naturalistic mode with obvious existentialist implications" (89), yet on another level, the narrative appears to function more as a play on the "naturalistic mode," underscoring the shortcomings of readings that purport the formulaic inevitability of bad environments and faulty genetics. At the beginning, Jones arranges a purposefully clichéd hospital hierarchy that conforms to the narrator's societal stereotypes and reader expectations with its white doctors and nurses and hulking black orderly (*WR* 77)—the stereotyped unthinking muscle at the bottom of the institution's power structure. Furthermore, as she does with Ricky in "The Coke Factory," Jones has her protagonist speak in a dialect that reflects her African American cultural identity as well as her specific mental and linguistic eccentricities—a language that basically invites the reader to view the protagonist as uneducated and possibly mad. In fact, several critics have advanced just such a reading. For example, Mary Helen Washington asserts the protagonist "is unable to defend herself with words" (126), while Laurie Prothro maintains that Jones's poor characters "communicate through shared hardship; dialogue is sparse because words are unimportant, and they go on living because there is nothing else" (485). On the surface, such readings appear quite accurate. For example, the protagonist has been institutionalized because she inexplicably urinates in front of her nephew's first grade teacher. When asked to write down why she did it, she responds with irrational obscenities that border on gibberish: "She [presumably the teacher] just sit on her ass and fuck all day and it ain't worth herself" (*WR* 79). However, the protagonist then elaborates her vulgar explanation to the reader: "I write that down because I know they ain't going to know what I'm talking about" (*WR* 79). Constituting anything but a verbally-inept sufferer, the protagonist, with her premeditated use and manipulation of words, subtly identifies herself as someone who understands how to use language to her advantage.

A degree of cleverness, of calculated posturing, appears to be functioning in the protagonist, which goes beyond the formulaic social milieu and naturalistic apparatus Jones establishes at the beginning of the story. Later, when the niece who has committed her comes to visit, the narrator, purposefully, it seems, attempts to disturb her: "I say I'm feeling real fine except everytime I go sit down on the toilet this long black rubbery thing comes out a my bowls" (*WR* 80). Having employed vulgar terminology consistent with mental unsoundness once again, the protagonist, as she had done earlier, undermines her own madness narrative by explaining her outburst: "I have scared her and she doesn't come back" (*WR* 80). Later, when the doctor asks her to tell him what she is thinking, she appears to play with him, asking, "*Is that the only way I can be freed?* [Jones's italics]" (*WR* 81). However, as Karrer notes, for the most part, the protagonist appears to have freed herself already: "The narrator of 'Asylum' does not necessarily look for harmony, nor does she live in her community. But she uses dialogue to assess knowledge claims as a means of empowerment" (100). Through her deployment of linguistic signifying, the protagonist finds herself in a circumstance where she controls the content and meaning of language and, subsequently, her situation. Furthermore, the more unusual things she tells the doctor, the more likely it is that she will remain institutionalized, which keeps her in what she considers a relatively comfortable environment ("I don't bother nobody and they don't bother me" [*WR* 80]) and saves her from returning to an unhappy domestic situation and the niece she detests. With everyone assuming she wishes to escape the proverbial briar patch, the protagonist maintains a formidable degree of agency and comfort by remaining there on terms of her own making.

As Karrer asserts, "Beneath the asylum tale lies the slave narrative" (96) and the specter of societal racism, which subtly manifests itself through the mental institution's hierarchy in "Asylum," serves as the central concern of "Legend" (1977), in which a white man orchestrates a grotesque act — the rape of his daughter by a slave named Eph Grizzard — in an attempt to achieve freedom from the guilt of racism. However, the grotesque repercussions of this event include madness for both his daughter (*WR* 151) and himself (*WR* 149) and the lynching of Grizzard, the response of a frightened and outraged white community. Grizzard is hung by a rope from a bridge and over the years the structure begins taking on symbolic, psychological implications, coming to serve as the physical manifestation of the macabre "legend" which constitutes the story's title. However, although the bridge's legacy is horrific, the community is reluctant to destroy it: "In all these years, the bridge has not collapsed. Men are afraid to tear it down. They are afraid to keep it up. They built another bridge beside it" (*WR* 149). Serving as a monument to the hate, violence, and madness generated by racism, the bridge endures since the black and white communities cannot imagine a world without it and, by implication, without racism. As the narrator notes, "White people, sometimes black, hold their breath when they go over" (*WR* 149), yet all are too frightened to take it upon themselves to destroy the edifice. For all its horrific connotations, in the end the bridge constitutes a grotesque stench the community can live with, albeit one it would like to ignore. However, the specter of race-based violence is not one to be disregarded. As the narrator asserts, "[Grizzard's] soul is a tongue that can't keep quiet" (*WR* 151), recounting his grotesque tale of hate, violence, and madness from beyond the grave and across time to people who would rather not hear it.

New Person, Same Subject

Jones's interest in various grotesque societal constructions of slavery and the madness that often accompanies them did not conclude with the stories in *White Rat*. In "Goosens" (1982), Jones relates the mental illness of Miss Goosens, who had been a child-actor in a plantation drama in which the slave-character, played by Goosens, was repeatedly ordered about and demeaned by her young white mistress. As a result of this experience, the elder Miss Goosens attempts to emulate a white, southern *grande dame* to the best of her ability, dressing in a pompously ridiculous ultra-feminine fashion, stating her opinions with a haughty righteousness, and repeatedly professing to deplore ignorance. "Goosens" is unique and ingenious in that its protagonist's race-based trauma proceeds not from a genuine slavery experience, but a media-constructed drama taking place in an idealized plantation South. Yet, for Goosens the psychological impact is just as destructive. Extremely fat, made-up, ribboned, and pampered (54), Goosens constitutes a physical grotesque even without the accompanying symbolic knowledge that she is attempting to emulate the oppressive leading lady from her childhood television program. As the young female narrator explains, "Suddenly, I understood. Miss Goosens was describing herself, but not her real self— not the real little girl she'd once been. Somehow she thought she was the other one. It was the little white girl she was describing and not the black girl" (57). Despite her mental illness and the grotesque nature of her charade, Goosens, still possessing the successful dramatic presence of an actress, has a powerful and impressive effect on the young narrator who muses, "I saw her as dignified, solitary, self-possessed[...]. I wouldn't have tolerated anyone calling her outlandish. I would have defended her against anybody" (58). Despite and perhaps even because of her grotesque behavior, Goosens inspires feelings of loyalty and protection in the young narrator, herself not much older than Goosens' childhood character. Comprehending the race-based, grotesque scenario before her, the protagonist responds with empathy rather than disgust.

Although "Goosens" was published in 1982 and constitutes a first-person narrative, Jones, in an interview the same year, professed:

> I've been moving into third person stories — to do it and to see what changes there are — the "voice" of them is different, sometimes less "natural" though I want to get more of a fluidity in them. Many of the stories in *The Straw Woman*— a new collection — are in third person, in fact, I think most of them are — the opposite of the *White Rat* collection just from that[4] [Rowell, "Interview" 37].

While Jones may have abandoned the intimate tone of her first-person narratives, in at least one of her new stories she maintained a thematic interest in the often grotesque interactions between society and mentally-ill African Americans. "The Seige"[5] (1982) introduces another character, Jean Zane, suffering from schizophrenia: "A twenty-two year old woman with a shotgun, barricaded in a room in Cleveland" (89). The narrator's initial description of Zane serves as a kind of euphemistic definition for schizophrenia: "Underneath her mask of defiance, there's another mask, and underneath that one another one, until one peels back the terror in anyone's soul" (89). Zane's paradoxical, schizophrenic references to herself symbolically align her with Joseph Corey in "The Return: A Fantasy" and "Version 2." Just as Corey relates that he can transform himself into Jesus or an ant (*WR* 173), Zane simultaneously likens herself to "a leopard and a mouse" (89). An additional connection between Corey and Zane exists in their relationship to food. Just as she had used grotesque food imagery to underscore Corey's misfiring perceptions (*WR* 173–174), Jones establishes a similar dynamic for Zane: "She chews a raw onion" (89). However, whereas the two respective versions of Corey's condition are rendered by himself and from the loving, sympathetic viewpoint of his wife, Zane appears to the reader through an anonymous, albeit partially sympathetic, third-person narrator, which enables the reader to maintain a certain objective distance from the story's mentally-ill protagonist.

Although "The Seige" mirrors "The Return: A Fantasy" and "Version 2" in its focus on schizophrenia, it is more thorough than either of those works in dramatizing the interaction between mental illness and society. Society's presence is felt through the police, who eventually charge her apartment, as well as her family, who have "traveled there to talk to her" (89), presumably at the authorities' request. Her mother calls to her, "I know you're no wicked girl" (89), aligning herself and morality with the practice of societal compliance. Yet, as the narrator remarks, "[Zane] knows she's not wicked, but she knows they've made up their own words for her" (89), underscoring society's problematic and demonizing construction of madness through a supposedly scientific language of deviance. Interestingly, a similar dynamic of scientific categorization also appears in the form of Zane's ill-fated lover, a mycologist and former ethics professor who had written an unsuccessful book on love and later become disillusioned with ethics (93). However, for all his interest in the classification of mushrooms, the scholar appears to possess a grotesque interest in entities, be they mushrooms or people, that do not conform to their communities and possess dangerous capacities. For example, he offhandedly informs Zane, "Benjamin Franklin used to write obscene novels that were banned by the government" (90). A symbolic association begins to emerge between Zane and the professor's mushrooms in which identification and death play key roles. Just as the scholar knows that Zane is schizophrenic and possibly dangerous but gets involved with her anyway, so Zane maintains that he ate a poisonous mushroom even though "[h]e knew it wasn't the right mushroom" (94). Yet, the reader also must weigh the credibility of Zane's claims with her obvious state of agitation, inability to reconstruct her time with the mycologist ("a jumble of events and fragments" [94]), and what appear to constitute guilt-ridden manifestations of self-reproach: "She feels that she's the antagonist in the story[…]. She's the oddity. If there are devils dressed up like human women, she feels she's one. She feels crowded and confused" (94). Afforded a distanced, third-person perspective, the reader is able to establish two possible readings: either Zane genuinely is distraught over what she claims to be the mycologist's suicide ("I would have followed him anywhere but *there*" [94]), or she is agitated and combative as a result of having murdered him. The story's clues tend to favor the latter interpretation, especially since Jones's narrator never provides any motive for the scholar's suicide. By contrast, the narrator reveals Zane's willingness to lie when the mycologist asks her about her medication: "She didn't tell him she'd forgotten it, left it in the car" (93). Through these devices, Jones performs a kind of twist on her earlier schizophrenic narratives. Whereas those first-person stories established a kind of empathy between narrative, reader, and mentally-ill protagonist, "The Seige" initially constructs a similar framework only to undermine it via the alternate readings afforded through third-person narration. At the end, readers are left with the likelihood that Zane is not so much a harmless, misunderstood victim of society but a violently insane murderer — a grotesque figure possessing the agency to kill.

The Grotesque and the Search for Identity

Although Jones's psychological tales constitute unique meditations on the intersections between madness, society, and the grotesque, not all of her short fiction is concerned with the dynamics of mentally-ill characters. In fact, some of her best stories invoke the grotesque while tracing the struggles of mentally healthy individuals as they attempt to achieve meaningful autonomy and identities in problematic communities. For example, in "A Sense of Security" (1973) a wandering male character subtly evokes himself in recounting "them people that jus' come over across the border and work[...]. People without a country" (87); while in her early autobiographical story "The Welfare Check" (1970), Jones dramatizes the difficulties of a young, educated African American woman "fresh out of college and doing what the black kids were supposed to be doing, or talked of doing, returning to the community" (67). Yet, perhaps the strongest representation of community-based adversity appears in "White Rat" (1975), in which the narrator, White Rat or Rat, is made into a physical and social grotesque by his marginal identity. Although he possesses predominantly Caucasian features such as blonde hair, Rat, culturally and linguistically, is an exclusive product of an African American community, which predictably gives rise to several awkward social episodes. In this way Jones takes her turn at the literary "passing" narrative, exemplified in notable works such as Twain's *Pudd'nhead Wilson* and James Weldon Johnson's *The Autobiography of an Ex-Colored Man*, among many others.

Jerry W. Ward, Jr. has identified entrapment as the paramount theme of Jones's passing story,[6] and Rat's physical appearance certainly does restrict and categorize him in that strangers consider him white, much to his fury, if he travels beyond the confines of his neighborhood (*WR* 6). For example, Rat is traumatized when he and his friends, all African Americans, are arrested out-of-town for drunk-driving and he is forced to stay in a cell with white prisoners (*WR* 7). Later, he has difficulties marrying Maggie because a court house official believes Rat is white and does not wish to perform an interracial marriage. However, the interpretive focus on physical appearance and race is not limited to white authority figures such as police officers and court officials. Indeed, Rat and his immediate African American community also define people largely in terms of their physical characteristics. For example, at one point Rat describes two police officers known to him and his friends as Fat Dick and Skinny Dick" (*WR* 7). Furthermore, the focus on physical appearance and skin color also is reinforced by his family. His mother informs him that when he came out he looked "just like a little white rat" (*WR* 5), which leads directly to his ambivalent naming. It is also implied over the course of the story that Rat hates white people more than his African American peers because he resembles them, which also was true of his light-skinned father: "My daddy hate hoogies (up North I hear they call em honkies) worser than anybody" (*WR* 5). The correlation between physical appearance, naming, and (self-)hate causes Maggie to resist Rat's suggestion that they call their son White Rabbit, fearing that the name will cause him to develop a complex when he grows up (*WR* 5). Of course, Maggie's fears are well-founded, based on the behavior of Rat, who laments, "I keep telling Maggie it get harder and harder to be a white nigger now specially since it don't count no more how much white blood you got in you, in fact, it make you worser for it" (*WR* 9). The combination of these problematic variables has resulted in remarkably contradictory critical readings of the story. Whereas Charles R. Larson labels Rat "a refreshing image of the black male" ("Uneven" D6), interpreting an acceptance of his deformed child and estranged wife, Carol Pearson believes he "can neither learn who he is nor love his light-skinned wife and club-footed child" (1678). Interestingly, Rat's confusing and ambivalent identity also appears to baffle critics. As an anonymous reviewer perceptively observes, the symbol of the white rat is "the sign of miscegenation and acculturation, which eats away black identity, manhood, and womanhood" ("Review of *White Rat*," *Choice* 1644). If the rat, as grotesque, debilitating symbol, confuses and erodes identity, then generating clear-cut meanings in the story becomes all the more difficult. In this way, Jones not only sets a "mouse-trap" for her protagonist, but by the reader as well.

Jones continues her meditations on identity development and race-based social conflicts in stories such as "Your Poems Have Very Little Color in Them" (1977) and "A Quiet Place for the Summer" (1977). The former narrative is unique in its use of grotesque humor as a catalyst for cultural commentary. As the story's protagonist — a female, African American, college student at a predominantly white institution — recounts:

Once I was making up funny songs and telling funny stories to the girls in the dorm. They thought they were very funny at first. But since I did it all the time and was never serious except with a few close friends, one close friend, they got tired of my funny songs and funny stories and dances. And so I am not funny anymore nor free. They were very disgusted and made me feel bad [WR 19].

Unable to connect with her white classmates, the speaker's attempts to fit in make her feel "not free" and carry negative psychological repercussions. More troubling though is the fact that the narrator's staged acceptance overtures involve a kind of signifying that borders on minstrelsy. She entertains her peers by attempting to embody an antiquated stereotype ("the ever-smiling, Negro entertainer"), only to have them reject her anyway. This dynamic is brought home symbolically at the story's conclusion when the young women view a movie on television in which Kirk Douglas's character forcibly kisses, and perhaps even rapes, a Native American woman. Her dormmates oblivious to the plight of the racial other, only the protagonist notices the film's cultural exploitation narrative — a theme to which she can relate.

Anticipating "Your Poems Have Very Little Color in Them," one of Jones's earliest published poems, "Tripart" (1970), records the challenges and pressures of an African-American protagonist attending a white college: "a very friendly/prison/this is —/white kids discussing politics/and suddenly your nerves have a finished/form (half-digested rage)—" (209). This preoccupation with adverse, cross-cultural adversity is more fully developed in "A Quiet Place for the Summer" (1977), in which the primary character — a female, African American writing student from Georgia — house-sits for her favorite professor, a middle-aged white man named Martin, over the course of a summer in Vermont. Jones uses the local groundskeeper, Coleman, to identify the protagonist with a transplanted tree. Coleman relates, "[T]his is a beautiful tree[...]. Some people would look at her and think she was deformed, but she's not[...]. I like her because I replanted her here[...]. A tree can be so still and have so much going on inside it. There are people like that, you know" (WR 157). Like the tree, the protagonist finds herself in an alien environment (a white New England community) where she naturally is perceived as a cultural other. She also suggests Coleman's description of the tree in that, as a writer, she constitutes a figure of internal contemplation ("so much going on inside it") while projecting a silent outward demeanor. The African American side of the protagonist's cultural conflict is articulated through Calvin, a fellow African American student and political activist, who is concerned about her affection for Martin and warns her that he may have unwholesome intentions (*WR* 158). Coleman, a member of the white community, wonders about her relationship to the professor as well, asking her what they are "to each other" (*WR* 159).

Through Coleman the protagonist learns of Martin's estranged wife, who is possibly insane and reappears at the house periodically for days at a time, only to depart again, sometimes in the company of a man. Coleman paints the professor's wife in dark terms before asking the protagonist if she's afraid "one night you'll be sleeping and a strange woman will come into the house and find you in her bed" (*WR* 161). Literally, the professor's wayward wife functions as a haunting grotesque; she tells Coleman, "I feel I must be crazy" (*WR* 163) and he notices, "Her fingernails were bit all the way down to the quick" (*WR* 163). However, she also constitutes a symbolic grotesque, looming over the protagonist and Martin, preventing — with the help of collective pressure from Calvin, Coleman, and the professor's New England community — the possibility of any romantic relationship between them. Unable to free themselves from their personal pasts and the cultural assumptions of others, their interaction remains spectral and largely imaginary.

Jones's narratives involving foiled heterosexual relationships — stories such as "A Quiet Place for the Summer," "The Return: A Fantasy," "Version 2," "Jevata," and "The Seige" — are countered, quite unexpectedly, by an early story entitled "The Roundhouse" (1971), the idea for which originally was conceived when Jones was in highschool as a romantic story about expatriate writers called "The Guitar." In "The Roundhouse" Jones focuses on a mysterious American immigrant rather than American writers journeying abroad. Employing romantic and sentimental fictional conventions and largely ignoring community, the story departs from the themes of grotesque societal pressures and personal freedom that inform the rest of Jones's short fiction. For example, the nearly mute drifter protagonist, Jake, functions as more of an attractive cultural other than a grotesque ("He looked like a foreigner, reddish brown. Maybe he was a

Negro, maybe he was Puerto Rican or something or maybe mixed" [*WR* 137]). After the central female character tends to Jake while he is ill, he leaves town only to return later to marry her — an unexpectedly straightforward and uncomplicated happy ending. Against the grotesque environments, personal angst, and occasional madness of Jones's other stories, "The Roundhouse" appears as a fictional anomaly, an abrupt and perhaps purposeful change of pace, unique in its portrayal of a largely conventional love story.

The heterosexual harmony of "The Roundhouse" is not duplicated in either of Jones's lesbian narratives, "The Women" (1977) and "Persona" (1977). The former story is the account of young Winnie Flynn's coming of age against the backdrop of her mother's numerous and constant female lovers. Jones's use of the grotesque first appears in the story through a nine-year-old boy, Freddy, who educates Winnie in society's vulgar categorizations of carnality before having sex with her. Freddy informs Winnie that her mother's lover, Miss Maybell, has "a pussy mouth" (*WR* 26) and warns her that she very well may develop the same condition: "When you grow up you gonna be jus' like your mama" (*WR* 27). As a result of Freddy's crude description of the human body and her mother's constant affairs, Winnie begins to reduce all social interaction to sexuality. For example, when she begins going to school, she informs her teacher, Miss Fletcher, that her mother had slept with another teacher named Fanny Bean, before asserting, "My mama sleep with you too" (*WR* 33). Her mother's example and Freddy's warning to her about becoming a lesbian also serve to mobilize her against the practice. During puberty she resolves, "I ain' goin' be like my mama when I grow up. I ain' goin' be a bitch's whore" (*WR* 43). Yet, her fascination with the female body and sexuality remain strong and unwavering. She calls her best friend, Retta Pace, "pussy" (*WR* 39–40) and the most important aspect of their relationship involves "who started bleeding first" (*WR* 42). When Winnie finally lends herself to a sexual encounter with Garland Morton in her mother's bedroom she resolves to determine her own actions in her sex-based universe. Yet, this resolution rings hollow since it is built upon the foundation of Freddy's grotesque constructions of lesbianism and her hatred and embarrassment for her mother's sexual practices. Until she is able to meaningfully confront these prejudices, she cannot genuinely explore her sexuality or truly be herself.

Jones shifts her perspective from a sexually-confused girl to a secure adult lesbian in "Persona" (1977). Professor King, a member of the faculty at a women's college, recounts her journey toward sexual identity over the course of the story while attempting to seduce one of her students, a shy young woman named Gretta. However, Gretta appears to sense King's attraction to her and is quiet and detached in return, resisting any possible overtures. When King invites Gretta and her friend, Susan, to dinner at her home Gretta is "uncomfortable" (*WR* 88) and the professor observes that "her knees were so close together" (*WR* 91).[7] However, Gretta's friend, Susan, is passionate, uninhibited, and intellectual. She criticizes the lack of eroticism in T.S. Eliot's poetry (*WR* 88) and, in the story's major twist, eventually becomes King's lover. As in "Jevata," Jones's protagonist is denied the thing she desires most, yet she is spared, like few of Jones's other characters, madness or perverse self-abnegation. Instead, she contents herself as best she can with Susan who in some ways suggests a younger version of herself. Just as King had gone to a female doctor when she was young and become aroused when the doctor examined her (to the point that she "kept going back to her" [*WR* 86]), so Susan discovers her sexual orientation through her repeated visits to Dr. King. In this way — and in direct opposition to "The Women"— the story serves as a favorable meditation on the liberation and assertion of sexual identity against a society that generally condemns it.

Voices of Freedom

Unlike the predominantly visceral and sexual narratives in *White Rat*, Jones's stories from the early 1980s that involve mentally-healthy individuals attempting to break free from restrictive personal and cultural relationships employ distanced third-person narration and exhibit a specific focus on creative and abstract aesthetic freedom. In "Those Rock People" (1982)[8] the protagonist, a popular performer of rock music, weighs her success and the joys of artistic self-expression against the condemnations of society and her reproachful ex-husband. To a child who sees her in the street she constitutes a kind of freakish grotesque in terms of appearance: "She remembered some kid pointing at her weird stockings. The mother, old enough not to be confused by oddities, explained, 'That's one of those rock people'" (59).⁹ The societal censure she feels from time to time is accompanied by her ex-husband's disdain for her career. A stern microbiologist, he had sought to inhibit her desire to become a controversial rock performer. Their problematic interaction over the course of the story is compared by the protagonist to the positive relationship between Carolina Tola and her husband, Abio. The protagonist likens herself to Tola, a Sicilian woman who "told them [her community] to bugger off and I went globe trotting" (63). However, unlike the protagonist, Tola enjoys a happy marriage based on the ability of her and her husband "to escape our very different terrors" (64). No such comfort or connection exists for the protagonist and her ex-husband. Although she has gained the expressive, creative freedom she desires, she lacks and envies the bond enjoyed by Tola and Abio, realizing that such a rapport is no longer possible between her and her former husband.

Although it appears in a more subtle form, the interaction between personal relationships and aesthetic expression also serves as a central concern in "The Day of the God" (1982), the title suggesting Paul Gaugin's 1894 painting of the same name, which depicts several nude women bathing, relaxing, and sleeping while a dark idol, the center of the work, looms over them. In Jones's story the painting hangs in the living room of John and Gloria. A gift from Gloria's first husband, Albert Wadsworth, the print functions as a silent symbolic sentinel, monitoring the couple and their son, Albert Jr.— Wadsworth's biological son. Just as Gaugin's dark idol subtly presides over the figures in the painting, so Wadsworth haunts Gloria's and John's marriage, infrequently appearing for the purpose of seeing his son. The tension produced by this situation has transformed John—who fears and resents Wadsworth—into a kind of grotesque, his petty hatred of Wadsworth manifesting itself in a number of ways. For example, he repeatedly offers Wadsworth drinks even though he knows he is combating alcoholism (74) and also insists on calling him "Mister" (75), accentuating and mocking that fact that he is fifteen years Wadsworth's junior. Furthermore, like Miss Goosens, he is physically grotesque, Wadsworth impartially remarking that John is as "hideous as he is handsome" (76). In the end, John's favorite expression ("Everybody's a bastard") is perhaps most applicable to himself. Although he is Gloria's husband and is raising young Albert, he struggles to enjoy his family while Wadsworth is still involved in their lives. While Gaugin's dark idol looms over a paradisal milieu, Wadsworth threatens and sours for John what should be an enjoyable and fulfilling domestic existence.

Less spectral and more explicit aesthetic dynamics haunt the protagonist of "Prophet Powers" (1982), Ezra, a sculptor who confronts the classic artistic dilemma between aesthetic impulse and societal expectations. Under contract to create a sculpture of Mary for a local church, Ezra's first attempt is rejected by the sect's leadership on account of her "funny grin and the wanton belly, the passionate black eyes" (80). What for Ezra suggests passion and vivacity constitutes disturbingly grotesque sensuality for the church hierarchy. In his second attempt Ezra asks a local bartender, called Marla or Jet, to serve as a model, yet his artistic vision is overwhelmed by sensuality again. For a time he wavers between the church's vision and his own: "He wants to do a real piece of her, to mold her breasts. But to the congregation the breasts are mostly fictions, as the other points of privacy. He broods over each stroke" (83). As he admits to Jet, in the end his own artistic inclinations win out: "Halfway through I stopped making it for them[...]. I started making it for you" (84).

Although it exhibits elements of societal conflict and the grotesque, "Prophet Powers," with its specific focus on cultural pressures and the artist, stands out from Jones's other short fiction in its aesthetic-minded self-reflexivity, while also resisting the temptation to stray too far into symbolism or myth — a criticism occasionally leveled at highly intertextual writers like Gloria Naylor. In dramatizing the artist's interaction with socio-political expectations, the story anticipates Jones's German novel *Die Vogelfängerin* or *The Birdcatcher*,[10] which recounts a struggling black female sculptor's decision to alter her work in order to avoid accusations that she is furthering racial stereotypes of blacks. Of course, the novel consciously draws upon the critical condemnations and political attacks that Jones received for her potently violent and sexual novels *Corregidora* and *Eva's Man*. Tragically and ironically, Jones herself appears to have undergone several of the cultural denunciations and categorizations dramatized by characters in her short fiction. With its penchant for shocking and upsetting conventional interpretive systems, the grotesque possesses the ability to jolt readers into the reality of a text, forcing them to produce meanings. That certain critics have attempted to paint Jones herself as a grotesque is a testament to the raw literary power — what one initial reviewer called "forcefulness" ("Review of *White Rat*," *Booklist* 140) — generated by her unique and sometimes distorted narratives.[11] Against protests from various corners of literary culture, Jones continued to write and — as in "Prophet Powers" and *Die Vogelfängerin* — even assimilated the critical attacks and underlying dilemma of art and politics into her fiction. Just as many of her characters escape grotesque conditions and discourses through language and the act of telling, so Jones continued to generate linguistic art and meaning, often employing grotesque vehicles such as madness and brutality, in the face of readings that wished to institutionalize her achievement, reducing and regimenting the rich dynamics of her work to various homogenizing agendas.

Notes

1. See, for example, Ivan Webster, "Really the Blues," *Time* 105 (16 June 1975) 79; and Jessica Harris, "Review of *Eva's Man*," *Essence* 7.2 (June 1976) 87. Also, in *The Afro-American Novel and Its Tradition* Bernard W. Bell characterizes *Corregidora* and *Eva's Man* as black feminist works with grisly gothic elements (267).
2. "Black Vortex: The Gothic Structure of *Eva's Man*." *Melus* 7.4 (1980) 93–101.
3. Jones specifically identifies the influence of these particular psychologists on her thinking in her dissertation, "Toward and All-Inclusive Structure," Brown U, 1973, 2–3.
4. *The Straw Woman* has not appeared in print to date. However, four of the five stories Jones published in the October 1982 issue of *Callaloo* are rendered in third-person narration ("Goosens" being the only exception).
5. It is unclear whether the alternative spelling of "siege" is purposeful or not.
6. "Escape from Trublem: The Fiction of Gayl Jones," *Callaloo* 16.3 (October 1982) 98.
7. Jones constructs a similar milieu with a different kind of sexual tension at a professor's house in "Sticks and Witches Brooms" (1978).
8. Details and descriptions from "Those Rock People" would appear later in Jones's novel, *The Healing* (1998).
9. This dynamic in the story also constitutes another example of Jones's interest in the problematic connection between culturally-influenced interpretations of appearance and genuine identity. For example, in an earlier story, "Sentences" (1975), the protagonist is troubled by her friend's identification of a woman as a prostitute: "I asked him how he knew. He said he could just tell. I asked him if he thought I was one" (47).
10. Hamburg: Rowohlt, 1986. The novel has not been translated into English.
11. For example, June Jordan attacked Jones by posing the question: "What does it mean when a young black woman sits down to compose a universe of black people limited to animal dynamics?" (37).

CHAPTER 3

Toward Feminine Mythopoetic Visions: Poetry

> *"The center of* Song for Anninho *is a love story and I also wanted to move beyond the 'blues relationships' of most of my earlier published stories to perhaps the 'spiritual mode.'"*
> — Gayl Jones in Rowell, "Interview" 41

Her distinguished body of fiction having received significant accolades and critical attention, Jones's comparably understated, yet formidable, corpus of poetry — three books and an assortment of uncollected published pieces — consistently has been overlooked, if not almost ignored, by readers and scholars of her work.[1] Yet, significantly, Jones's first publication appeared in verse[2]; and her literary production from 1969 through the early 1980s includes nearly as many poems as short stories, betraying a formative and consistent involvement with poetry. Furthermore, Jones's serious interest in the intellectual and cultural legacies of African American verse in particular is confirmed in her critical study of African American literature, *Liberating Voices*, in which she makes the important general observation, "African American poetry from the turn of the century to the present shows a movement toward the freeing of African American character and voice in literature" (17). Jones's critical summary of the genre in which she practices has consequences for her creative work as well. In its own particular development across the decades of the 1970s and 1980s Jones's poetry, on a smaller scale and over a much more compressed period of time, reflects a similar narrative aesthetic shift, from a concern with separate single voices involved usually in problematic personal relationships to viewpoints and utterances articulating cultural issues across time and place — a shift that would eventually become palpable in her fiction as well with the publications of *The Healing* (1998) and *Mosquito* (2000).

Jones's lack of critical recognition as a poet is at least partially traceable to her documented ambivalence regarding genre boundaries and her own artistic identity: "I've never really considered myself a poet. I've written what I call poetry but I've always thought of myself as primarily a fiction writer and so I write poetry from the viewpoint and interest of a storyteller — the concern with character and event" (Rowell, "Interview" 39). Consistent with this self-conceptualization of her creative output, Jones's critical observations regarding the work of other poets often are based on the execution of techniques traditionally associated with distinguished fiction writing. For example, she believes Sherley A. Williams's "Someone Sweet Angel Chile" is an important poem because "She makes the character/singer speak for and identify herself, take authority over her own story, and recreate her song. In the multitude of other voices we have listeners/witnesses become storytellers and storytellers become listener/witnesses" (*LV* 43). For Jones, narrative and its rendering usually appear to outweigh the various poetic conventions of prosody and form. While reviewing the work of Sterling Brown in a critical capacity, Jones provides a checklist of what chiefly attracts her in poetry: "The variety and quality of characterizations, the interplay of voices, dramatic forms, histories, scenes, portraits, the range and integrity of voice" ("A Review of the Collected Poems of Sterling Brown" 43). Again, characterization and narrative voice appear in the foreground, accompanied by such fictional structural concerns as dramatic forms and scenes, all of which come together to reveal a sensibility interested primarily in formulating a poetics of effective storytelling.

Also listed among Jones's poetic concerns is an interest in "histories," the implications of which hold a special significance for African American poets. Lorenzo Thomas, speaking for a multitude of scholars, describes the persistent inability of African American writers to be aesthetically insular in the face of their collective histories: "[E]ven had black poets wished to create within the pristine seclusion of a 'dark tower,' their color made it impossible for them to avoid involvement in the turbulent racial politics of the United States" (8). Expanding her historical interest in race beyond the boundaries of the United States, Jones's work is unique in its specific, repeated meditations on historical, race-based oppression in Brazil. Perhaps this foreign focus is not altogether unusual since, in the very broadest of terms, contemporary Brazil shares with the United States a climate of race-relations generally governed by class status, in which prejudice against African ancestry often is outweighed by respect for higher class status. Yet, the fact that Jones imports the overwhelming majority of her historical material from South America significantly differentiates her from most other historically-minded African American writers working in the United States. As the Brazilian scholar Stelmaris Cosner summarizes, "Jones's research on slave history in Brazil informs a kind of work that is original and unique" (122). Coser also correctly observes that in Jones's first book of poetry, *Song For Anninho*, she, "with an identification and a solidarity based on gender and race, brings out of forgetfulness voices of black women abused in the Brazilian past" (123)—an endeavor that separates the work from the verse Jones produced in the early-to-mid 1970s, poems dealing primarily with romantic and philosophical relationships between African Americans in the contemporary United States.

As Jones notes, her shift from contemporary African American relationships in the United States to those historically-situated in Brazil was accompanied by an overarching philosophical transition: "The center of *Song for Anninho* is a love story and I also wanted to move beyond the 'blues relationships' of most of my earlier published stories to perhaps the 'spiritual mode'" (Rowell, "Interview" 41). Seeking a "spiritual mode," Jones appears to have attempted to forsake the overtly visceral, violent, and sexual concerns of her earlier work for the more abstract corridors of international history and legend. In other words, she sought to evolve her art past her successfully-realized, relationship-based, blues poems to the more ambitious imagined historical domain of mythopoetic forms. As Susan Sellers notes at the conclusion of her book, *Myth and Fairy Tale in Contemporary Women's Fiction* (a study that includes discussions of works by A.S. Byatt, Angela Carter, Anne Rice, Michele Roberts, Emma Tennant and Fay Weldon), Jones is not alone in attempting to aesthetically transmute traditional history and myth: "Myth, it would appear from the wealth of women's adaptations and reworkings, is a potent force in contemporary feminist fiction. Yet as the discussions in this volume show, women's rewritings frequently alter the form of their source-myths and set them to very different purposes" (128). As her Brazilian poems clearly indicate, Jones is interested in dislocating and reinventing the forms of what Sellers calls "source-myths," recovering — partly through research, partly through the poetic imagination — muted voices across time. In this endeavor, Jones's approach is necessarily mythopoetic, creating nuances and legends to accompany and augment the history of an all but forgotten people. Essentially, mythopoesis is the production of myths, or mythmaking. Whereas mythology, in the broadest sense, studies and analyzes the mythic patterns of people and their cultures, mythopoesis involves the creation of new myths either through gradual cultural changes or by the work of those in the arts, or both. Taking Brazilian slave history as her subject, Jones uses her artistic imagination to confront and fill in the gaps of "objective history," constructing a memorial to a silenced culture and providing a moving conceptualization of it for readers in the present.

Blues Poems

Early in her career, Jones did not possess the necessary poetic tools to attempt mythopoetic renderings of historical cultures beyond the United States. Instead, like most young poets, she worked with more immediate materials such as dynamics of personal relationships and the African American culture that surrounded her and of which she was a member. A particularly fine example of the latter subject is her poem "Deep Song," published in 1975 but written much earlier in graduate school. One of Jones's professors at Brown University, the poet Michael Harper, recalls, "I remember asking Gayl Jones what she was listening to, and she said Billie Holiday, so I said why don't you write me a poem on Lady, and Gayl just smiled; she seldom said much, but a few days later I got a copy of 'Deep Song' under my door, dedicated to 'B.H.'" (Rowell, "Down" 798–799). "Deep Song" is an important poem in the way it explores the pain, love, and general ambivalence of romantic relationships while incorporating stylistic elements of the African American blues tradition — most notably, varied verbal and rhythmic repetition. The speaker sings a song that is part-celebration, part-lament, culminating in an intimation that the love and depth of feeling in her relationship flows equally from the evil and endearing aspects of the man she loves: "Deep Song" also reflects Jones's strong interest in narrative, her belief that the speaker and the listener must strive together for meaning. As Jones infers, this guiding dynamic also informs the poem's authorship: "I was listening to Bille Holiday when I wrote the poem—while I was writing it, I mean. I was writing it and listening at the same time" (Harper 700). Simultaneously functioning as hearer and speaker, reader and writer, Jones plays with the idea of narrative translation and interpretive layers of meaning. As she hears the song, she writes her poem, witnessing and passing it on to other listeners, most notably "B.H.," to whom it is inscribed and to whom she had originally "listened," in another sense, when he asked her to write the poem.

Jones's concern with tension-filled blues relationships in her poetry also dominates much of her fiction and drama from the 1970s: the novels *Corregidora* and *Eva's Man*, the plays *Chile Women* and "Beyond Yourself (The Midnight Confession) for Brother Ahh," and numerous short stories. And Jones was quite cognizant of the blues as a stylistic and philosophical catalyst across the different genres of her work. Commenting on a specific poem and novel, she asserts, "There is a relationship between 'Deep Song,' which is a blues poem, and *Corregidora*, which is a blues novel. Blues talks about the simultaneity of good and bad, as feeling, as something felt" (Harper 700). Not surprisingly, the poignant immediacy of what Jones conceptualizes as blues sensation or "something felt" functions most powerfully in her early poems, several of which share with "Deep Song" the tragic sense of pain and ambivalence in relationships between men and women. For example, in "The Lovers" (1974) the female protagonist is willing to give everything to her man, but in doing so "she is blind/she does not know he nibbles/slowly/at her heart" (89). Occasionally, the emotional ambivalence at the cores of these heart-rending relationships come to resemble Jones's second novel *Eva's Man* in their flirtations with psychological elements of the perverse. In "Jasper Notes" (1975), for instance, the female speaker relates a troubling interior monologue: "'But you must learn to love and not look for love/in return,' my mind said. 'Feel affection but not seek the consequences of affection'" (28). As in "The Lovers" the speaker gives of herself in a way that puts her heart in jeopardy while adding the depraved caveat that she should never expect anything in return for her love. In an important respect the poem constitutes a meditation on nihilism and negation, the speaker assuring her male counterpart, "'I'll never be to anyone what I couldn't be to you'" (33). Just as *Eva's Man* travels beyond the blues-narrative of *Corregidora* to investigate the debilitating psychological dynamics of sexuality, so poems like "Jasper Notes," while still containing blues elements and revolving around romantic relationships, essentially are comprised of psychologically-based statements of self-identity.

One of Jones's lighter and more successful blues poems is "The Cup" (1975), which portrays the juxtaposition of intimate and working worlds by recounting the journey of a peripatetic coffee cup. Thinking of the cup helps the female narrator, still at home in an intimate domestic sphere, to formulate how she and her lover "made love/all the sweet night long" (48). Bridging the worlds of work and pleasure, the cup functions as a reminder of private, personal bliss in "that world afterward," the separate and impersonal existence of the work place. Like "The Cup" and much of Jones's fiction, many of Jones's early blues poems employ physical objects, bodies, and actions in order to deliver their philosophical implications. "Party" (1976), for example, is loaded with strong images of diarrhea, heavy drinking, and sex, all functioning as grotesque signifiers of the poem's troubled male character, who feels compelled to drink excessively in order to have sex with the female protagonist. The poem's physical action makes its symbolic and psychological consequences all the more troubling. His expression before he has sex with her is "hateful" (56), yet she pulls him to her nevertheless. Jones continued to explore this dynamic of adverse ambivalence, narrated by uncertain and possibly abused female protagonists in a repetitive blues mode, into the late 1970s in poems such as "Alternative" (1979) and "Chance" (1979). In the former poem the female character suggests physical action (a walk) as a means of addressing the roadblocks in their relationship: "'Come, let's go for a walk,' she says./'No, *I'll* go,' he says [Jones's italics]" (111). Often Jones's male figures appear to remain enigmatic and emotionally distant, or even antagonistic, as a means of manipulating, dominating, and ultimately controlling the feelings of their female partners. When the woman in "Alternative" suggests a walk, the man makes an alternative imperative statement which rejects the woman's suggestion as well as her company. Developing the rejection theme further, "Chance" involves a female protagonist who is psychologically terrified of losing her man, resulting in an unhealthy one-sided relationship in which the woman is obsessed with constantly placating her lover: "She kisses him with fear/ ... afraid he'll think she wants something" (112). Blending tenuous physical fear and sexuality with a hint of psychological perversity, Jones again offers an association riddled with uncertainty and misplaced desire, demonstrating that the power of blues relationships proceeds as much from their real and immediate pain and suffering as from love.

Mythopoetic Groundwork: Abstractions and Prophets

Jones's collective blues poems involving visceral relationships are accompanied by a smaller group of pieces from the 1970s that comment on abstract, philosophical subjects in conjunction with African American culture and often involve prophets—subjects that lead, seemingly inevitably, to her eventual preoccupation with slavery and its consequences across national boundaries. In the poem "Part IV of *Journal*" (1979), Jones employs contemporary African American fashion and marketing as catalysts for a meditation on what constitutes cosmetic beauty and identity. Her speaker comments, "I think how in the black fashion/magazines they are using the/darker girls now" (208). Operating here is an affirmation of African American culture's movement away from European standards of physical beauty, while also acknowledging the ominous power of the media, both African American and mainstream, to manipulate the most basic and superficial ideals of the masses for good or ill. Removed from such dynamics of pop culture yet still involving African American history and contemporary identity, Jones's poems involving prophets seek to destabilize and reinvent notions of African American cultural and spiritual concerns, past and present. As early as 1970, having not yet received her undergraduate degree from Connecticut College, Jones, perhaps partially inspired by her teacher Robert Hayden, was investigating and interpreting African American history in poems involving prophetic figures and wide-ranging religious terminology. For example, in "Satori" (1970) the speaker springs "from the Buddha's forehead,/black as Jesus" (210), blurring the distinctions between the figureheads of different religions and their assumed ethnicities, which ultimately calls into question the conventional interpretations of their messages as well. Similarly ambiguous, in "Salvation" (1970) the protagonist believes she has become a Christian but still, "The African wind chimes tingle in the wind" (94), persistently reminding her of another and, in many respects, conflicting faith and culture from which she can never, and should not wish to, escape. Skepticism regarding established religions and cultures is accompanied by doubt of a self-proclaimed African American prophet in "The Gathering" (1976), in which the twenty-year-old, female speaker converses with Brother Eliot, a forty-year-old man who "thinks he's a prophet" (54). Refusing to romanticize the prophet figure as an idealized African American man, Jones uses "The Gathering" to explore the tension between the need for cultural and spiritual renewal and self-indulgent delusion and exploitation. Even at the poem's conclusion, the narrator is uncertain whether Eliot is a genuine avatar or merely a clever and mischievous man, a player, who cultivates an eccentric, sorcerous image (signifying, as it were, on the idea of true prophecy) for the purpose of attracting curious young women. In "The Gathering" Jones adroitly demonstrates that rediscovering one's own culture and spirituality, especially if the searcher is overly romantic or sentimental, often is accompanied by dangers and doubts.

In "Many Die Here" (1970), another poem from her undergraduate days, Jones has her speaker lament that her people have been allowed to "die without a name" (211), expressing a genuine concern for a perceived lack of identity among African Americans (a defining *logos* from which meaning may be derived). Developing from the seeds of historical identity in "Many Die Here" and accompanied by an increasingly palpable concern with spiritual abstractions and prophets, Jones's poems from the mid-to-late 1970s began demonstrating more international and cultural themes. In the historical narrative "Más Allá" (1975), Jones's first distinctly South American poem, her prophet narrator explains that his people are living in "a place where they kill you for dreaming" and that "they are afraid our dreams might break into flesh" (54). Significantly, the "they" in the poem, the slaveholding oppressors, fear the dreams of their chattels more than the immediate prospect of manifest rebellion. Yet, ever the unsentimental storyteller, as in "The Gathering," Jones generates dramatic tension by calling into question the prophet's legitimacy and even sanity. The poem's elderly male soothsayer carries a basket which he says contains onions and sardines, which the speaker describes as prophet's food, since only prophets may truly see (54). While the mystic may in fact possess a second sight derived from perceiving things not readily apparent, Jones simultaneously leaves open the possibility that he may simply be mad or delusional, imposing whatever compelling meanings he wishes on the nothingness surrounding him.

Journey to Brazil: Song for Anninho

Just as Nikki Giovanni's poetry moved from overtly and politically charged concern with "Black Revolution" toward a more universal style and content, so Jones eventually began too seek larger cultural and aesthetic milieus. Building upon her piquant prophecy-based narratives and researching South American history, she began paving the way for an extended poetic foray into the Brazilian past. The "The Fur Station" (1980) serves as a kind of theological precursor or prelude to *Song for Anninho* as the mixed-heritage hunter/protagonist attempts to contemplate and balance his cultural background and knowledge of the land with the Christian faith to which he clings. He claims he "don't believe in fantasisms and enchantments,/but ... you can't answer everything with logic" (23). At the center of this statement is the assumption that European Christianity, with all its self-assured links to knowledge, constitutes an inadequate world view for Brazil, a country with its own specific characteristics and set of seemingly fantastic legends. *Song for Anninho* (1981) is not so much concerned with this pre–European Brazil and its original people as with the implications of European colonization — physical, theological, philosophical — and, especially, the distinctive implementation and perpetuation of slavery by the Portuguese. The book's central social focus, the Palmares society — founded almost entirely by escaped slaves and based in Macaco, Brazil — had successfully resisted, evaded, and withstood Portuguese attacks for almost a century, when on February 6, 1694 Domingos Jorge Velho's seasoned mercenaries effectively assaulted, plundered, and burned the settlement. In the aftermath, thousands of Palmares men from Macaco and other nearby villages were slaughtered. Women and children generally were left unharmed, at least physically, although many mothers resolved to murder their own children and starve themselves rather than become Portuguese chattels. As Coser recounts, "Letters and records reveal that Negro Women who did not breed as often as they should had breasts amputated or sexual organs mutilated" (209), a horrifying prospect — hauntingly conveyed in *Song for Anninho* — to which self-inflicted death perhaps was preferable.

Against such a brutally violent historical background, Jones sought to evoke the implacable will and spirit of the Palmares people to endure while relating their experiences to those of all African-descended slaves and their respective descendants across time. As Richard Jackson accurately observes, *Song for Anninho* is "a spiritual journey through memory over time, a remembering beyond Palmares that establishes a place for blacks in the world. In the same larger sense, *Song for Anninho* is a story of hope and freedom, of perseverance and the will to survive" (138). In her discussion of the poem and the unpublished prose version of it, "Palmares,"[3] Jones verifies Jackson's reading, while also describing at great length her overlapping use of myth, history, and imagination in creating the book-length poem:

> *Song for Anninho* is a poetic fictional account whose focus is on "spirit" and interior landscape — the landscape of imagination and dream and memory. The characters are certainly living in an "oppressive time and space," the battles with the Dutch and then the Portuguese to maintain their freedom in Palmares, the state formed by fugitive Brazilian slaves in the 17th century. But even in my book *Palmares* that the poem is adapted from, I don't even focus on the final battle — because it is the consequences to character and circumstance that is the "significant event." If Anninho rather than Almeyda had told the story, the focus would have been the battle, I think, and the raids and spying expeditions and the trading, etc. Perhaps it's a flaw that I don't focus on the battle. Perhaps I bend the idea of the "significant event"[...]. But neither *Song for Anninho* nor *Palmares* — as I've written them — neither one is political social documents of the time. On one page of the book, Almeyda describes what it is and what it's supposed to be when she says — "But it's not the actions I wish to capture but the spirit!" Of course, the fictional version has to capture more events — but the focus is "personalized, psychological" [Rowell, "Interview" 43].

The "personalized, psychological, spiritual" elements Jones evokes conspire to allow the poem to transcend its self-appointed place in history — "neither one is political social documents of the time" — and serve as a timeless philosophical meditation on slavery. As Trudier Harris perceptively summarizes, it is "through Almeyda's sights and values, we come to see the strength of her people, and we come to hope — with her — that they might one day establish a spiritual and physical unity that will withstand all oppressors" (103).

In order to forge the compelling spiritual unity capable of resisting brutally violent oppression, Jones first had to convincingly present the nightmarish physical suffering which paradoxically fueled both the Portuguese ability to oppress and the Palmares determination to resist. Before *Song for Anninho*, seemingly as a kind of exercise, Jones had sought to investigate this visceral dynamic in "The Father" (1975), which explores a parent-child bond forged and problematized in the process of an agonizing flight from slavery. The child-narrator says of the journey with her father, "His wife carried me ... till the pack cut her shoulders/but their footprints were still kisses" (4). Mingling physical suffering and abstract affection, Jones uses the images of lacerated flesh and the prints of exhausted feet to underscore simultaneously the pain of the family's journey and the love that accompanies it. Significantly, the physical anguish fills an important emotional and structural function, the broken skin serving as an entry point for love and the footprints forming a palpable trail of kisses. Jones mingles similar images of slavery-related physical tribulations with historical implications in her early fictional renderings of episodes involving Almeyda and Anninho — scenes that were never translated over into the story's poetic version and provide important insight into Almeyda's and Anninho's relationship. In "From Almeyda" (1975) Almeyda describes how falling in love with Anninho was irrevocably marred by the historical conditions of their time: "I remember when we came to each other. And we both had heavy smiles, Anninho, because this was not the time or place for a man and woman" (32). Oppressed by historical forces beyond their control, Almeyda and Anninho feel the inevitable nearness of pain and tragedy even as they fall in love. Fulfilling their prophetic sense of sorrow, Almeyda is unable to conceive, explaining, "My womb was angry" (34). "Angry" at the limitations and suffering imposed by the institution of slavery and its accompanying horrors, Almeyda's body is unable to perform as she wishes. Implied here is the idea that her body is not really her own, affected by and belonging to the Portuguese even though they are not physically present. Almeyda's symbolic psychological fears later are fully realized in "Work in Progress" (1976) which contains a brutal sequence — part reality, part dream — in which Almeyda and Anninho are captured by the Portuguese, who rape and torture them, cutting off Almeyda's breasts. Even though the bulk of the writing concerns the terrible visceral aspects of their torture, Jones maintains that Almeyda's and Anninho's most humiliating disservice is rendered by history: "After it is all over and everything but history has touched us. (The pain has touched us, but they deny us the history.)" (46). More devastating than the agony they endure is the (fore)knowledge that none of it will be chronicled, that their suffering may very well mean nothing to the generations that follow.

As Trudier Harris says of Almeyda and Anninho, "Their health reflects community health" (103) and, preceding Almeyda's account of their violent trials, the beginning of *Song of Anninho* celebrates the flourishing of African-descended slaves in Brazil, most notably through their close affinity with the land. At the outset of the poem the women are singing and an important connection is made between South America and Africa. Almeyda observes, "This is a good place,/because it is like the place/we lived before;/like our own country" (*SA* 1). Taking the connection a step further, Almeyda explains to Anninho the bond between herself and the earth, which has strong and obvious postcolonialist implications in the general sense that the Portuguese appropriate, develop, and abuse the Brazilian landscape. Early in the book Almeyda establishes the philosophical groundwork for condemning this process by relating the earth to history as well as herself. According to this interior logic, when the Portuguese change the land and abuse Almeyda they are not only committing crimes against nature and humanity, but history as well. For Almeyda, none of these elements are mutually exclusive — thus when she is made to bleed not only a woman is maimed but also a country and a history.

Further delineating her primary mythopoetic variables, Jones adds a powerful spiritual element to her physical association of blood, land, and history through the character of Zibatra, a mystical scholar. Zibatra's

Chapter 3—Toward Feminine Mythopoetic Visions: Poetry

prodigious mastery of African, Brazilian, and Christian spiritual concepts makes her an ideal commentator on the metaphysical conditions of Almeyda and Brazil. Combining Christian and pagan imagery and language, Zibatra possesses the ability to express things beyond language, functioning as an ideal healer and muse for Almeyda, who strongly desires to transmute the memory of personal and cultural pain into words that shape and empower the spirit. Almeyda's task, mirroring Jones's, is to verbalize the horrific destruction of Palmares, establishing it in memory and spirit so that it may continue.

Why this task should fall to Almeyda, a maimed woman, is established over the course of the book through scenes that dramatize the specific and complicated trials of slave women. For example, what Almeyda and her grandmother interpret as a mark of prophecy or intelligence — the strange and affecting quality of their gazes — is construed by the men around them as licentiousness or seductive witchery. And a similar anxiety-laced misinterpretation also appears in Agostinha, a white woman who becomes jealous of Almeyda after her husband purchases her to work in his shoe shop (SA 31). A year after *Song for Anninho* appeared, Jones published "The Shoemaker and the Sadism of the Senhora" (1982), which renders the same sequence in prose at much greater length. As Capao, a male slave, explains to Almeyda, Agostinha "is afraid of you. She wonders of what her husband might come to see in you" (46). The misguided interpretations of Agostinha and the men in the poem, white and black, highlight the well-documented and seemingly inevitable historical propensity for identifying female slaves purely as sexual beings, objects of carnal conquest for men and Jezebels to be feared and loathed by white women.

In *Song for Anninho* Jones works against such negative, traditional interpretive constructions by having Almeyda establish her identity in abstract, ontological terms. Almeyda's grandmother informs her that she is a granddaughter and inheritor of Africa (SA 37) — a legacy that defines itself in intellectual and spiritual, as opposed to physical, terms. When Almeyda attains womanhood her grandmother hides something in her with her eyes (SA 63). Significantly, Almeyda's coming-of-age is not accompanied by the revelation of carnal knowledge but rather a kind of spiritual transmission across generations, an exchange through the windows of two souls. This ethereal transference across time has a powerful and perhaps defining impact on Almeyda's identity, for she links her existence in the present to an idealized — a mythopoetic — woman, invented and lingering in the shadows of the mind and spirit.

Almeyda's imaginative and spiritual identity also informs her narrative impulse to record the history of Palmares in which she seeks to seeks its spirit rather than its empirical action. While Jones seeks to translate and reclaim the literal horror of the Palmares massacre and slavery in aesthetic terms, Almeyda transforms her physical injuries into constructive imaginative catalysts for narrative. Zibatra tells Almeyda that as her breasts are being healed, the memory of Palmares is experienced through Anninho, as well as the desire to share it — to sing the tale in its entirety. Anninho informs Almeyda that Palmares women captured in battle, were forced to forget themselves, abdicating their free spirits and identities as they returned to a condition of bondage under the Portuguese. Almeyda's ambition, not unlike Jones's, is to recapture the poignant, simultaneously free and doomed aura of Palmares through her relationship with and memories of Anninho. Almeyda recounts that when the Palmares leader Zumbi initially freed women, they marveled at and celebrated the new dignity with which they were treated. Jones, working through Almeyda, attempts a similar artistic catharsis over the course of *Song for Anninho*, transmuting the despair of pain and bondage into a new feeling of dignity and self-worth — establishing narrative myths and cultural systems of self-identity which celebrate the historically neglected freedom and love of Palmares amid the brutality of the Portuguese slave system.

Brazil Revisited: The Hermit-Woman *and* Xarque and Other Poems

In *Song for Anninho* Jones uses Almeyda's account of her relationship with Anninho as a catalyst for exploring the larger historical dynamics of African bondage. "Fiction Study," a poem from her next book, *The Hermit-Woman* (1983), functions as a kind of blueprint for how Jones effectively goes about relating personal relationships to larger cultural and historical phenomena. An exercise in self-reflexive metafiction, "Fiction Study" literally involves the speaker and reader as they endeavor to construct a narrative out of Jones's notes for a story. After expressing her intention to introduce an institutionally-discharged, insane wife into the narrative, Jones writes, "Each time he brings/her home she tries/to kill him" (*HM* 17). Introducing the fragmented events and characters she hopes to portray, Jones leaves it to the reader to imagine how they might develop and interact while observing certain ground rules she lays out. Specifically, she wishes to capture a feeling of hysteria while blending the sexual and the historical. Although the possibilities of the story inevitably take on different shapes for different readers, the notes that constitute the poem establish what Jones hopes to achieve: a psychological meditation charged with sexuality and carrying with it the potential for larger historical implications and commentary.

The other poems in *The Hermit-Woman* generally follow the rough compositional formula Jones establishes in "Fiction Study" while portraying personal relationships in South American milieus — usually involving mystical prophetic figures — and relating them to larger cultural concerns. In "Ensinanca" the male protagonist is literally half-black, half-white, a result of having ignored his mother's advice to develop his true gift and become a healer. Instead of cultivating his mystical talent, a product of his family's culture, the speaker has endeavored to become "a modern man/ ... scientific, rational" (*HM* 12). As becomes symbolically apparent, "Ensinanca" is a poem about divided cultural loyalties, the protagonist excelling in the rational, modern, western world while the gift of his culture persistently haunts and plagues him.

A sense of displacement and divided cultures also informs "Wild Figs and Secret Places," which portrays an extended encounter between a European explorer and a South American native woman who has been banned from her tribe. Although they are from drastically different cultures, both characters are, by necessity, independent wanderers of the wilderness. The female narrator explains that she was banished from her tribe, "for learning the language/and religion of devils" (*HM* 43–44). Although the protagonist has been excluded from her people for openly learning about and communicating with European "devils," the European man describes her in bestial terms, acknowledging her intelligence but attributing it and her other positive characteristics to her contact with the Catholic church. His diary entry reads, "*I have met a native woman./At first I thought she was/one of those river monsters/we have read about*" [Jones's italics] (*HM* 29). "Wild Figs and Secret Places" is a meditation on cross-cultural misinterpretation and exchange, accompanied by the female narrator's assertion of personal autonomy. Lacking knowledge of the woman's culture, the European interprets her according to his didactic, theologically-based value systems and thus never fully realizes the kind of remarkable person he has met. On the other hand, having encountered other Europeans, the female speaker understands and predicts the man's actions. Later, when he asks her to translate the words she is singing in her native tongue, she replies that it is not possible (*HM* 47). Realizing the irresolvable differences between their cultures and the unavoidable prejudices and limitations of single cultures, the woman contemplates a future identity devoid of memory. Trapped by her biological identity, the woman nevertheless flirts with a mythopoetic awareness beyond memory and awareness that remains completely hidden to her European companion.

Like the woman in "Wild Figs and Secret Places," the female protagonist of the of "The Machete Woman,"[4] is a social outcast. However, whereas the wandering woodswoman has been banned for conversing with Europeans and violating tribal authority, the speaker in "The Machete Woman," Destinaria, an abused female slave, has horrified the governing European community by hacking her cruel mistress to death with a machete before taking refuge in the local Catholic church among nuns who consistently seek to educate and convert her. Developing a strong relationship with the nuns, Destinaria initially embraces their religion but later develops doubts after the arrival of an African sorcerer, a powerful and charismatic man whom the nuns aggressively attempt to convert, "parading around *him,*/repeating words of salvation" (*HM* 61). Irritated by the nuns' pride in their work and contempt for the African man's indomitable beliefs, Destinaria singles out Sister Juana's faith-based arrogance (*HM* 61). Over the course of the poem, Destinaria and the sorcerer each become ill and are forced to heal each other using their own arts since the nuns possess no useful medical knowledge and their persistent prayers prove ineffective. Nevertheless, the nuns inevitably attribute their recoveries to their Christian god, dismissing the "pagan" herbal remedies as "devilry." In the end, a predictable dialectic emerges in terms of freedom. When the African sorcerer escapes, the nuns mourn that they have lost a soul, while

Destinaria rejoices and romantically dreams of the freedom he enjoys. Forming a band of "wild black men" (*HM* 69) and becoming a revolutionary, the sorcerer leads frequent attacks on white gold miners exploiting the land. Combining African religious tradition with revolution in the New World and rewriting Catholic conversion narratives, Jones establishes the sorcerer as a heroic mythopoetic figure who draws on his extensive African knowledge to generate freedom and meaning in a new land. However, as in "Wild Figs and Secret Places," the true value and identity of the prophetic figure remains obscured to the poem's Europeans. Sister Juana laments the sorcerer's flight and informs Destinaria that heaven wants to liberate them (*HM* 69), which — ironically — is precisely what the African sorcerer is literally attempting to do for his people.

In Jones's third collection, *Xarque and Other Poems* (1985), she finally closes the chapter on colonial South America by introducing Almeyda's daughter, Bonificia, and granddaughter, Euclida, before continuing to move forward temporally into more contemporary milieus. As in *The Hermit-Woman*, mystical prophetic figures serve as symbolic catalysts for the poems' larger concerns. In fact, the title poem, "Xarque" (1979), essentially constitutes an initiation narrative about developing spiritual perceptions and becoming a prophet, Almeyda's granddaughter, Euclida, learning the foundations of the art from her mother, Bonificia, who also educates her about her grandmother. Bonificia recounts to Euclida that Almeyda fed her "strange plants,/so I could see and hear and taste and smell/new things in the world" (*XQ* 11). She maintains that Almeyda possesses the ability to apprehend phenomena that go unnoticed by others (*XQ* 33). Yet, this is a gift Bonificia never successfully acquires, though she does function as an important link to the past, a bridge to Euclida's cultural roots, the free society of Palmares, and her destiny of becoming a healer.

Their story unfolding almost half-a-century after the destruction of Palmares, Bonificia and Euclida live in a time of slavery, when the imaginative and mythopoetic significance of Palmares is essential to the dream of freedom. Jones effectively underscores the immediacy of slavery through a series of symbolic exchanges between Bonificia and Euclida. For example, Euclida asks why stray cattle are killed, to which her mother insinuates that it is not unlike tactics employed for runaway slaves. Before the initial publication of "Xarque," Jones had dramatized a conversation between Euclida and Almeyda in prose format under the title "Work in Progress" (1977), in which Euclida describes the Portuguese man who purchases her, preferring her for her "silence and detachment" (125). However, despite her youth and tranquility, Euclida has no illusions about the system that keeps her in check and repeats the expression, "Come to the land of gold and women" (124), a testament to her knowledge of the ambitions that drive Portuguese men. In "Xarque" the literal presence of a different kind of oppression is conveyed through the figure Tirana, whose name embodies songs women sing about the oppressive qualities of love (*XQ* 8). A victim of love as well as slavery, Euclida becomes a healer, entering a role of servitude to the suffering people she cherishes. At the end of the poem, she is off to take care on a maimed woman who is alone, a scenario that echoes the sorceress Zibatara's care for Almeyda throughout *Song for Anninho*. In a sense then, using similar imagery Jones comes full-circle from Almeyda's story of love for Anninho and Palmares to Euclida's decision to give of herself for her people. Functioning as culturally-affirming, mythopoetic figures across generations, these women provide a means of recording and confronting oppression that celebrates and reinforces their culture throughout time.

Jones's interest in cultural dynamics and prophetic figures across historical eras — a commonality her work shares with that of Sherley Anne Williams (who was publishing her historical slave-centered work around the same time) — is confirmed in the poem that immediately follows "Xarque" in *Xarque and Other Poems*. "Composition with Guitar and Apples" (1982) takes place in contemporary Brazil and, anticipating the character of Joan "The Bitch" Savage in Jones's third novel, *The Healing*, involves a rock star protagonist who flies to Brazil in order to recover her voice and spiritual energy.[5] Fascinated by the landscape of the country and the elderly woman with whom she stays, the speaker begins to feel a strong connection between herself as a musician and the mystic women of the Brazilian past. She imagines herself and her senescent host "in other landscapes,/timescapes,/spacescapes" (*XQ* 54) and recalls Jimi Hendrix as a kind of sorcerer or mystical figure who helped her to discover the essence of music beyond its formal properties. The old woman keeps peacocks in her yard against an old superstition that they are bad luck. Providing a kind of symbolic path for the protagonist to follow, she forms a spiritual and cultural connection across time; the speaker ostensibly will resume her career with a renewed voice and an new appreciation for and confidence in the mystical essence at the heart of music.

Jones's final poem in *Xarque and Other Poems*, "Waiting for the Miracle" (1982), contains an epigraph from Günter Grass: "*For still the saint answers questions* [Jones's italics]" (*XQ* 55). The protagonist, an unnamed religious witness, spends much of her time defending the poem's saint, Black Mary Jane, against the claims of a heckling doubter. Grass's epigraph comes into effect in the sense that even in a contemporary world, full of unprecedented science, doubt, and secular rationalism, there remain questions and needs only saints and prophets may effectively address. Furthermore, Jones contends that the answers, as well as the needs, ultimately must flow from the believers rather than the avatar. In the poem, Black Mary Jane does nothing but laugh while the energy of the people appears to perform the miracle. As the witness/narrator explains, it is "in the air, and spinning./The saint is the axis./The saint is sitting still,/and laughing" (*XQ* 65).

A highly self-conscious formalist, Günter Grass creates narrators acutely aware of their art of storytelling, and his poetic style often flirts with elements of surrealism. In "Waiting for the Miracle," the witnessing speaker argues for the legitimacy of the saint, a kind of self-important justification narrative, only to have the saint's actions undercut her claims — it is not the saint's powers but the peoples.' In this sense, Jones establishes a kind of mythopoetic, anti-mythopoetic poem in which the speaker's myth of the prophet is stripped and reduced to the participation and energy of the people, a myth of a different kind. Symbolically, this concept also may be interpreted as a kind of culminating aesthetic statement — a meditation on the poet, a kind of prophet herself, and her audience; for without an audience, without readers, there can be no poetic power. "Waiting for the Miracle" also serves to remind us that behind Jones's various aesthetic catalysts (her compelling speakers and gripping narratives), behind the blues laments and historical reimaginings, sits a formidable craftswoman and storyteller. In poignantly singing the songs of her people, African-American and Brazilian, across time, Jones creates and establishes a compelling logocentric historical authority — a poetic miracle of sorts from which we, the readers, may generate meaning and witness it to others.

Notes

1. The book-length *Song for Anninho* (1981) is the only poem to date which has been discussed at length by scholars and in two notable cases (Coser [146–162] and Jackson [137–139]) it appears in a subordinate role to other texts. Howard Ramsby II's "Things Deserving Echoes: Gayl Jones's Liberating Poetry" considers some of the poems from Jones's three poetry books, but does not address her large body of uncollected pieces from the 1970s. These poems remain altogether neglected and largely unread.

2. "Night of the Leopard: Theatre Poems," *Silo* (Bennington College) 16 (Winter 1969) 15–38.

3. Jones conceived of and worked on "Palmares" before writing *Song for Anninho*. Although it has not been published as a completed novel, portions of it appeared in various literary journals under the titles "From Almeyda," "Work in Progress," and "The Shoemaker and the Sadism of the Senhora" (all listed in bibliography).

4. A decade later Jones published an extended prose version of the poem under the title "From *The Machete Woman*: A Novel," *Callaloo* 17.2 (Spring 1994) 399–404.

5. In *The Healing* Harlan Jane Eagleton reminds Savage, "[Y]ou lost your voice. But then you got it back in Brazil" (*HE* 212).

CHAPTER 4

Afrocentric Recolonizations: 1990s Fiction

"She's sorta a Afrocentric feminist, though. I don't think that's the same as a feminist feminist."
— Harlan Jane Eagleton, *The Healing* 197

"We has spiritual perfection and we has the capacity to reverse the fables that the enemies of our peoples say about us and to attain the truth of who we is and who we wants to become."
— Monkey Bread, *Mosquito* 540

In his ambitious study, *The Ideologies of African American Literature: From the Harlem Renaissance to the Black Nationalist Revolt*, Robert E. Washington makes the important historical observation that:

> Black literary culture, over the past several decades, has evidenced a conspicuous absence of protest oriented works. A staple genre of the rigid caste era of race relations, black protest literature has virtually disappeared. In fact, if the new black literary culture has any one distinguishing feature, it is its postpolitical orientation, which is revealed in its tendency to focus on black communal experiences rather than black-white racial conflicts [336].

Taking as a given the idea that African American aesthetics have become highly self-reflexive and self-contained, Adam Lively, in his epilogue to *Masks: Blackness, Race, and the Imagination* summons hip-hop music in wondering "whether the extreme expressions of 'blackness' in rap music are a sign that divisions are growing greater or, rather, a healthy indication that demons from the past are being exorcised" (285). Whether or not the contemporary collective African American artistic scene ultimately is congealing or fragmenting, cultural observers such as Washington and Lively see contemporary African American art forms as chiefly being about themselves and the specific ethnic experience that ostensibly generates their aesthetic difference. As Washington summarizes:

> Influenced by the identity movements and celebrations of cultural diversity fostered by American Third World minorities (e.g., black Americans, Asian Americans, Hispanic Americans, and Native Americans), as well as women and homosexuals, black literary culture has assumed the function of an identity discourse, seeking to explore, to define, and to affirm a distinctive black American ethnicity [336].

For good or for ill, scholars like Washington perceive African American aesthetics as vigorously attempting to demarcate itself amid a chorus of other minority discourses as well as the looming American cultural hegemony which constantly threatens to pervade them all.

Gayl Jones's Afrocentric Fiction

Long before ethnic identity politics became a pervasively fashionable avenue of aesthetic inquiry, Gayl Jones was exploring the complexities of African-American culture through heavily psychological and tension-filled blues narratives. Over the course of the novels *Corregidora* (1975) and *Eva's Man* (1976), the plays *Chile Women* (1974) and "Beyond Yourself (The Midnight Confession) for Brother Ah" (1975), the short story collection *White Rat* (1977), and various poems, Jones established a powerful and sometimes problematic dialectic between aesthetic experimentation—a highly unique combination of clinical psychology, eroticism, and applied African American musical elements (ritual, myth, repetition)—and the cultural investigation of what it means to be a modern African American woman. Like contemporary gangsta rap, Jones's early fiction, drama, and poetry unflinchingly consider and portray violently negative aspects of African American culture alongside its beautiful qualities, which differentiated and occasionally alienated her texts from much of the highly-idealistic, self-affirming work of the Black Arts Movement of the 1970s. Yet, despite its tendency to portray violence and abuse within African American culture, Jones's early work remains essentially Afrocentric in the sense of Manning Marable's "everyday language" definition: "*Afrocentrism* has come to mean a positive black consciousness that is anchored in the knowledge of African culture and history [Marable's italics]" (18). Although they confront and combat troubling cultural themes and dilemmas, Jones's early narratives nevertheless are concerned with the important and constructive tasks of earnestly exploring and defining African American consciousness.

Jones's aesthetic is also Afrocentric in the sense that she does not limit her concerns to African Americans or contemporary American culture. In the 1980s she published three books of poetry (*Song for Anninho* [1981], *The Hermit-Woman* [1983], and *Xarque and Other Poems* [1985]), two of which are entirely historical narratives and all of which portray South American, particularly Brazilian, milieus. This trend toward an increasingly international poetics continued into the 1990s with the novels *The Healing* (1998) and *Mosquito* (1999), books that contain international characters of African descent as well as lengthy cultural ruminations on other ethnic groups and the imaginative role of Africa. Anticipating these novels in a 1992 interview, Jones expressed a desire to capture the international or universal black experience while also explaining her ongoing, formative interest in Brazilian history:

> I'd like to be able to deal with the whole American continent in my fiction — the whole Americas — and to write imaginatively of blacks anywhere/everywhere. In one of my short stories I've even brought two contemporary Brazilians to Kentucky to visit a friend there, mingling place and historical moment. But going to the Brazilian history and landscape helped my imagination and writing. I also wanted to write about someone and a time distant from my own. It was also a way of getting away from things that some readers consider "autobiographical" or "private obsessions" rather than literary inventions — that they don't accept as imagination from a black woman writing about black female characters in a certain American world [Rowell, "Interview" 40].

Hoping to escape the restrictions of a portrayed "certain American world," Jones sought to build upon her compelling historical Brazilian narratives — the novel *Corregidora* as well as several uncollected stories and the three books of poems — in an effort to construct a contemporary black consciousness without national boundaries.

In her essay "From *The Quest for Wholeness*: Re-Imagining the African-American Novel: An Essay on Third World Aesthetics" (1994) Jones provided a kind of blueprint for her cross-cultural aesthetic agenda. Written in the first person, the essay's speaker is a precocious African American novel: "I am an African American novel. Like all novels, I deal with two kinds of action, real and symbolic. Like all novels — or most novels? — I am literature, though as an African American novel, I am more likely to be read — If I am indeed read — as sociopolitics, socioculture, or sociopsychology" (507). In conceptualizing itself, Jones's African American novel provides some defining assumptions about literature and interpretation. It asserts, for instance, that "all" "or most" novels are literature, a distinction that does not provide hallowed ground for canonical western literary works. Instead, all or most novels have within them literary qualities worthy of serious consideration. Yet, in terms of interpretation, Jones's novel perceives a problematic tendency on the part of readers to process African American novels through various reductive sociological lenses. In fact, the novel asserts that if it is read at all, it will likely be constructed in such limiting terms. Jones hopes to liberate the African American novel from these strictures, an ambition made evident in her definition of Afrocentrism, which does not limit itself to people of African descent:

> In Afrocentric novels, such as I am, (some might prefer to see me as a pamphlet or in the pages of a periodical or read/listen to an abridged or censored edition), marginal people step from the margins into the center of their own worlds, of their own texts and fiction, invent and re-invent themselves (as I invent and re-invent me) and begin to see themselves for themselves and not as subordinates ["From *The Quest*" 508].

Defying overarching sociological distinctions which occasionally border on profiling groups, Jones places an emphasis on developing unique marginal characters who are neither subordinate to the dominant culture nor to the expectations of their own groups. Jones's application of Afrocentric themes to other people and ethnic groups is most evident in *Mosquito*, portions of which might be labeled Latinocentric or even "non-centric," many of the various ethnic individuals having transcended or successfully signified upon the stereotypical characteristics often associated with their respective cultures. In *Mosquito* the special friendship between Sojourner

Nadine Jane Nzingha "Mosquito" Johnson and Delgadina reflects a kind of unusual and rewarding blending of African American and Latino world views, each woman coming to see herself and each other through related and shared experiences. Significantly, Jones's imaginative cultural aesthetics also speaks to inevitable demographic trends. With the U.S. Latino population having grown to supplant African-Americans as the largest ethnic group in the United States, cross-cultural political and artistic dialogues have become critical to both groups. Anticipating the prospect of ever-increasing cultural interactions between African-Americans and Latinos, *Mosquito*, in one important respect, constitutes an interesting imaginative handbook on how ethnic cultures may account for and respect each other while striving for common goals.

Although Jones's two 1990s novels are concerned with the overlappings and mergings of various cultures, the experiences of Africa-descended people remain at the center of each book, making her conceptualization of Afrocentric theory among the most useful avenues for establishing their respective and collective implications. In employing Afrocentrism here, specifically to Jones's two later novels, I wish to avoid the intensely problematic nature of the theory as a whole across various disciplines — its tendency, for example, to construct unscholarly histories that are more or less rooted in wishful thinking about the past. However, both Jones's use of the term and its most basic assumptions make it useful in this particular case. In his influential essay "Locating an African American Text," Molefi Kete Asante lists three criteria for formulating a literary work's purpose: attitude, language, and direction. He says of the first term:

> Attitude refers to a predisposition to respond in a characteristic manner to some situation, value, idea, object, person, or group of persons. The writer signals his or her location by attitude toward certain ideas, persons, or objects. Thus, the critic in pursuit of the precise location of the author can determine from the writer's characteristic or persistent response to certain things where the writer is located [Asante].

For Asante attitude is an unavoidable byproduct of the writer's conscious or unconscious self-reflexive poetics. Fictional speakers and narrators may be stripped away methodically to reveal the author's core beliefs: her essential cultural attitude toward the "ideas, persons, or objects" of everyday life. Asante goes on to remark that the most useful and crucial tool for tracing attitude and locating a text is language:

> Language is the most important element because it is the most easily manifested in the text. One sees words on paper. If one sees a reference to Africans as primitives or to Native Americans as "a bunch of wild Indians" or Latinos as "greasy," then one knows the cultural address of the author. While it is true that authors might use irony, sarcasm, and other techniques of language to deliver a certain point or perspective, the Afrocentric critic is sensitive to the persistent and uniform use of pejoratives as demonstrating the author's location. When an author uses pejoratives unknowingly to refer to Africans, the critic often is being confronted with an unconscious writer, one who is oblivious to the social and cultural milieu [Asante].

Asante's concept of pejoratives resonates with Jones's work, which often utilizes negative stereotypes for the purpose of critiquing or signifying. More important, however, is her Afrocentric rendering of narrative, which makes use of traditional African oral techniques such as myth, anecdote, temporal disruption, and repetition. In fact, in "From *The Quest for Wholeness*," Jones's speaking novel remarks, "Am I being repetitious? I am being deliberately repetitious. Some storytelling traditions, and hence some novels, use repetition more than others" (509). Celebrating its use of repetition, Jones's novel leaves little doubt as to the cultural storytelling legacy from which it is derived. Also pertinent to her Afrocentric conceptualization of narrative form, Jones has praised Gwendolyn Brooks's poem "In the Mecca" for its effective use of formal and colloquial language: "It is an eclectic poetic tradition that manages to move both away from and toward the language of (heightened) everyday speech. It is an aggregate language that runs the gamut of 'elevated' and 'street' without devitalizing either" ("Community and Voice" 195). In *The Healing* and, especially, in *Mosquito*, Jones, like Brooks, "runs the gamut" of formal and colloquial speech, often mixing and blurring the forms. Using language in this manner, Jones plays with and confuses the reader's linguistic assumptions regarding supposedly educated and uneducated, eloquent and seemingly illiterate, characters. In her Afrocentric world, speakers and characters play with, signify on, and create language without suffering the reductive connotations of appearing merely streetwise or ignorant.

As it implies, Asante's third term for locating an African American text, direction, suggests, "The line along which the author's sentiments, themes, and interests lie with reference to the point at which they are aimed[...]. It is the tendency or inclination present in the literary work with regard to the author's objective. One is able to identify this tendency by the symbols which occur in the text" (Asante). Tracing a work's symbols, direction projects the writer's intended objective for her work. In Jones's case, the purpose most notably is a portrayal of the African-American's relationship to the homogenous culture that surrounds her and a roadmap for how she will achieve personal agency. In "From *The Quest for Wholeness*," Jones's talkative Afrocentric novel relates that:

> Novels like people can be colonized or decolonized. A novel is colonized, for example, when patterns of stories and patterns of ideas in stories and how stories are made from one storytelling tradition are imposed upon another storytelling tradition; that is, when the storyteller from the dominant culture says that you must tell stories the way I tell them, or when one storytelling tradition is seen as the mere subgenre of another. What is a colonialist? A colonialist controls [511].

Although Jones's novel sees most Afrocentric novels as existing against or within a colonized cultural milieu, it does not conceptualize itself as postcolonial, using instead the term "decolonizing":

> This is a chapter not on "How I Became Decolonized" but "How I Am Becoming Decolonized," for no matter how much I imagine or re-imagine my own decolonization, most all Third World novels are in the process of becoming decolonized, but decolonization like independence itself is a multiplex demanding physical, spiritual, and economic independence. All these elements of decolonization are necessary for complex artistic decolonization before we can achieve the full decolonization of any novel ["From *The Quest*" 514].

Rather than conceding a legitimate postcolonial or genuinely global contemporary aesthetic climate, Jones's novel argues that such an atmosphere is, instead, still in the tenuous process of coming about. As a result, Jones's protagonists in *The Healing* and *Mosquito* combat vestiges of colonial hegemony even as they progressively liberate themselves, decolonizing and redefining their immediate surroundings.

A limited example of how Jones addresses the theme of decolonizing appears in her short prose piece, "From *The Machete Woman*: A Novel"

(1994). Based on an earlier poem, "The Machete Woman,"[1] "From *The Machete Woman*" is the first-person account of Destinaria, an abused Brazilian slave who horrifies the local governing European community by hacking her cruel mistress to death with a machete before taking refuge in a Catholic church, among nuns who consistently seek to educate and convert her. The story begins with Destinaria's impressions of the colonizing tactics employed by the Catholic church in rewriting history. She observes, "They've got palimpsests, new manuscripts written over old ones. Sometimes the old ones show through, though. And there's one the nuns say shows a text written in the 6th century — probably a nun's diary or a monk's journal" (399). Implicit in Destinaria's description is the idea that texts, history, and meaning are forever in a state of flux, producing layers of portrayed logic and culture that stretch back into antiquity. She explains the process as, "New reasons written over old ones, and sometimes the old ones showing through the new. And you don't know how many layers of reasons there are" (402). Having established the fluid and tenuously-constructed nature of history and meaning, Destinaria then specifically applies it to the Catholic colonization of South America: "New Spain they call it, though the Indians have got another name for it, and it's as old a world as any other. Tlatelolco, the Indians call it. Tlatelolco. Tlatelolco, I've heard them say, clicking the roofs of their mouths, just like I've heard Africans do" (399). Informing Destinaria's account is the close relationship between Africans and native South Americans, each using similar-sounding language to identify their home despite their having come under the colonizing yoke of the Europeans.

Destinaria's decolonizing of her status in Brazilian culture, in addition to the violent decapitation of her mistress, takes place partially through her acquired knowledge of it — an inevitable irony since it is her slave master and then the nuns who educate her. A fellow slave, Fulana, says of Destinaria's master, "'He knows how to treat his slaves to liberty. But it's good he teaches you your alphabets and numbers, girl. That's enough liberty for you, eh?'" (402). However, as we learn more about Destinaria it becomes obvious that her education is not "enough liberty" for her, serving instead to fan the flames of coveted autonomy. Jones symbolically establishes Destinaria's difference early in the story when her name is given — a word possessing powerful futuristic connotations — by Fulana against the Señora's custom of using Greek names for slaves. Later, literally having forged her own identity and applied her education toward an analysis and realization of her role in Brazil's chattel system, Destinaria concludes, "The logic of the master — or the mistress, as the case may be — always turns topsy turvy when applied to the slave" (404). An ironic wild-card catalyst in the formula of European-enforced slavery, Destinaria functions as a living, breathing decolonizing agent, cutting off her mistress's head (the seat of skewed colonial rationality and logic) before fleeing and receiving protection from the Catholic church. In a final irony, the colonizing institution (the church) resolves to protect a decolonizing agent hostile to its own ideological tactics, further underscoring the doomed, "topsy turvy" rationale of Christianity-endorsed slavery.

Decolonizing American Culture: The Healing

Not unlike Destinaria in her historical setting, Jones's *The Healing*, her first published American novel in twenty-two years, functions as a kind of decolonizing agent — in terms of content, form, and attitude — amid late twentieth-century American literary and popular culture. Initial reviewers of the book were quick to note its resistance to ordered western notions of the novel, Marcie Hershman explaining, "What in [Jones's] earlier work was bull's-eye directed and tersely expressed now comes across as expansively detailed and moving in circles away from its subject — deceptively, of course" (E1). Jones's layered minutiae and deceptive movements, so radically different from the techniques of her spare 1970s prose narratives, generally were viewed with qualified favor. As Valerie Sayers remarked, "In loosening the tight control she exercised over her earlier fiction, Jones risks all kinds of gaps in logic and development. Sometimes she leaps the chasm and sometimes she takes a nose dive, but on the whole the dares are worth her trouble and ours" (E4). Just how Jones specifically loosens her tight control in *The Healing* is most effectively articulated by Bernard Bell: "After establishing the authority and viability of the black female faith healer in the initial two chapters, the dialect becomes more elastic and complex as the story within a story shifts in flashbacks and increasingly shorter chapters to the relationship between

Harlan and Joan" ("Liberating" 253). Bell is very perceptive in noting the novel's overall thematic shift from the relatively formal initial portrayal of the faith healer to the short, informal vignettes recounting her friendship with a female rock singer. Yet Jones uses this transition only to point out that the content of characters' experiences and observations is ultimately more important than their relationships with each other. As Candice Jenkins remarks, "The facts of women's lives are open to interpretation. Indeed, the actual events of each woman's story may be less important than whatever lesson she, and we, can glean from her experience" (366). The experiences of *The Healing*'s main characters being highly unconventional—often decolonizing American cultural assumptions and stereotypes—Jones's figures frequently convey lessons that constitute critiques of the society around them and even call into question the fundamental nature of how culture is created.

Molefi Asante's assertion that attitude and locating a text are most readily achieved through considerations of language is certainly applicable to *The Healing*. The book's attitude, one of progressive decolonizing, is revealed most notably through the complex linguistic techniques of its protagonist, Harlan Jane Eagleton, a figure whose highly fluid identity is reflected in her manner of speaking. Although Eagleton is extremely curious, open-minded, and socially-transcendent, occasionally she is ridiculed for her humble origins and lack of conventional education. For example, when she attends a lecture on Nietzsche a philosophy student belittles her once she discovers that Eagleton is studying cosmetology (*HE* 130). Despite having to negotiate occasional episodes of intolerance, Eagleton's unconventional, fluid identity ultimately is one of international semantic proportions. She is called Dottoressa in Milan and Curandera in Brazil (*HE* 13), each name carrying with it slightly different linguistic meanings and identity traits. Eagleton herself is very aware of these variations, manipulating and nuancing her identity at will in various situations. For example, she maintains that as a healer she speaks "more folksy than I naturally am, 'cause when you's doing the healing you's got to talk about the healing yourself, 'cause among some that lends as much credibility as the healing itself, but like I tell the scientific-minded people or them media people that wants to write up they own confabulatory stories about faith healing in America, I'm mostly there to do the healing" (*HE* 12). Realizing the importance of language in legitimizing her discourse, Eagleton alters her voice accordingly, frequently playing to the listeners' expectations for the purpose of strengthening her credibility.

Beyond the linguistic tactics she employs in performing as a healer in the text, Eagleton, as the novel's narrator, also uses her "folksy" voice symbolically in an effort to reach and heal the reader, which, in fact, constitutes part of the book's overarching direction. Yet, in order for her to attain this goal, Eagleton must gain agency and acceptance for her healing narrative, which she achieves partially through self-deprecating descriptions of her gift:

> Some look at me in pure wonder, others are looking at Nicholas in pure wonder, others are looking like they still gotta see to believe. Even if Nicholas a believable-sounding man, even if he a powerfully believable-sounding man. But a lot of them's looking at us like it one of them confabulatory tales of them UFOs, like it one of them confabulatory UFO tales that Nicholas telling [*HE* 32].

Even as Eagleton builds the case for her healing power, she acknowledges its fantastic similarity to other suspect phenomena, thereby underscoring her own grounded, commonsensical world view. This stable, humanistic aspect of Jones's protagonist stands in stark contrast to the fragmented, psychologically-tortured characters in much of her early fiction. And, in fact, *The Healing* constitutes a very conscious and distinct shift in direction with regard to Jones's *oeuvre*. As Jones bluntly put it in a *Newsweek* e-mail interview, "*The Healing* is meant to be a rejection of those earlier novels" (Chambers 68). Even had Jones not made this remark, the book self-reflexively bears her out in an episode where Eagleton heals Sally Canada, a schoolteacher who has been accused of being related to Eva Medina Canada, the troubled protagonist of Jones's second novel, *Eva's Man* (*HE* 38–39). Just as Eagleton heals Canada, so Jones hoped to confront and relieve in her new novel the fragmenting tensions she so skillfully had produced in her earlier fiction.

Also distinctive from her early fiction and indicative of her shift in direction is Jones's newfound preoccupation with popular culture, the intricacies of which must be catalogued and interrogated if genuine understanding is to take place. Of particular interest to Jones and Eagleton are the ideas of cultural elitism and relativism which either ignore Afrocentric cultural contributions or assimilate and repackage them in terms of the dominant American culture. As Eagleton points out, "But them Americans on the cover of the *Popular Culture* magazine with they tatoos and nose rings and sculptured and painted hairdos kinda looks like the kinda folks you usedta just see in the *National Geographic*-type magazines, ... and not just the so-called primitive peoples" (*HE* 5). Perceiving the ironies and contradictions of American popular culture, Eagleton remains dubious of culturally-sanctioned phenomena such as beauty and aesthetic value, choosing instead to make her own judgments. Eagleton's interrogation of and skepticism about American culture are augmented by the more pointed and extreme observations of her musician friend, Joan "The Bitch" Savage. For example, Eagleton says of Savage:

> She hardly ever reads the great writers, the great books. I mean, she reads the Great Books, she's got shelves of the Great Books. She reads them, but she also reads the trash, not just the trash, but she likes to read a lot of that obscure nonfiction, but she says the trash, the tabloid journalism, the tabloid novels, have more to do with the modern world, the trashy nonfiction, the trashy novels, the tabloids [*HE* 187].

Although Savage reads canonical western texts, her appreciation of them is hindered by the fact that she believes they have almost nothing to do with contemporary American culture, a milieu best left to the genre of "trashy" writing. While she is never wholly explicit, Eagleton appears to entertain a similar opinion, referencing canonical western texts for the purpose of pointing out their numerous shortcomings and lack of applicability to her life. For example, she critiques Henry James's failure to successfully imagine female characters while interpreting *Portrait of a Lady* as a book about an "American lady in Britain and the American lady ain't the same type of lady as the British lady, 'cause in Britain you's got to be a true royal to be a lady" (*HE* 28). To Eagleton's contemporary thinking, such effete class distinctions seem trivial in a world where drastic inequalities along ethnic and cultural lines result in extreme poverty, abuse, and death. In her literary critiques, Savage tends to read authors in terms of gender dynamics, arguing, for example, that Shakespeare is "good at portraying bitches, but even they're a man's idea of a bitch." However, she is more sympathetic toward Chaucer and his portrayal of the Wife of Bath since it articulates the simple notion that "A woman wants to be her ownself, just like a man wants to be his ownself" (*HE* 103). Though their critiques of high culture remain largely negative, Eagleton's and Savage's distinctive commentaries on artistic phenomena, high and low, situate the women as serious, albeit unconventional, thinkers who believe that comprehensive knowledge of culture is essential to understanding the society around them and their places in it.

Jones's cultural indictments through Eagleton and especially Savage inevitably lead to larger considerations of gender and feminism. Eagleton remains inconclusive about feminism, pointing out her problems with adopting a traditionally feminist identity: "I've always been kinda ambivalent about that feminism. Them women that don't wanna be on no pedestal ro say they don't want to be on no pedestal, 'cause seem like to me a lot of them wants to keep the perks of womanhood, is kinda different from the women that ain't never been on no pedestal" (*HE* 53). Commenting upon gender in her own way, Savage uses her performing identity, Joan "The Bitch" Savage, to signify upon "bitch" as a sexist term. Eagleton says of her, "Joan a rock star. Well, she ain't exactly a star. And ain't exactly a bitch. She just likes to call herself a bitch, you know. She likes being a woman, you know, but she doesn't like women being judged by different standards than men are judged, you know" (*HE* 78–79). Specifically implicit in Joan's signifying is her commentary on the term's prevalent use among hip-hop artists. As Eagleton tries to explain to her grandmother, Jaboti, "A lot of the male rappers refer to women as bitches, excuse my French, so she's sorta signifying on a bitch's, excuse my French, version of that type of music. It's supposed to be a satire, you know" (*HE* 208). Selecting parody instead of openly hostile critiques, Savage uses her art to implement her own feminist agenda by appropriating and mocking the offensive terminology of her musical male counterparts.

Just as Savage combats the gender-insensitive colloquialisms of her fellow performers, so she also must justify her decision to be an African American performer against charges of minstrelsy and selling out. For example, she relates that her highly-intellectual, former-husband Jamey "thinks enough of us jigs are singers and dancers anyway. That I'm just another stereotype. Playing the Nigger Entertainer" (*HE* 151). Although Savage's satirical music and highly-independent personality demonstrate that she is anything but stereotypical, Jones's account of Eagleton's and

Savage's meeting with a music industry promoter demonstrates the very real dangers of minority exploitation in the entertainment business. A music executive who specializes in exploiting ethnic performers, the promoter, Mr. Schacter, sponsors artists who look "like carnival acts, but a multicultural carnival, even a Native American among them" (*HE* 176). Despite the promising ethnic diversity, all of the performers have been assimilated to varying degrees by the homogenizing guidelines of Schacter and the corporate music industry, resulting in several bland, albeit marketable, styles. In the hip-hop genre for example, Schacter stays clear of gangstas and promotes only "bubble-gum rap," periodically infusing new blood into a low-risk, marketable musical formula.

In his role as an agent of soul-killing exploitation, Schacter functions as a kind of representative cultural foil against which Savage and, in fact, all of Jones's women must stand firm. As Jaboti wisely maintains, "Some people think that freedom is to manage everybody but theyself. Learn to manage yourself. That is the key to freedom" (*HE* 209). In *The Healing*, conducting oneself successfully demands a constant awareness of one's sexual and ethnic identity, as well as an understanding that the larger culture is constantly looking to colonize and exploit one's cultural differences. Identifying one of Norvelle's academic colleagues, Eagleton remarks, "She's sorta a Afrocentric feminist, though. I don't think that's the same as a feminist feminist" (*HE* 197), a comment which emphasizes her belief that gender considerations alone are insufficient signifiers for establishing identity. More important to Eagleton is a conceptualization of the world based on people of color's involvement in it. When she tries to remember whether or not Nicholas is from Colorado she rules out the town of Boley while noting that it is "supposed to be a town originally chartered by African Americans, one of they own towns" (*HE* 11). Otherwise irrelevant, Boley remains significant in Eagleton's mind because she conceives of it as a creation of African Americans. While historical ethnic references serve to help her understand and appreciate her own place in contemporary American society, they have ambivalent connotations for some of the book's other characters. For example, Jaboti's husband, like many African American military personnel, had elected to stay in Korea after serving in the American military because he "had more freedom there" (*HE* 223). More disturbing, however, is the debilitating paranoia suffered by the wealthy

African-German horse trader, Josef Ehelich von Fremd, who takes extravagant security measures to protect himself from white rival horse dealers in Kentucky. Pain-wracked victims of American racism, figures such as Fremd and Jaboti's husband cannot share Eagleton's bemused, holistic view of American culture, opting instead for such drastic measures as building small security armies and going into exile.

In Jaboti's husband's defection to Korea and Fremd's Afro-German heritage, Jones demonstrates a preoccupation with international, cross-cultural African themes. This concern also extends into her succinct portrayal of Savage's lead guitarist, Jimmy Cuervo, a Mexican described as possessing strong African features. Eagleton remarks that he "ain't the sorta Mexican you see in the movies. Look more African than Mexican," before going on to note the existence of "whole towns of Mexicans that look African" (*HE* 84). Through Cuervo Jones briefly contemplates race beyond the African American experience, using him to work against Mexican stereotypes both in terms of his appearance and guitar style. After hearing him play, Eagleton compares him to Jimi Hendrix, as opposed to Carlos Santana, before bringing him into the studio to work the pentatonic scales on new Savage numbers such as "Big Dick from Boston" and "Randy Dandy." An African-Mexican heavily influenced by American rock music, Cuervo slides through and incorporates different cultures in a manner Eagleton can admire and respect.

Jones's and Eagleton's interest in tracing African characteristics across international borders inevitably leads to a concern with contemporary Africa itself, the most literal manifestation of the book's Afrocentric agenda. Troubled by American portrayals of Africa, Eagleton ruminates at great length on the myths of Africa versus its realities:

> On television and in the movies you always saw the little African villages and the African bush, or the people on safari, or the native African medicine men and women, but you never saw the cities with their modern buildings and the bustle and automobiles and rumble and bicycles and mixtures of type and dress. My husband referred to these city Africans as "detribalized." But I liked them, the African businessmen I saw in the hotels, the market women, the college students, and I liked the tastes and sights and sounds and smells of the cities, but especially the islands off the coast of Africa, the islands of Zanzibar and Pemba [*HE* 117].

Eagleton's construction of Africa as a bustling, fully-developed entity complete with extensive commerce and skyscrapers works against the romantic pastoral or savage stereotypes entertained by many Americans, white and black. Even Savage, for all her hard-nosed cultural critiquing, idealizes Africa and belittles Eagleton for her realistic assessment of the continent: "I still can't believe you've been to Africa. I can usually tell people who've been to Africa" (*HE* 155). For Savage, a trip to Africa leaves a literal mark or aura on a person, a sentimental manifestation she tends to imagine probably because she has never been there herself. In fact, when it comes to traveling and touring Savage looks down contemptuously on having to perform in poorer countries. She scoffs, "A first-rate gig in a fourth-rate little country is a third-rate gig" (*HE* 215). Jones, then, uses Savage to underscore a central problem with contemporary perspectives on Africa among people of African descent. Though many understandably tend to romanticize their heritage and the continent of their ancestors, most remain simultaneously derisive of and repulsed by the poverty associated with it. Ignoring Savage's distaste, Eagleton acknowledges the cultural and economic realities of Africa while emphasizing that these considerations necessarily must give way to the importance of its place in the imagination. She explains:

> You know, Africa's a bigger continent than's on the map. When you see a map of the world, they got it so that Europe and America is the center of the world and the biggest continent, but Africa's a bigger continent than it is on the maps. They just do the maps like that, 'cause they want to believe in Europe and America, and we's supposed to consider them more important, you know, in the history of the world. But none of the maps you look at is the true maps of the world. Norvelle he got him a true map of the world, that shows Africa as big as it is and it dwarfs them other continents. That's the true Africa and I been there [*HE* 159].

For Eagleton the factual Africa, its dimensions in terms of square kilometers, is less important than the "true Africa," the continent whose people have come to populate and influence meaningfully many of the world's cultures. In this way, the idea of Africa has become the central dominant catalyst by which Eagleton conceives the world. Yet, this is not to be confused with romanticism. As a child, the magic realist transformation narrative of Grandmother Jaboti (*HE* 134) fascinates Eagleton, but as an adult she no longer finds it useful. Just as Jones had moved away from mythopoetic readings of African experience (most powerfully evinced in her three books of poetry), so Eagleton has grown up to reject sentimental notions of Africa while holding on to the ramifications of its imaginative power — a power which fuels her Afrocentric worldview and critiques of American culture. Remaining true both to her ideas and ideals, Eagleton marks the direction by which she will navigate the complexities of contemporary culture, imparting the gift of wisdom, as well as healing, to the injured and oppressed people she encounters.

Ethnic Self-Constructions: Mosquito

The cultural endeavor Eagleton begins over the course of *The Healing*, deftly critiquing and resisting American hegemony in an Afrocentric context while aiding its victims, continues in *Mosquito*, in which Jones renders her characterizations, ideas, and general literary techniques in increasingly layered and ambitious terms. Consisting of 616 pages written in a colloquial, conversational, anecdotal style, all but ignoring traditional structural notions of the novel, *Mosquito* baffled initial reviewers even as it intrigued them. Eleanor Bader called it "by turns exhausting and exhilarating" (152), while James Miller warned that for some readers "this work, like a mosquito, will buzz along — nagging, irritating, provoking, exasperating" (E3). Having increased the volume and frequency of both the cultural cataloging and philosophical debates which informed *The Healing*, Jones cultivated a style which readers such as Greg Tate characterized as "long-winded, disassociative, plotless, cutesy, full of hair-splitting deconstructive debates" (Tate). Tate and others also were troubled by Jones's authoritative depictions of Latino culture, accusing her of problematically "speaking on behalf of our Latin American brothers and sisters too and doing it at a length that might kindly be called self-indulgent, if not incredibly demanding of even her most sympathetic readers' time, tolerance, and intelligence" (Tate). What in *The Healing* had been celebrated as a fleshing out of Jones's previously sparse style and meager cultural concerns became for some readers of *Mosquito* an excessive and ill-considered meditation on topics about which she might better have remained silent.

As Tate's obdurate, albeit representative, reading implies, *Mosquito*'s uneven, jive-laced narrative style failed to gain the sympathies of most reviewers. Among the unconvinced, Tamala Edwards dubbed the book "a frustrating detour on the road to better storytelling" (72), while Henry Louis Gates Jr. observed, "It's as if Jones wanted to deliver a dissertation about orality in literature by transcribing hours of tapes from a loquacious storyteller" ("Sanctuary" 14). Gates's point aptly captures the problematic nature of the book's narrative presentation: ambitiously hoping to get as close as possible to informal oral phrasing in a written mode of expression, Jones runs the risk of drowning the reader in informal recorded chatter — talking them to death with written words. In fact, this is exactly the fate to which Gates succumbs, ultimately characterizing the book as "a sprawling, formless, maddening tale" ("Sanctuary" 14). Yet, much of the problem here stems from readers' conventional expectations of the rules to which novels should ascribe. As James Miller asserts, "It may also be misleading to call *Mosquito* a novel, since this is a work that steadfastly resists not only any sense of a linear narrative but also the qualities we often associate with well-made fictions" (E3). Stretching the genre paradigms of the novel, *Mosquito* makes its own laws and breaks new ground in its unconventional storytelling techniques, abandoning or radicalizing the novel form at the risk of inviting censure.

Mosquito's disdain for the accustomed structural standards of fiction is matched by its unflinching confrontation of stereotypes and interactions across cultures. As Deborah McDowell summarizes, "Full of spirit and adventure, burlesque and caricature, *Mosquito* eludes the literary border guards and fingers the new commissars of culture" (10). McDowell's general observation is especially telling in its evocation of "the new commissars of culture," the book's non-white, ethnic characters who shape language, meaning, and — increasingly — the world around them. As Carrie Bramen notes, *Mosquito* is an important book in the sense that "[s]tereotyping in this novel is explored not primarily through the conventional perspective of white people objectifying nonwhites, or the postcolonial emphasis on colonizers representing the colonized, but rather as a cultural practice within and between minority communities" (126). Subordinating the invasive presence of the dominant culture, Jones instead interrogates interactions among African Americans and Latinos, symbolically maintaining that their mutual discourse is of greater importance than their shared dialogue with white America.

At the center of these cultural dynamics is the book's narrator, Sojourner Nadine Jane Nzingha "Mosquito" Johnson, whose directional storytelling unfolds, according to reviewer Alma Luz Villanueva, "in the 'nonnegotiable' spirit of a warrior class woman (who don't take no shit)" (107). Like Eagleton in *The Healing*, Johnson is presented as an everyday, commonsense African American woman who possesses extraordinarily independent and intellectually adventurous ideas about culture and life in the United States. Her commentary early in the book on race and the American Dream sets the tone for many of the observations she makes over the course of the ensuing 600 pages: "Them that can't play white in America or refuses to play white is the niggers" (*MS* 9). Johnson's commentary here partially is meant to be self-reflexive for the benefit of the reader. Refusing to "play white" and becoming increasingly desperate through her involvement with the Sanctuary Movement, Johnson identifies herself as a contemporary manifestation of the true American Dream. Also significant in Johnson's characterization of the "true dream" is the fact that she does not limit the term "nigger" to people of African descent. For her it applies to anyone who desperately resists the rules of white society — a politics of perspective and thought rather than singular ethnicity.

Another participant in the true dream of America is Johnson's iconoclastic Latino friend, Delgadina, who resists American hegemony mostly through her writing. As Johnson remarks, "Delgadina say they ain't no such things as law. That law is them that makes the laws. That law is discretionary, when it ain't arbitrary" (*MS* 10). According to Delgadina law functions as a safeguard for American gringo power and, as such, generally is damaging and irrelevant to ethnic peoples — something to be resisted. The same is true for dominant intellectual discourses. As Johnson says of historical narratives, "I ain't like to hear the white man's version, 'cause everybody know that. I likes to hear the other people's eclectic stories of the Southwest" (*MS* 14). Defying the law as well as accepted and established versions of history, Johnson and Delgadina generate their own meanings drawn from their exclusive and shared experiences, as well as those of their respective ethnic groups.

Inevitably, the fact that Johnson and Delgadina are women enters into their intellectual considerations and world views. Johnson considers herself a believer in romantic freedom while also insisting that she is not a hoochie woman: "I'm romantically free, but it ain't no hoochified romantic freedom, and I believes in the old-fashioned kind of romance myself" (*MS* 16–17). Johnson's firm assertion of romantic love and her preoccupation with hoochie women becomes evident a few pages later when she recounts how a marine guide once had looked at Delgadina "like he thought she were one of them hoochie women, you know, the stereotypes they has of them women they considers exotic looking" (*MS* 21). Essential to the established portrayal of her sexual self is Johnson's declaration that she is free and uninhibited but also careful and reserved, holding out for the monogamous heterosexual pleasures of traditional romance while resisting stereotypes of exotic licentiousness. Also central to Johnson's conceptualization of herself as a woman is a belief in what she calls "true feminism." Using her truck-driving occupation as an example, she recounts, "Man, he be driving a eighteen-wheeler he supposed to be a ordinary man, just a ordinary working mans, but woman, she be driving a eighteen wheeler and she ain't no common woman" (*MS* 49). At the core of Johnson's visceral political position is a belief in equal respect for equal work. To her thinking a woman who receives special praise for doing construction or driving a big truck is celebrated unnecessarily since she is merely competently performing the task of an ordinary man. Yet, as Johnson points out, her hard-nosed position largely is a result of the special challenges she faces as an African American female: "[Y]ou ain't just colonized you's precolonized and recolonized" (*MS* 36). Having individually resisted and overcome these colonization attempts and become a successful trucker in spite of her gender and ethnicity, Johnson has no respect for women who pridefully call attention to themselves for inferior accomplishments.

Race also problematizes Delgadina's occupational aspirations for being a writer. Johnson recounts that Delgadina "say once when she was in high school she wrote a story about a Chicano descriptive geometrist — I think they call them geometrists, don't they? — and all the people did when she read it was laugh" (*MS* 118). Having serious intellectual ambitions, the young Delgadina faced special challenges when sharing her ideas with her gringo peers, most of whom could not imagine a Chicano mathematician or a female Latino writer. This problem continues to haunt Delgadina in the book's present-tense narrative, forcing her to rebuke her fellow community college writing students who believe she "should write universal stories or some shit. Gringo stories, that's what they mean by universal, or gringa stories, even gringa stories can be universal now" (*MS* 487). Like Johnson Delgadina believes that dominant American society and culture are flawed fundamentally in their adherence to the tastes and expectations of gringos. Yet, Delgadina also shares with Johnson the charitable philosophy of not ascribing the damning gringo label to all white Americans. Using her acute writer's eye, Delgadina enjoys "specifying" or identifying different people and their beliefs. And over the course of this exercise she comes to the realization, "Not all gringas are gringas. Gringoism is a state of mind" (*MS* 285). Although ethnicity often functions as an inevitable marker of identity, Delgadina ultimately believes that it is based more on imagination and psychology than biology — a distinction which also informs her literary agenda. As Johnson explains, "Delgadina is writing what she calls a border novel for her borders art project. She has a long and involved first chapter because she want it to be like the people who reads the novel has to cross a border to get into the novel. I tells her that they's a lot of people that ain't going to wants to cross that border to get into her novel" (*MS* 562). Structuring her border book in such a way that readers must cross an ideological boundary in order to enter and understand it, Delgadina indicts gringo culture while firmly placing her aesthetic critique in an imaginative, rather than literally ethnic, context.

Delgadina's preoccupation with gringo culture and its precarious effects on Latinos is complemented and overlapped by Johnson's observations on African American identity, particularly in terms of stereotypes. For example, at one point she humorously projects racial awareness onto captive ocean animals, remarking, "I poke my nose up against that glass and be looking at them marine animals and some of them marine animals be looking back at me like they ain't never seen a African nose. I know it's my African nose they's looking at. I should call it my West African nose, 'cause them East Africans, most of them, they ain't got noses like that" (*MS* 19). Playfully using sea life to point out the divergent physical characteristics of Africans, Johnson underscores the physical stereotypes associated with people on the African continent while also demonstrating the personal, physical self-consciousness she has developed over the course of growing up as an African American woman in the United States. Later, expanding upon Eagleton's observations on Africa in *The Healing*, Johnson remarks, "When most people think about Africa they don't think about them cities, and they always be more interested in them animals than they is in them human beings. And like I said they know the names of all them animals and don't even know the names of them human beings" (*MS* 288). In her own distinctive way, Johnson makes the familiar assertion that misconceptions about Africans largely are a result of ignorance about them, their culture, and their continent. As a result, Africans are dehumanized in terms of their appearance and culture, the importance of which often is tellingly subordinated by highly-educated people to the characteristics and value of the continent's animals. Furthermore, accompanying and underlying these racist perspectives and questionable ethics is the colonizing incursion of the western imagination, which threatens to blight further people's conceptualizations of Africa. Despite Johnson's strong independent mind, this is a force which affects even her. As she explains, "I be standing there thinking about the African jungle, but seem like every time I be thinking about the African jungle Tarzan and Jane and Jane's daddy and some other man that I just calls Bwana in that jungle" (*MS* 360). Although Johnson partially is signifying here on a manifestation of cultural misrepresentation, her comment underscores the deceptive and dangerous ease with which one's culture may be stripped and reinvented.

At the respective and mutual cores of their discourses, Johnson and Delgadina fundamentally are searching for methods by which to meaningfully locate their imaginations and voices in a disingenuous society that hopes to silence or alter them through economic and political means. Johnson quotes Delgadina in remarking "that most modern colonization is economic. That's how the modern colonialists, the neocolonialists, colonizes, she say. Then they can pretens they ain't colonials. 'Cept they knows who they are. Least them in power does" (*MS* 55). In possession of an economy-driven media, the neocolonialists dictate their collective cultural vision to their various ethnic consumers, often in their own language, accompanied by a seemingly benign, though ultimately bogus, political message. As Johnson explains, "Delgadina say them whites that's all for multiracialism just want to use the multirace as a buffer, you know" (*MS*

27). Yet, the attempt to generate dialogic meaning is just as much an endeavor of ethnic cultures, which hope to repudiate and heal their legacies of subjugation. For example, Saturna's regional anecdote concerning Chief Nigger Horse serves to transform the meaning of a racial epithet by employing repetition: "But it like when he say that Nigger in Chief Nigger Horse, it like that word ain't got no power" (*MS* 89). The linguistic struggle for legitimacy and power between white American culture and ethnic interests is one to which Delgadina and Johnson both remain acutely attuned, especially when cultural transmissions have been subtly manipulated. For example, Johnson interprets the phenomenon of French braids as a form of linguistic colonization: "I guess the French musta got that style from them Africans in France and then the Americans they be seeing the French with that style and be calling them French braids. Or maybe they know they African braid and just call them French braids 'cause they don't wanna call them African braids" (*MS* 48–49). Recognizing a historical legacy of literal and linguistic colonization, Johnson contemplates the phenomena as a means of repudiating and moving beyond it in order to more fully establish her place in the contemporary world.

In addition to historical knowledge, *Mosquito* also employs aesthetics and politics as means for confronting oppression. The most notable manifestation of the former is Lucille Jones's play, *Blessing for Coliene* (*MS* 448–463), which tellingly reverses stereotypical class and gender hierarchies. On the political front Jones develops two subversive organizations that confront oppression and colonization: the Sanctuary Movement and the Daughters of Nzingha. As the leader of the Sanctuary Movement, Ray Mendoza, says of his group, "We're sort of like a modern Underground Railroad" (*MS* 225). Although the group has historical underpinnings and performs literal acts of subversion, language is its dominant weapon and concern. Indeed, the fact that liberation takes place along linguistic lines reflects back on the text of the novel itself. Mendoza reveals, "Even I myself was schooled in the language of the oppressors. The language of the oppressed has always been a different language. But, like I said, we weren't there to politicize the people. But people know that truth is them. That's why all governments want to turn people into things" (*MS* 231). Just as *Mosquito* asks readers to jettison their preconceived notions of culture and the novel form, so the Sanctuary Movement attempts to exorcize the language of the oppressor in favor of recognized self-value — "people know that truth is them." Considering Johnson's talent for identifying and resisting colonizing discourses, it is not surprising that Mendoza asks her to be a "hidden agenda conspiracy specialist." As he explains, "Sometimes we receive letters from various people, but because of the regimes, the lack of free speech, we have to be able to decode what's in the letters" (*MS* 550). Since she effectively has deciphered various ethnic, cultural, and political discourses over the course of the novel, Johnson is well-suited to this position, which also constitutes a skill to which the reader might aspire.

More specialized in its concerns than the Sanctuary Movement, the Daughters of Nzingha conceptualizes itself as a political and economic organization designed primarily for the benefit of African American women. One of its most distinguished members, Monkey Bread, describes its main foundation: "African women should be economically independent if possible" (*MS* 391). Consistent with the non-discriminatory philosophies of Johnson and Delgadina, although the Daughters of Nzingha name can "be used only by descendants of the victims of the African Diaspora Holocaust" (*MS* 413), it is not exclusively for women, a distinction which separates it from exclusively gender-based organizations. As Johnson explains, "'Do not submit to your own ignorance': the motto of the Daughters of Nzingha is actually derived from a speech given by Malcolm X. That is what is different about the Daughters of Nzingha. They don't just includes wisdom derived from Afro-womanhood but also includes Afro-manhood wisdom books in they archives" (*MS* 613). Made up entirely of different types of women, the Daughters of Nzingha, nevertheless, is not averse to utilizing male knowledge in its quest for a better way of life. Like Johnson, the organization sees its visceral ends as being much more important than the nature or politics of its political means. Whatever collectively gives African American women increased economic and cultural legitimacy is worthy of utilization, regardless of its ideological source.

In a Daughters of Nzingha newsletter we are told that Joan "The Bitch" Savage, the erratic rocker from *The Healing*, has become director of the Nzingha Foundation and financier of the New Palmares Settlement in Brazil (*MS* 429, 431). Although these unsubstantiated details initially may appear gratuitous in terms of the overall novel, they are very significant in the way they reflect Jones's use of the Daughters of Nzingha to reference her work as a whole. Although Savage appears in *The Healing*, the character makes her debut much earlier in a 1982 story called "Those Rock People."[2] Furthermore, the New Palmares reference summons up Jones's poetry books, all of which contain allusions to Brazilian history. In fact, in a functional sens, as much as the Daughters of Nzingha works toward redefining the cultural roles of African American women, Jones uses *Mosquito* as a means of recontextualizing her earlier work. A passage during one of Johnson's reveries effectively describes both endeavors: "*We has spiritual perfection and we has the capacity to reverse the fables that the enemies of our peoples say about us and to attain the truth of who we is and who we wants to become* [Jones's italics]" (*MS* 540). Using the Daughters of Nzingha to revisit her earlier work, Jones underscores her desire to use *Mosquito*, a spiritual meditation, as a self-reflexive means of demonstrating where she "is" and who she "wants to become."

Jones also frequently appears to speak self-reflexively through the novel's respective storytellers: characters such as Delgadina, Monkey Bread, Lucille Jones, Saturna, and Johnson. For example, Monkey Bread says of her writing, "Well, I keeps trying to get freer. You know, mixing my words with whatever I wants to mix them with" (*MS* 433), a sentiment that embodies the overall style of *Mosquito*. Speaking through Johnson, Jones elaborates that this freedom is partially a result of associating jazz with storytelling: "I be wondering if it be possible to tell a true jazz story, where the peoples that listens can just enter the story and start telling it and adding things wherever they wants" (*MS* 93). Like a free jazz solo, *Mosquito* conveys things "wherever they wants," skipping from anecdote to anecdote and character to character, asking or perhaps even forcing readers (story organizers both inside and outside the text) to "tell it theyselves"—to put together the fragmented pieces and establish the connections in a way that makes them part of the book. Much like improvised jazz, the narrative also remains fresh through the tone of its performance: mainly the colloquial voice of Johnson. Through the character of Ray Mendoza Jones partially anticipated negative reactions to the book's narrative format. As Johnson recounts, "He said corrupted English or corruptible English or maybe even incorruptible English. I ain't sure what he say, but I know he talking about my language. What that have to do with my intelligence? I'm asking" (*MS* 110). Just as Mendoza has trouble reconciling Johnson's dialect with her formidable intelligence, so readers must wade through the book's realistically excessive colloquialisms in order to detect its richness.

Mosquito's structure, an additional concern of initial reviewers, also is addressed indirectly by Jones in the text. In the midst of her storytelling, Johnson remarks, "I spent so much time telling y'all about Delgadina, y'all probably forgot about that priest. But that's the way true stories is" (*MS* 121). Sacrificing formal design for the sake of realistic telling, Jones throws the reader into a rambling tale that jumps, without warning, forward and back. Yet, understanding the challenges this presents to conventional readers, Jones has Johnson sympathetically admit, "I knows there's a lot of y'all that ain't used to hearing conversations that jumps back and forth between real time, the past, the future, and virtual time" (*MS* 421). However, whereas Johnson understands and concedes the complexities of her narrative style, she remains unwilling to change it, convinced that the telling is essential to the content and the meanings she wishes to convey.

Although Jones plants passages in her novel to explain her stylistic and structural decisions, the reader ultimately must remain slightly wary of both her and her narrators. At one point she tells Mendoza, "You talking 'bout race being a myth. Well, it seem like to me that language is a myth too" (*MS* 242), a comment that later has implications for her own storytelling: "I's told y'all the truth about most of the peoples in this story, although I ain't told y'all the whole truth about none of the peoples in this story" (*MS* 601). Although Johnson appears to be telling us a genuine story, it is most likely muted and exaggerated in places so as not to compromise the Sanctuary Movement, as well as to call into question the complexities of narrative truth. At one point Delgadina tells Johnson, "You're not an ignorant woman. You don't look like an ignorant woman. You look too cunning and clever. I think you're a trickster, a jokester" (*MS* 312). A manipulative master of storytelling, Johnson retains important information in weaving her tale, which becomes an important aspect of the overall novel. Deprived of all the details, readers are left to trust the general direction of Johnson's tale, which is not difficult to do given her laudable principles and achievements. Destabilizing a nationalist gringo subjectivity, Johnson, along with Delgadina, suggests an alternative, liberating vision of American and world culture while reaffirming the overall importance of cultural experience. This endeavor also remains the aim of Jones. Working from an Afrocentric core, Jones stretches out in *Mosquito* to establish an ambitiously inclusive portrayal of gendered and ethnic subjectivities — one that may encourage readers to reexamine and liberate their own views on and roles in an increasingly boundary-less and cross-cultural global existence.

Notes

1. *The Hermit-Woman* (Detroit: Lotus, 1983) 50–69.
2. *Callaloo* 16.3 (October 1982) 59–65.

CHAPTER 5

A Quest for Wholeness: Criticism

"I take for my focus everything."
—Gayl Jones, "From *The Quest for Wholeness:* Re-Imagining the African-American Novel: An Essay on Third World Aesthetics," 510

Perhaps because she is a writer and storyteller, wedded to the expressions and rhythms of word and voice, Jones evinces a more practical, application-based criticism than the academic formulations of her more scholarly academic contemporaries. Eschewing jargonized theoretical frameworks and lengthy footnotes for the joy of discovering what resonates, what works, in a given literary creation, Jones's is a criticism wholly arrived from the imagination of the working artist–delineating what is to be celebrated in the achievements of other writers while wondering, all the while, at how the tenuous boundaries and distinctions of literature may be pressed ever further.

The critical endeavor, the effort to explain, can be a contradictory foil to both the creative process and, more generally, the creative writer, especially when applied within the context of storytelling and oral play. Academic interpretive approaches cannot help but restrict and formulize — bind and mark — the printed word, whereas the dynamics of the oral tradition afford life and possibility to texts — indeed, are experience personified — making their perusal an active event for the beholder, who in critical disposition often remains as much a listener as reader. As evinced in slave narratives up through some of the best literary works of the twenty-first century, the African American oral tradition inherently resists definitive explication and assimilation. Even when it appears to play a eurocentric game or conform to a new methodology, there usually may be identified some form of critique — a counter logic or rhetoric — at work as well, lurking just beneath the surface.

From the very beginnings of her writing career, Jones has been fascinated by the grand, interlocking process which draws both on creative techniques and forms, as well as the mysteries of the authorial self, in somehow managing to translate lived experience into a performed literary medium. In her 1973 dissertation, "Toward an All-Inclusive Structure," Jones recounted, "I've been concerned not only with a linguistic flexibility, but with a flexibility of consciousness: a way of using language as a means of meeting experience, both private and communal, external and internal" (1). The focus here — large and complex, as it would remain decades later — is on a psychologically and linguistically informed poetics of totality, an aesthetic wholeness — what she would identify in the dissertation as an "all-inclusive structure":

> This structure is one which would theoretically include *everything*: experience and imagination, autobiography, history, legend, myth, ritual, metaphor, dream (essentially all forms both linguistic and experimental); it would make use of specifically black forms, both musical (blues, jazz, work songs, spirituals) and linguistic (the sermon, playing dozens, signifying, jive); it would see the erotic as an authentic method of expression [1].

Grand and perhaps even inherently self-defeating in its conception, Jones's ambitious critical program nonetheless remains a remarkable one in its attempt to evoke the entirety of artistic creation rather than draw it beneath the yoke of a fashionable, limiting framework.

According to Jones, the key to the achievement of artistic wholeness — or the "all-inclusive structure," as it initially was termed — lay in the establishment of a highly flexible narrative structure that would allow for rhythmical and modal shifts across language and consciousness. Critical here is the functional exchange of art and psychology across blurred boundaries of experience — an exchange that creates ripples or other forms of distortion in the presentation of fictional events. In her dissertation Jones specifically recorded an indebtedness to "the synactical innovations of Gertrude Stein and the orthographical innovations of James Joyce" (2). Of particular note, she was fascinated by the ability of portions of Stein's and Joyce's respective work to embody pathological speech patterns: "to put their language disturbances down on paper in that amorphous form we give the name genius to" (2). "Amorphous" might also partially describe the actual deployment of the "all-inclusive structure," for the lack of systematic elements in its workings leads one to suspect that it is was as much Jones's literary genius, her traceless writerly talent — one thinks here of Poe and his "Philosophy of Composition" — that fueled its successful execution as the realization of a discernable and easily repeatable pattern.

It is worth pointing out that Jones's dissertation was penned during and shortly after the early 1970s explosion of demands for and the establishment of hundreds of Black Studies programs at universities and colleges across the United States. Though usually supported by liberal white faculty, such programs often were constructed on foundations of traditional curricula and scholarly approaches. In other words, many of them were designed in such a way as to muffle the political activism and revisionist claims that had served as the catalysts for their founding. Jones surely was aware of these trends, yet her decision to focus primarily on aesthetic and imaginative formal elements rather than political issues in her "all-inclusive structure" and dissertation seem to have had more to do with her necessary development as a young writer than a lack of sensitivity to the political issues of that era involving African Americans in higher education.

Nearly a decade later, however — by the time she had completed the manuscript for her first book-length work of criticism, *Liberating Voices: Oral Tradition in African American Literature* — Jones, as an established writer and college professor, would demonstrate a recognition of and interest in social forces in the African American literary tradition, albeit translated through works of high formal complexity and achievement. Indeed, to some extent *Liberating Voices* marks a measured embrace of the ethnic and political aspects of literature that largely remained unremarked in her dissertation. In the spirit of its times, the book is a "corrective" work of African American criticism, seeking to destabilize the eurocentric framework upon which earlier critics had argued the African American literary tradition was based.

Liberating Voices asserts that authentic African American literature is contingent upon altogether throwing off the yoke of European and American literary traditions, or transforming them into something unrecognizable through the utilization of African-based oral and musical techniques: "This artistic liberation movement links the writers of African American literary tradition and is common to all literatures which have held (or assumed) a position of subordination to another literary tradition" (*LV* 178). Such assertions of aesthetic and intellectual cultural liberation were quickly becoming cliché in the early 1990s, as postcolonialism and African American studies flowered and thrived in all manner of institutions and scholarly venues. As a result of this wide-ranging and highly visible trend, more than one critic was quick to take Jones to task for not having surveyed more thoroughly the intellectual climate and landscape into which Harvard University Press had launched her book. In his review of *Liberating Voices* renowned essayist Sven Birkerts deadpanned that the study is "neither particularly liberating nor revelatory" (168). Apparently unconcerned with appearing to defend the eurocentric status quo, Birkerts asserts that Jones inaccurately arranges European and American literary traditions into a kind of overly simplistic and exclusionary, bad-guy "strawman figure" (169) against which African American literature must dutifully and sympathetically struggle. For Birkerts, Jones fails to capture the complexity and ambivalence between cultural traditions — a dynamic that sometimes oppresses the subordinate culture, yet also possesses the capacity to enrich it. Concluding that Jones did not give enough credit to the positive aspects of European-based modernism, namely its formal innovations, Birkerts maintains that she instead employs it as a self-evident variable for African American resistance and innovation. For Birkerts, at least, this simplifies and reduces the process of literary transmission to a level that is problematic and, in the end, unsatisfying.

Though Birkerts ultimately found Jones's book wanting in some of its most essential areas, he is sympathetic to the questions it raises and affords its claims a high measure of seriousness and respect. At least one other reviewer was considerably less willing to meet Jones a portion of the way. In her review of *Liberating Voices* Belinda Edmondson smugly pokes fun at what she perceives as Jones's "rather effusive prose" and overly simplistic glossary of terms at book's end: "It would appear that Jones anticipates a remarkably ill-informed audience for this work — or a very young one" (129). Edmundson also ventures beyond drawing attention to these largely cosmetic matters to discern specific problems in Jones's portrayal of African American music: "Jones bases her assessment of black music's aesthetic superiority in part on its ability to develop its own standard and thereby judge other musical forms, thus setting the stage for racial one-upsmanship" (128). Edmundson particularly laments the fact that the study's musical one-upsmanship includes no mention of rap. However, in pointing to this perceived shortcoming Edmundson reveals an interpretive flaw of her own: that she either failed to read or misread the book's postscript and thus remained wholly unaware of its 1982, pre-mainstream rap composition date.

Considering the vast growth and evolution of African American studies between 1982 and 1992, the book's early 1980s composition frame is an important fact for the reader to bear in mind, and indeed does much to explain the presence of what some reviewers have taken to be deficiencies or redundancies when measured against other works of early 1990s African American criticism. As reviewer Gay Wilentz has pointed out, the book "would have been much more useful and appropriate had it been published when it was first written" (141). In fact, Cheryl A. Wall explicitly observed that *Liberating Voices* anticipates many of the voice-based arguments established during the second half of the 1980s by Houston Baker, Henry Louis Gates Jr., and others. However, because Jones did not choose to revise her study to account for the works that preceded it in print if not in conception, Wilentz cannot help but find flaw with the fact that "the lack of attention to critics, both cursorily named in the postscript and unnamed, seems to deny what has transpired in the last decade. Creative writers often write critical works with their own impressionistic style, but in this case, the work of criticism is an extremely conventional one and therefore needs to be appraised in this context" (142). Sympathetic in her appreciation of Jones as a creative writer and her assessment of the manuscript as chronologically passe, Wilentz nevertheless is forced to echo some of the overarching concerns of Birkerts and Edmundson.

Wilentz differs from other reviewers, however — Birkerts, most notably — in her assertion that Jones sometimes inadvertently valorizes the European models from which she is seeking to liberate African American texts. Whereas Birkerts perceived the book's portrayal of European writers as that ascribed to an overly simplified villain, Wilentz detects an underlying admiration for their methods. One important dynamic these differing observations seem to reveal is that *Liberating Voices* is more formally-oriented in its concerns than its title and various descriptions imply. As Jones herself explains near the beginning of the introduction, "[T]he book focuses on technique" (*LV* 2). Consequently, at the very end of the introduction she again hones in on the study's formal considerations and how they might prove useful to working writers; how they might "show technical developments in oral tradition and their uses in creative writing, uses which may be as broad and varied and complex as those derived from written traditions in the ways of representing and developing character, structure, language, and dramatic moments" (*LV* 14). This assertion, ignored by many of the book's reviewers, does much to explain the preponderance of ambivalent assessments that greeted the book upon its publication. Too often the expectation seems to have been for academically-oriented critical innovation when in fact Jones predominantly was seeking to demonstrate creative literary functionality in terms of the texts she utilized. This pragmatic approach perhaps condemned the study conceptually within the context of its time, yet it is this very characteristic which, ironically, makes the study still viable and instructive now. As reviewer Elon Kulii pointed out, the book promised to be accessible and useful to "folklorists, students of literature, writers, and critics" (107). Perhaps the study did not situate itself to the extent expected by most working literary critics, but this was justified in the sense that it promised to be useful beyond the boundaries of that era's criticism. For the interpretive critical fashions that surrounded the book's 1992 release have long since changed, but the fruits of Jones's functional criticism — established, as they are, by one of the late twentieth century's best working writers — are as relevant and useful today as they were in 1982.

Though it would not appear in print for another decade, the composition of *Liberating Voices* was receding in Jones's literary rearview mirror by the end of 1982. So it is that her essay "About My Work," which appeared two years later in 1984, may serve as a reflection of Jones's intellectual evolution beyond her 1992 book-length study and, indeed, aids in contextualizing the perspective from which it was generated. Among the things revealed in "About My Work" is a professed predilection for telling the story in just the manner and style it demands at any cost — even if that means violating the taboos of politics or consciously ignoring politics altogether. Jones explains at length:

> I do not have a political "stance," but I am interested sometimes in the relationship between history, society, morality, and personality. I believe that all literatures can have political uses and misuses. Sometimes politics can enhance, sometimes it can get in the way of the imaginative literature. Sometimes politics or political strategies, like any kind of strategy and system, can be useful in the organization and structuring of one's work, the selecting of character, of event, the choosing of ideas, but it can also tell you what you cannot do, tell you what you must avoid, tell that there's a certain territory politics won't allow you to enter, certain questions politics won't allow you to ask — in order to be "politically correct." I think sometimes you just have to be "wrong"; there's a lot of imaginative territory that you have to be "wrong" in order to enter. I'm not sure one can be a creative writer and a politician [234].

As evinced by much of her early fiction — perhaps most notably *Eva's Man*— Jones is not afraid to be what she ironically characterizes as "wrong," even at the risk of alienating reviewers and critics who favor political context over good storytelling. Necessary to her writing technique is the freedom to journey wherever the story leads without restriction — a liberating approach that privileges by necessity the unfettered imagination. Thus, storytelling remained the primary consideration for Jones, regardless of the political context. As she maintains in "About My Work," "I notice people more than landscape. I notice voices ... I like to write about imaginary people — become their 'voices'" (234). What is said and the persona that utters it always remain front and center in Jones's work. The truth of utterance and characterization consistently function as the primary variables upon which the rest of Jones's work depends.

Jones's focus on voice and the formal elements that constitute its successful establishment is perhaps best demonstrated through her critical work on the poet Sterling Brown, a renowned reader and literary performer. Jones would discuss his work in *Liberating Voices* and then return to it in a book review of his collected poems a year later. What seems to have fascinated her most about Brown's verse is the freedom, the liberation, afforded by its colloquial qualities. For example, she describes Brown's poem "Uncle Joe" as a kind of "open-ended folkspeech capable of any reflection, any sort of expository and narrative strategy" (*LV* 34). Indeed, much of the poem's success seems to arise from the tension between its poetic structure and the powerful voice of the main character, Uncle Joe, which threatens to disrupt that structure. As Jones points out, "Uncle Joe's voice, in keeping with the folk character as the key figure, is more fluid and has more tonal intensity than the narrator's; it is more immediate, more vibrant, reproducing real emotions and varieties of them in a small space" (*LV* 35). For Jones, the energy of the teller and what is being told takes precedence over the formal strictures that seek to frame it.

At the end of her discussion of Brown's poetry in *Liberating Voices* Jones proclaims that as a result of Brown's work, "more voices with broad range and conceptual complexity were waiting to be heard" (*LV* 37). This assertion meshes nicely with the first sentence of her review of Brown's collected poems a year later in 1983: "Sterling Brown's poetry must be heard to be wholly experienced" ("A Review" 43). Jones's emphasis on the voice of the poet/storyteller is complemented here by a focus on the hearer and what precisely is heard. Thus, Brown's is not so much a poetry to be read, but rather experienced in an auditory capacity. This dynamic underscores the underlying influences on Brown's work, which, in fact, is very similar to the sources that have shaped Jones's aesthetic. She says of his method in her review, "Brown combines traditional literary forms with artistic forms derived from oral culture: spirituals, blues, jazz, worksongs, sermons, ballads complicate and broaden the sound devices as well as maintain the imaginative integrity of these traditions" (44). This passage easily might describe Jones's artistic concerns as well. Sound and the various conventions of its conveyance conspire to create an approach that appeals to the senses but also takes part in and helps to record and transmit oral traditions not readily evident in print art forms. Traditions are enriched and transmitted even as they are performed.

Beyond his formal approach to his variety of performance poetry, Brown also is notable to Jones for his understated method of dealing with social issues and politics — his ability to infuse them into his work without making the appear polemical or dogmatic. She observes, "Brown's vision is full and acknowledges the social, historical, political and economic dynamics but these are never 'frozen' as statement but always 'carefully' and 'lovingly' in tune with voice, memory, song, and speech of whole persons" (44). Central here is an achievement of melody between artistic subject and social context, which in turn helps to create fully-realized characters and stories — a degree of wholeness which completes the work at hand. Four years later, in her 1987 essay on Gwendolyn's Brooks' "In the Mecca," Jones would celebrate a similar overarching quality in her description of Brooks' composition: "There is something circular in even the vertical and horizontal progressions of this poem" (202). For Jones, the great curving abstract message of Brooks' verse transcends its rigid lines and general placement upon the page. The telling seems almost to become a different form, breaking loose from its visual rigidity in print and revealing its underpinnings in a grand circle of meaning.

Probably because she primarily is a creative writer, Jones embraces a method of telling which remains always central in her consciousness, even with regard to her scholarly works. In an interview she pointed to her narrative decision-making in terms of the critical manuscript that would become *Liberating Voices*:

> I'm currently working on a book entitled *Oral Tradition in Afro-American Literature* and among other things it attempts to speak about how Afro-American writers invent linguistic worlds and structural and dramatic procedures using elements of the Afro-American oral tradition. In the telling of it there are also problems of language that I have to work through — for instance, avoiding the "dissertation voice" and still making it a scholarly work [Rowell, "An Interview" 33].

One need only crack the pages of a contemporary literary journal to discern that considerations of narrative and language often are overlooked by academic writers in favor of theoretical exposition. And there exists within literary culture very different venues for literary criticism, the essays one peruses in a top literary quarterly — the *Sewanee Review*, for instance — generally demonstrating a greater attention to language and style than the more jargonized work one typically encounters in a periodical with a focus that is purely academic and theoretical. Rare is the scholar who publishes in both sorts of venues, for they are, to notable degrees, aimed at very different audiences and discursive communities.

Central to this discussion of literary periodicals is Jones's long and fruitful relationship with one of the best literary quarterlies, African American or otherwise: *Callaloo*. Celebrated for its publication of the best African American writers and critical works about them, the journal long has enjoyed an innovative and enviable run in the capable editorial hands of Charles H. Rowell. Having published more than a dozen works by Jones since 1979, *Callaloo* has functioned as the primary artistic outlet for Jones outside of her books, particularly during those long, silent stretches when she has elected to publish little or nothing anywhere else.

It should come as little surprise then that it is to a 1994 number of *Callaloo* we must turn in order to peruse Jones's most fascinating work of criticism: an essay lengthily and provocatively entitled "From *The Quest for Wholeness*: Re-Imagining the African-American Novel: An Essay on Third World Aesthetics." In its narrative approach, "From *The Quest for Wholeness*" firmly and brilliantly breaks free from traditional criticism altogether by allowing itself to be articulated by a speaker who is, in fact, a vivacious make-believe novel:

> I am a novel of the Third World, and so you would expect me to ... have a different aesthetics, to revise (or rewrite genre), characterization, style, theme, structure, viewpoint, values, and so I do. Paradox and ambivalence may be seen in the margins of this marginal text, and may be read in and between these lines. Satire and irony is plentiful here, for it's part of my tradition. Sometimes I may support or challenge your sense of logic or rationality; depending on who you are, I may be a novel full of contradictions [508].

Unlike specialist scholars, Jones, as a gifted renderer of fiction, has the ability to generate, to *be*, the novel of which she speaks. Yet her essay does not claim to be a prescription for all African American novels, rather it confidently purports what it is doing in its own voice, insinuating that other works may or may not choose to do likewise. And there are echoes of Jones's assertions from earlier works, as when she has her novel assert:

> [D]on't mistake me for politics, or economics, or sociology, or history — which folks like to mistake for, or mere folklore when I tell my stories in vernacular, pidgin or creole. But since I'm literature and more specifically fiction, though not always fictitious fiction, I may contain every sort of implication: political, economic, sociological, anthropological, historical [508].

In its open-ended and liberating philosophy, this passage is vintage Gayl Jones, subordinating politics to the vernacular story at hand while attempting to grope and account for a wholeness that encompasses "every sort of implication."

"From *The Quest for Wholeness*" arrived at a time during which the awareness and production of scholarship on other ethnic groups in the

United States had compelled many African American thinkers to narrow their identity discourses, many of which focused on defining and affirming a unique African American form of personality among other ethnicities. Whereas *Liberating Voices* might have been slightly out of step with the contemporary critical fashions of its release year, "From *The Quest for Wholeness*" was dead on. Establishing its own definition of Afrocentrism in asserting what it means to be African American, Jones's bold novel asserts, "To be free, to be liberated, an aesthetic must come from oneself, be defined by oneself, not others.... My aesthetic(s) is Afrocentric, then, and I may challenge or confirm your ideas of beauty, value, and form, depending on who you are" (509). The concept of Afrocentrism, championed perhaps most notably in the academic realm by Molefi Asante, had reached the apex of its popularity by the time Jones penned her essay. At the center of the term is a preoccupation with making African ideals, aesthetic and otherwise, the prime basis for acquiring knowledge, much in the way the "western tradition" had been accused of measuring works by its own hazy, collective cultural standards. Ironically, as with eurocentrism, one of the popular attacks leveled at Afrocentrism emphasizes the concept's rigidly prescriptive structure and inability, or unwillingness, to account for diversity and pluralism within African American communities and in relation to other ethnicities. Yet Jones is delivered from this pitfall by her ongoing attention to aesthetics and her embrace — perhaps most notably revealed in the late 1999 novel *Mosquito* — of the interactions between African American cultures and other communities and ethnicities, be they specifically Brazilian, broadly Latino, or even Afro-German. For Jones, the perspectives of Afrocentrism and what she identifies as "Third World Aesthetics" are more or less identical in their celebration of the identity of the culture from which art actively emerges and their resistance to the colonizing interpretive frameworks of the cultures that would seek to forcibly influence them.

In moving from the inward toward its outward expression in a manner that acknowledges culture while refusing to be dominated by it, Jones repeatedly evokes and approaches the all-inclusive structure she brazenly articulated in her 1973 dissertation. How much more vividly the elements of fiction and criticism alike shine when they focus upon the fundamental rudiments of identity and existence while also devoting time and attention to the very nature of their telling and transmission. Jones maintained in *Liberating Voices* that "Oral tradition offers continuity of voice as well as its liberation.... Each writer in his or her own way resolves the tensions between orality and literature in the quest for the restoration of self as whole personality" (*LV* 180), whereas in "From *The Quest for Wholeness*" Jones's novel recognizes and acknowledges that "[e]very group and nation wants to be able to pattern its stories. Pattern its ideas, and handle space, time, and perspective in its own unique way" (511). These concerns with self and culture coalesce in one of the 1994 essay's most important sentences, which reads as though it might have been drawn from her dissertation more than two decades earlier: "I take for my focus everything. Theme, style, structure, character, story. You ask where's the story: I'm the story, me/you, myself/ourselves. I am a complex blending of every story element and non-story" (510). For Jones, the essence of such expressions as "wholeness" and "everything" arrive from an integration of modes of communication (primarily, in Jones's case, the oral and the literary) along with a secondary, though increasingly palpable, recognition of social context. More than a basis for her successful fiction and poetry, it informs the very essence of her unique and valuable body of criticism. Like the creative work, it seeks to set us free.

Conclusion: Liberated Voice

Creator of a wide and progressively changing body of work, Gayl Jones has demonstrated that her liberating voice consists of many different tones and utterances. Having stated, "I think my language/word foundations were oral rather than written" (Harper 692), Jones has not hesitated to build upon those original rudiments with new varieties of language and voice, keeping innovative modes of oral expression at the center of her written work — variables to be read, heard, traced and delineated with great reward. At the end of his influential study *The Contemporary African American Novel* Bernard Bell asserts "that a systematic, rigorous inquiry into the use of African American vernacular forms by novelists offers readers the most illuminating, challenging, and effective method of assessing the complex relationship of language, power, and knowledge in their interrogations of the distinctive correlations of literature to life, fiction to fact, and myth to reality in the tradition of the contemporary African American novel" (388). Singularly encompassing and embodying the tropes in Bell's recommended critical approach for current and future readers and scholars, Jones's work collectively constitutes a unique and remarkable model of the African American vernacular functioning in a complex literary medium.

In her dissertation, Jones had proclaimed her ambitious intention of constructing an "all-inclusive structure," a comprehensive arrangement of experience, imagination, autobiography, history, legend, myth, ritual, metaphor, psychology, dream, black forms (musical and linguistic), and the erotic as an authentic method of expression. Among others, James Coleman has suggested that the "African American imagination is conceived in the individual struggle and the historical travail created by the horror of the past of slavery and racism" (3), and over the course of her early plays and novels Jones mixed and deployed her numerous dissertation themes with notably dark and violent results, all the while hoping to establish an elusive variety of cultural and aesthetic hope for the future. Jones's remarkable ability to interweave and reconcile her "all-inclusive" themes, to impressively meet the demands of her own demanding theoretical structure, constituted an impressive achievement for a young writer, even though her vivid depictions of the negative aspects of African American culture — her abstraction of tropes such as madness and evil into monocultural black milieus — resulted in various derogatory appraisals of her work. In hindsight, we may discern that Jones's subject matter and her rendering of it were very much ahead of their time. In his Foreword to *Making Callaloo*, a collection of that celebrated journal's best writings, Percival Everett recounts that the African American novel of decades past was "novel: a people's statement about black life, about being black in a racist, oppressive society. It all fit neatly into the rehearsed rhetoric of the 1960s and 1970s" (xvi). Jones, to her credit, did not suffer the rhetorical mold of those times and, against protests from certain corners of literary culture, continued to develop her agenda, assimilating, over the course of several short stories and the German novel *Die Vogelfängerin*, the critical attacks and underlying dilemmas of art and politics into her work. Just as many of the characters in her short fiction escape grotesque conditions and discourses through language and the act of telling, so Jones herself continued to generate provocative linguistic art and meaning, all the while employing grotesque vehicles, such as madness and brutality — elements she believed to lie at the painful and truthful core of contemporary African American existence.

The major shift in Jones's cultural and aesthetic themes occurred with her three books of poetry during the 1980s, which constituted a collective transition from a concern with separate single contemporary voices involved usually in problematic and violent personal relationships to viewpoints and voices articulating cultural issues across time and place. Her catalyst for this endeavor was the history of slavery in Brazil, a violent, yet distant, phenomenon which allowed her to explore the complexities of temporality and oppression from a more objective, though equally heartfelt, perspective — ultimately establishing a compelling logocentric historical authority that provided overdue utterance to a wronged and silenced dead. A powerful gendered element informed this idea as well since the history of slavery fundamentally threatens the existence and continuity of femininity and motherhood. A writer like Jones combats such a debilitating cultural condition by confronting it and affording it utterance — a rehabilitative and liberating process of reconceptualization described by Venetria Patton in *Women in Chains* as "rememory" (150). Although she eventually would return to the milieu of the contemporary United States, Jones remained firmly focused on international culture in her 1990s novels. The protagonists of those books present liberating visions of American and world culture, for African-descended people and others, while reaffirming the overall importance of cultural experience, and conceptualizing healthy futures containing healing practices and evaporating cultural boundaries.

Works that attempt to articulate and reconcile ethnic identities across cultures face a number of challenges; they are struck with the task of simultaneously establishing new modes of authenticity and calling them into question — a wavering, searching process both liberating and destabilizing. Ethnicity itself continues to constitute an evasive distinction, different from race, which is itself a shifting cultural and political construction. The undertaking is complicated further when its primary taskmasters are ethnic women, since their historical roles as stakeholders in national identities often have been delineated as small — meaning their defining endeavors are as much recoveries of traditional authentic identities as they are rejections and reconfigurations of the popular hues those identities take in the present. Jones's women burst the representational bonds that confine them to private, non-public spaces and seek to gag and otherwise muffle their voices. They desire not only to participate in but to define new concepts of place and nationhood that allow for their identities as meaningful variables, free from the restrictive masculine formulas traditionally associated with the nation state. Jones's women and their stories offer free and frank revisions to the imperial nature of history and contemporary cultural hegemony, conspiring to generate autonomy and voice — independent yet overlapping — where before there had existed only an enforced silence.

Metaphorically, culturally, and literally, Jones's women shatter barriers and cross borders in establishing their identities, their narratives serving as ready-made embodiments of "border-theory"—a vein of cultural inquiry based predominantly on United States–Mexico border exchanges. However, extending beyond these important North American concerns, Jones's preoccupation with a truly global cultural perspective has uniquely anticipated and embodied the tensions inherent in such relevant larger early twenty-first century theories as diaspora studies and globalization. On the one hand rests the ongoing interest in tracing specific traditional cultures as they spread out, taking note of their significant variations, and reimagining the supposed single past from which they have journeyed. On the other hand is the encroaching sense of global community, ever pressing closer, that increasingly blends and confuses cultures, diasporas, and racial identities—the blurring of which makes tracing or mythologizing a shared history all the more difficult. Yet, both the discourses of global postcolonial theory and traditional African American literary studies turn upon arguments drawn from alternative cultural views of dominant cultures. Bearing this distinction in mind, scholar John Gruesser has urged early twenty-first century "postcolonial and African American critics to emulate, expand on, and, where appropriate, emend [Paul] Gilroy's bold attempt to bridge postcolonial and African American studies, embracing the black Atlantic's stress on movement through space and intercultural connections" (133). Indeed, moving beyond American literature, matching and contextualizing its racial and cultural connotations on the other side of its nation-state boundaries, appears to have become the most relevant avenue of inquiry for studying American literature—the trajectory of the national charted in the process of attempting to map the contemporary global moment.

Jones's 1990s fiction clearly prefigured the endeavor of globalizing African American concerns, as demonstrated by the ability of her more recent protagonists to see themselves existing both in a specific cultural tradition and an evolving world where that tradition is likely to become (be made into) something else—addressing, significantly and singularly, the identity crisis that will confront progressively larger numbers of people in the twenty-first century. And in anticipating and confronting this cultural dilemma, Jones herself does not cling to traditional notions of racial and national heritage but rather addresses them with an openness and naked honesty suggestive of the hard psychological case studies informing her early work. In a 2003 essay, Jones proclaimed her admiration for "the good man and good woman, people with a nobility of spirit, as New World African" ("From *Stop Dat Moda*" 723). Over the long course of her serious and unrelenting investigations of African-descended identity — not all of them positive and affirming — Jones demonstrates an aesthetic and cultural variety, an authorial manifestation, of the "nobility of spirit" of which she speaks. In this sense she is a "good woman," a liberated voice meaningfully and singularly attempting to relate and define the ongoing experience of both New World Africans and the cultural others, here and everywhere, with whom their future will be forged.

Appendix I

An Interview with Gayl Jones, by Claudia C. Tate

Gayl Jones's first novel, *Corregidora*, appeared when she was twenty-six years old. It is a bizarre, romantic story which exposes the intimate family history of three generations of black women residing in rural Kentucky from the early- to the mid-twentieth century. Jones's second novel, *Eva's Man*, is about a young black woman's recollection of the events leading up to her confinement in a mental institution. Her third work, *White Rat*, is a collection of short stories depicting brief encounters with seemingly ordinary black people in rural Kentucky.

All of Jones's work is characterized by carefully wrought narratives in which the process of communication develops from the author's determination to relay the story entirely in terms of the mental processes of the main character, without any authorial intrusion or judgment. Although this technique has made many reviewers uneasy, Jones insists that her task is to record her observations with compassion and understanding and not to be judgmental. Her stories, moreover, reflect her mastery of combining improvisational storytelling with sophisticated formal concerns without making the story appear contrived or relying on obtrusive narrative devices.

Born in 1949 in Lexington, Kentucky, where she continued to reside until she first went to Connecticut College and then to Brown University, Jones is now Assistant Professor of English at the University of Michigan. She refuses to divulge additional biographical information, contending that her work must live independently of its creator, that it must sustain its own character and artistic autonomy. But while she will not discuss her private life, she did, in the interview that follows, share some insights into her artistic endeavors and about her perceptions of American literary history.

Jones and I met at noon in the Michigan Union on the campus of the University of Michigan in Ann Arbor on August 2, 1978. While I reminisced about my days as an undergraduate there, Jones pointed out changes that had occurred in the English Department. As we leisurely strolled about the campus, she told me that she was currently revising several short stories and poems written years ago as well as working on another novel. That novel, entitled "Palmares," is set in seventeenth-century Brazil and is, at this writing, finished. Jones expects it to be published in the not-too-distant future.[1]

TATE: Gayl, you said in your interview with Mike Harper l that you didn't know what mysterious act Great Gram had performed on old man Corregidora until you got to the end of the novel [*Corregidora*]. Does this mean that your writing is somewhat spontaneous, somewhat open-ended? Would you elaborate on your writing process?

JONES: In the interview with Michael Harper I said that I didn't know what Great Gram had done to Corregidora at the time that I first mentioned her "mysterious act" in the novel. When I asked myself that question I didn't know what it was going to be, or even if I was going to resolve it in the book — whether it was going to remain a "mysterious act." But "in the process of writing" the question was resolved. Or rather it was resolved in the process of the character, Ursa's acting out a new situation.

My writing is mostly open-ended, though I will make somewhat loose outlines — lists of events, themes, situations, characters, and even details of conversations — lists of items that I want to include. I'll make notes before and while I'm writing. I find that I make more of these notes now, than when I was writing *Corregidora* or *Eva's Man*, though this kind of "loose" outlining started with these novels. I think that I like the word "improvisational" rather than "spontaneous"; I think that it better describes my writing process.

Corregidora, as it appears in the Random House edition, is mostly my first version, although there is a minor revision. It consists of having added information about Ursa's past, her relationships with Mutt and her mother.

My revision method generally consists of asking questions, and then I try to answer those questions dramatically. In the case of *Corregidora*, my editor, Toni Morrison, asked the unanswered question: What about Ursa's past? This question required that I clarify the relationships between Ursa and Mutt and Ursa and her mother. So I added about one hundred pages to answer those questions. Now before I submit anything, I'll ask myself the questions that have not been answered in the course of the manuscript, or perhaps pose new questions. I then answer them; and, of course, I prefer to answer them dramatically rather than just to make statements.

Eva's Man went through several writings: It was a kind of lyrical novel, then it was a short "dramatic" story, then it was the *Eva's Man* as it is printed in the Random House edition. The handling of time in the novel is most improvisational; what I mean by that is that the ordering of the events is primarily improvisational. I wanted to get the sense of different times and different personalities coexisting in memory. I was also trying to do something else that I don't think comes across very well. I suppose that I can call it "social realism." I was trying to dramatize a sense of the "real" and the "fantastic," or fancied and real episodes, coexisting together in Eva's narrative. The question that the listener would continually hear would be: How much of Eva's story is true and how much is deliberately not true; that is, how much of a game is she playing with her listeners/psychiatrists/others? And finally how much of her story is her own fantasy of the past? I try to suggest this in the manner that the story begins, and also by the repetition of the same events/situations but with different people involved.

TATE: The second question is related to the first in that I am interested in having you label yourself as either a fiction-maker or a storyteller. The process that you just described seems especially well-suited to someone who is telling a story because a story seemingly doesn't have to concern itself with extremely formal aspects. The story seems to unravel, and the structural concerns are, in fact, much more subtle. Thus, do you consider yourself to be primarily a storyteller? And what then does that involve as you think in terms of your listener, your evolving story, and especially the narrator for whom you shape ideas?

JONES: I think of myself principally as a storyteller. Most of the fictions that I write that seem to come across, that seem to work, have been those in which I am concerned with the storyteller, not only the author as storyteller, but also the characters as storytellers, those who are very conscious of speaking either to a particular person or to particular people. I think there's also that sense of the hearer as well as the teller in terms of my organizing and selecting events and situations.

At the time that I was writing *Corregidora* and *Eva's Man* I was particularly interested, and continue to be interested, in oral traditions of storytelling — Afro-American and others — where there is always that consciousness and importance of the hearer, even in the interior monologue where the storyteller becomes the hearer. That consciousness or self-consciousness is important in terms of the selection of significant events.

TATE: When I was reading *Corregidora*, I had the sense that I was hearing a very private story, and that Ursa had especially selected me to hear her story. I felt her consciously trying to select events that she would relay to me in her narrative. I also felt that it was not just my job to listen to her, but to become so involved in her story that I would be able to put the pieces together in some fashion, a fashion that she, too, was struggling to achieve. In *Eva's Man* I sensed that Eva's character was not going to be violated by anyone, not even by her selected listener. She would tell her story, a story that she had previously refused to tell anyone. But still in her act of telling, she refused to divulge something that would give coherence to her story.

JONES: Well, I think that in the Corregidora story I was concerned with getting across that sense of an intimate history, particularly a personal history, and also to contrast it with a varied, broad kind of impersonal telling of the Corregidora story. Thus, one reason for Ursa's telling her story and her mother's story is to contrast it with the "epic," almost impersonal history of Corregidora.

In *Eva's Man* I guess that there was not the same kind of straight, confiding telling of a history as in *Corregidora*. Although Eva rendered her "intimate history," she chose to do so only in terms of horrific moments as a kind of challenge to the listener. I also wanted the sense of her keeping certain things to herself, of her choosing the things that she would withhold. But I also wanted the reader to have a sense of not even knowing whether the things that she recalled were, in fact, true, that she might have been, perhaps, playing a game with the listener.

TATE: One quality that I like about first-person narratives, especially first-person narratives that are concerned with self-revelation of experience, is that the process of characterization is dynamic. A lot of stories, especially about black males (I think of *Invisible Man*; I think of *The Autobiography of an Ex-Coloured Man*...), never tell you anything about the intimate self. They tell you about the self in conflict with external institutions. They don't seem to have any genuine personal relationships. Your work, and also most of that by women, seems to be concerned with revealing the character's intimate sense of self through very complex relationships. These situations not only teach that character about the other people involved, but also provide a kind of learning experience in the self. Thus, your stories seem to focus on the revelation of the inner character rather than on reporting head-on confrontation with social issues.

To turn to a related concern, last year I taught a course in Black literature. I have taught the course before, but last year it became apparent that black male characters are almost singularly concerned with defining the self in social roles with respect to political and/or economic power. Black heroines, on the other hand, are not concerned with defining themselves because they always seem to know who and what they are. They seem to be more concerned with realizing their potential. Do you understand my point? Remember when Sula [in Toni Morrison's *Sula*] says that she felt like she was a medium for art, and she was going to make something of herself? I see that too in Ursa in *Corregidora*. She is not overly concerned with the external; she is trying to realize an extreme state of self-conscious womanhood. Do you have any sense of such a dichotomy between black male and female characters?

JONES: Yes, I've been thinking about that; I guess I've been mainly thinking of it in terms of something that I just call significant events in fiction. There is a difference in the way that male writers select significant events and significant relationships, and the way that women writers make these selections. I've noticed oftentimes that those events and relationships that are treated as significant by women writers aren't treated or presented as significant by the men.

APPENDIX I

I find that with many women writers relationships within family, community, between men and women, from slave narratives by women writers on, are treated as complex and significant relationships, whereas with many men the significant relationships are those that involve confrontations — relationships outside family and community. These are the significant relationships, and the complexity of experience as well as the "dilemma" is there. In the slave narratives by women, for instance, one often finds the relationships treated by women are the personal, particular, "intimate" relationships, whereas those by men are the "representational relationships." Also when men create heroines, often the relationships selected or given significance are the "representational" rather than the personal.

For example, let's compare Gaines's *Autobiography of Miss Jane Pittman* and Walker's *Jubilee*. The relationships in the former that are given attention are those that have some kind of social implications. On the other hand, we really don't have a sense of any kind of personal history for Miss Jane. Her attention is always directed outside of herself, and those events that are described in detail are those that are external or those which have some kind of social implications, rather than personal or intimate implications. You don't really have any sense of her relationship, let's say, with her husband.

Perhaps the question of one's identity, the power to act, works in the same way. Women writers seem to depict that essential mobility, that essential identity to act within the family/community, but perhaps for male writers that "place" as well as those relationships are insignificant (or not so significant), restrictive, circumscribed.

But the question of significant events/actions/relationships in fiction and how one's sex, one's history, one's culture, and one's geography influence them has been something that has interested me not only in terms of writing, but in terms of how it affects one's critical response to a work.

I guess a question that comes from this is: Would the women's actions be considered "significant actions" by the men? Would the consequences of a man's actions be different from those of a woman? How do the historical consequences of the men's actions present themselves in the works?

If you compare the slave narratives written by men with those written by women, you have a sense of very delicate and complex interpersonal relationships in the former, whether they be among members of the same race or between races. Again with men there's a kind of focus on external social grievances, and there is little sense of intimate relationships between the slaves precluding the desire for freedom.

TATE: Black male characters always seem to define themselves in terms of white expectations and power, in terms of their attempt to possess, whether it be material goods or people, whereas the women don't seem to be at all concerned with material aspects, they seem to be focusing in on relationships which result in a kind of crystallization of their own doubts and speculations. The men don't seem to want to face that kind of troubling reality. This brings me to another issue. The women always seem to be pragmatic. Now, granted there is conflict, but they almost always resolve that conflict.

Yesterday I was talking to Mary Helen Washington about this, and we had to laugh because we were talking about Helga Crane in Nella Larsen's *Quicksand*, who must determine the kind of woman she is going to be. Now, at the end of the novel she ends up in symbolic green pastures with her husband Pleasant Green, a name suggestive of a cemetery. She resolves her conflict, though not too well, but she resolves it nevertheless. The men, however, never seem to resolve anything. They're always playing "Jack-the-bear," as in *Invisible Man*, getting ready to act. The analysis is overly simplified, but I think that there is some basis of truth in it. Do you agree?

JONES: Yes. But I guess that another question which enters is probably whether the historical consequences of men's actions and women's actions have carried similar weight.

TATE: Are you saying that women's actions have not carried similar consequences?

JONES: Well, I don't want to say this, but it seems to be true. I'm working on a story now in which a man and a woman participate in the same action and the consequence for the man is, let's say, death, whereas for the woman it isn't that.

TATE: Is it that the burden or consequence of the action rests more heavily on the male than on the female?

JONES: Yes, I think so.

TATE: Let's turn to another concern. Do you have any mentors? Who or what has had the greatest influence on your work?

JONES: My mother, Lucille Jones, and my writing teachers, Michael Harper and William Meredith, have been the most important influences on my writing, and also the "speech community" in which I lived while I was growing up. I can never really say particular ways that writers have influenced my work. I think my storytelling writing style was influenced first by the people I've heard talk.

I'll list writers: Hemingway, Joyce, Gaines, Cervantes, Toomer, Chaucer. I think these were probably the first influences on my writing. Hemingway, Gaines, and Chaucer for me are the "storytellers"; Joyce and Toomer, the "fictioneers"; Cervantes, both. I say "in terms of writing" because now a new kind of concern has been added: the teaching, particularly the course in Afro-American literature that I teach. As a teacher of Afro-American literature, one has to look at the writers, the work, literary traditions in a way one doesn't have to as a reader/writer. As a result of this different perspective, certain themes, concerns of the writers crystallize in ways that I don't think they would otherwise. For example, classroom discussions about "psycho-historical influences on characters" sharpen this theme and particularly so when one must discuss how it enters Zora Neale Hurston's and Jean Toomer's works, or Alice Walker's or Toni Morrison's. So that having to discuss works in this manner forces one to see them very differently.

For instance, when I wrote *Corregidora* "psychosexual ambivalences and contradictions in the American experience" wasn't a self-conscious theme, but now it would be, as well as its connections in works by Baldwin or Walker or Toomer. Cervantes also has different implications now. When I read Cervantes now, I make connections between *Don Quixote* and the picaresque Afro-American slave narrative, and consequently *Don Quixote*, which is a favorite book, becomes even more important. Hurston interests me because of her use of folklore and storytelling, but I think she's important if one wants consciously to crystallize an idea of a heroine. Not in a self-conscious way, but in a conscientious way. None of my women are really heroines except in the sense that they're the storytellers and the central figures.

There are also unconscious ways that people are influenced by speakers and writers, or by an environment or landscape.

I realize that I am rambling, and I think that is because I hesitate to "analyze" influences. I think the earlier writers — the ones I read at an earlier age — influenced me more stylistically and perhaps the influences now go beyond style, to how style can manifest theme, how it contributes to or enhances idea.

TATE: Alice Walker said in the interview with John O'Brien that she was committed to exploring the oppression, the insanities, the loyalties, and the triumphs of black women.[2] And I was wondering if your commitment to writing has assumed a definite pattern, or whether you are just telling stories that happen to be in your head.

JONES: Well, I'm mainly telling stories that happen to be there. I guess I can look at things that I've written up to now and see a kind of pattern in terms of things that I'm interested in. I will probably say relationships between men and women, particularly from the viewpoint of a particular woman. And I'm also interested in psychology of women, psychology of language, and personal histories.

TATE: When I first started reading reviews of *Corregidora*, the reviewers talked incessantly about sexual warfare. At first, I agreed, but I kept reading the novel over and over again. After a while, I didn't see the sexual warfare anymore. What I saw is something I'll call, for lack of another term, the dialectics of love. Everybody in our society expects love to be pleasant. Everything that is supposed to be positive and pleasurable is supposed to be all positive and pleasurable. You're not supposed to have any pain mixed in with it. The more that I read *Corregidora* the more I started to see that in love there is a combination of pleasure and pain, serenity and hostility. The warfare to which the reviewers responded was merely symptomatic of this dialectic operating within Ursa's and Mutt's love. In this regard, I remember one particular image that you use maybe two or three times in the novel about the calluses on the hands that are soft underneath, a symbol that becomes associated with the pleasure and pain in love. Ursa tries to develop some kind of shield to lessen her pain, but on the inside she is very vulnerable. Do you observe this dialectic at work in the novel? And what is your response to reviewers who say *Corregidora* is a dramatization of sexual warfare?

JONES: I didn't think that Ursa was involved in sexual warfare. I guess I was interested in and I'm always interested in contradictory emotions or emotions that coexist. I do think that there is probably a kind of sexual tension in *Corregidora* both in the historical and in the personal sense.

TATE: Love, especially Ursa's love for Mutt, seems to be a very contradictory emotion. And I think that's the reason why no one can explain precisely what love is. It is entirely too ambiguous, elusive, contradictory. Love seems to be something that's held in suspension, something that is both positive and negative. And the reason that we can't get at it is because we're compelled and repelled at the same time. Do you find that relationships which involve contradictory emotions reveal more about human character?

JONES: Yes. I also think that people can hold two different emotions simultaneously.

TATE: It's often been said that art is a process of ordering our environment, that art makes sense out of chaos. Does your work attempt to make sense out of chaos, or does it record the chaos?

JONES: Well, I think it attempts to record that chaos, but at the same time the artistic process becomes a kind of order for the storyteller and also a way of dealing with the experience.

TATE: Can you say what inspired you to write *Corregidora* and *Eva's Man*?

JONES: Aside from my mentioning that I saw myself outside of conventional roles, that of wife and mother, that I was particularly interested in Brazilian history and wanted to make some kind of relationship between history and autobiography, I cannot. I could never really think of any reason to say why I wrote *Eva's Man*. It is easier to talk intellectually about, to try to articulate about, *Corregidora* than *Eva's Man*. The only kind of correlation between the two is I generally think of *Eva's Man* as a kind of dream or a kind of nightmare. It's something that comes to you, and you write it down. The novel went through a number of stages before it took the last form, although the basic story was there as a whole from the beginning.

TATE: You had the essential core including the violent act at the end? Did the core include Eva's history?

JONES: There was nothing of her past in the very first version or even in the short stories formed before it became a novel. It was just her meeting Davis and their going to the room. There was only one incident from the past, that when she knifed the man in the bar. The main idea that I wanted to communicate is Eva's unreliability as the narrator of her story.

TATE: When I read the story, I became immediately aware of three pervasive symbols: Queen Bee, Medusa, and Eve biting into the apple. These three symbolic personages have been very detrimental to men in our cultural history. How did you happen to relate these three images?

JONES: Well, they're the kind of images that I would say worked themselves into the story as I was writing it. I think that when I was first writing the novel there was Eva's concern that she was different from the way others perceived her as being. She was bothered by the fact that men repeatedly thought she was a different kind of woman than she actually was.

TATE: Davis thought she was a whore, didn't he?

JONES: Yes. She began to feel that she was. I put those images in the story to show how myths or ways in which men perceive women actually define their characters. Eva, of course, eventually associates herself with Medusa and the Queen Bee.

TATE: I am wondering about the neurotic, the psychotic characters. Oftentimes, people who don't have to stay within the boundaries of sanity reveal more than those who are supposed to be rational. When you selected Eva to tell her story in a rather obviously incoherent fashion, did you think that a character who was not bound by sane responses could tell a story with greater sensitivity, could tell something of her relationships with a man, something about life in general, that a sane character could not?

JONES: Well, I think such characters' stories affect the proportions of incidents, observations, perceptions, things that maybe an ordinary, sane teller might treat more or less insignificantly or brush over or compress into a brief narrative package. The person who is psychotic might spend a great deal of time on selected items, so there might be a reversal in the relative importance of the trivial and what's generally thought of as significant. In Eva's mind time and people become fluid. Time has little chronological sequence, and the characters seem to coalesce into one personality.

TATE: You're describing a process that requires the psychotic character to be more concerned with those things which are more important to the personality than trying to impose rational or chronological ordering on experience. For example, if something happened when he or she was growing up, then that event is going to be a primary obsession, which is in turn going to keep surfacing throughout the narrative.

JONES: Yes. There is an "irrational" process of selecting incidents to be related in the story. In this regard, there was one critic who talked about my not having included incidents to round out Eva's life, to make it into less of a horror story. Those things might have happened in her lifetime, but they wouldn't, given the situations that she was in, have been the things that she would choose to tell you.

I'm also interested in "abnormal" psychology, psychology of language. I think that abnormal psychological conditions affect sensitivity to certain things, change proportions, affect "significant events/relationships, etc." There are some critics who can't separate or don't want to separate the "persona," the character's neurosis/psychosis, from the author's psychological autonomy. They feel that the character's preoccupations are those of the author. I don't think this would be so true if the stories were written in third person and if there were some sense of the author's responding to the experiences, directing how they're to be taken, or if the author weren't also female and black. There have also been more responses to the sexuality, or the "neurotic sensuality" in the books, than to the lesbianism. I don't recall the lesbianism entering into any critical discussions except as an overall part of the sexual picture.

I think also what the critics feel missing is that sense of authorial "judgment" which the works don't have.

TATE: What kind of response have you gotten from readers concerning your writing about characters who do not conform to positive images of women or black women? Do they want to cast Eva and Ursa as some sort of representative black female?

JONES: Yes. And even if they're not bothered by those things, they're bothered by the fact that the author doesn't offer any kinds of judgments or doesn't show her attitude toward the offense, but simply has the characters relate it.

For example, Eva refuses to render her story coherently. Controlling what she will and will not tell is a way of maintaining her autonomy. Her silences are also ways of maintaining this autonomy. "Autonomy," I find, is easier to use with her than "heroism."

I like something that Sterling Brown said, that you can't create a significant literature with just creating "plaster of Paris saints." "Positive race images" are fine as long as they're very complex and complicated and interesting personalities. I like the idea of a heroine, though none of my characters are. That's something I can see working with. Right now I'm not sure how to reconcile the various things that interest me with "positive race images." I think it's important to be able to work with a range of personalities, as well as with a range of personalities within one personality. For instance, how would one reconcile an interest in neurosis or insanity with positive race image? I think Ernest Gaines can create complex, interesting personalities who are at the same time "positive race images." But other "positive race images" can be very simplistic, so can negative images.

TATE: When I read your short stories, I thought about the manner in which James Baldwin tried to vindicate homosexuality. In your works, however, there is no effort to vindicate lesbianism. That it exists seems to be the only justification needed for artistic attention. Is this assessment accurate?

JONES: Yes. Lesbianism exists, and that's the only way that I include it in my work. I'll have characters respond to it positively or negatively, or sometimes the characters may simply acknowledge it as a reality.

TATE: Have you heard black critics contend that lesbianism/homosexuality has nothing to do with black folks?

JONES: No, I've never heard that comment from critics. I've been around people who are curious about my personal life because I have characters who are lesbians.

TATE: Do you consciously write yourself out of the story, or is it something that you just do as a matter of fact?

JONES: I just do it. When I write in first person, I like to have a sense that it's just the character that's there. Judgments don't enter. If judgments enter, I like them to be the judgments that a particular character would make. And oftentimes, that character's responses may not be what mine would be in the same situation. Also, as much as possible, I like to have that character as the storyteller without involving myself. It would be, perhaps, more interesting if my position were known. But, perhaps, there would be the same kinds of problems in terms of critics who do not want authorial intrusion. Maybe some of these problems could be avoided if there weren't also elements of identity between the characters and myself as a black female. Critics frequently want to make certain correlations.

TATE: When I read *Corregidora* and *Eva's Man*, I felt as if I were placed in a puzzle, and there were no directions. I was just supposed to read the books, and if I wanted to sit down and figure out something that was all well and good. If I didn't want to figure out something, that was all well and good too. Basically, I didn't feel a burden of theme. In some books, where the author is always intruding to tell you something, there is a burden that the author feels which he or she is compelled to share with the reader. The author's got to make the reader see the importance of certain ideas, so he beats the idea to death. But I didn't feel a burden of theme in your story. Did you feel compelled to relate some theme or just to dramatize situations?

JONES: I mainly dramatize situations, and I guess my main interest is in characters in relationship with other characters. Theme for me now is a kind of background thing but not something that I'm overly concerned with.

TATE: Do you have any theories about the human condition which you dramatize in your work?

JONES: Well, I don't really have any kind of theory of the human condition. I think what comes out in my work, in those particular novels, is an emphasis on brutality. But I think that something is also suggested in them that will perhaps be pursued in other works, namely the alternative to brutality, which is tenderness. Although the main focus of *Corregidora* and *Eva's Man* is on the blues relationships or relationships involving brutality, there seems to be a growing understanding, working itself out especially in *Corregidora*, of what is required in order to be genuinely tender.

TATE: Can you realize tenderness without experiencing brutality?

JONES: Perhaps brutality enables one to recognize what tenderness is.

TATE: Do you take delight in the unusual in telling these stories, or does the unusual event just sort of happen?

JONES: I think it's something that happens, but I'm also interested in characters who are unusual. I'm not interested in normal characters. I think this is also related to the whole question of positive and negative images. What does a black writer do who is not interested in the normal?

TATE: Do you observe any kind of evolution in the writing by Black Americans, especially that by black women? It seems that black women are now concerned with a kind of folk heroine. Do you think that eventually black women writers will characterize a college-educated black woman who is, by fact of her education, encountering all kinds of additional problems?

JONES: Yes. I think it will probably take another generation of black women writers. I've read some work by some of my students whose characters are not folk heroines but are college-educated heroines.

TATE: If you had an ideal interview, what questions would you like your interviewer to ask you, be it about your work or your personal opinions? What would you like to have them ask you about *Corregidora*, or what would you like to have said about *Corregidora*? In short, how does it feel to know that critics are dissecting your works?

JONES: Well, my first response to interviewers or to critics was kind of difficult because of the kinds of questions that I would be asked. The questions seemed to have very little to do with what was for me the process of telling the story.

TATE: Do you like critics to write articles about your work? Is that something you entertained when you wrote the novels?

JONES: No, I hadn't entertained it. I guess I was surprised by the number of reviews that the first novel got.

TATE: How does it feel not to be just a storyteller but actually to be written down in the annals of literary history, to have people dissect your stories like I'm attempting to do?

JONES: It feels strange. There's something about it that I'm not sure about. I don't know what kind of effect or what possible path my writing might have taken had there not been critics. I think they do make me think of my work in a more self-conscious way. As I write, I imagine how certain critics will respond to various elements of the story, and I force myself to go ahead and say, "Well, you would ordinarily include this, so go ahead and do it."

TATE: But you do stop and think.

JONES: I know. I have a sense of how certain people will take aspects of character, style.... Also, I find myself, though not directly, maybe dramatically, responding to certain kinds of criticism, not in ways that you might recognize as responses, but perhaps in terms of certain kinds of themes that might enter which are related to various critical responses. I find that I probably take more notes in terms of the things I'm doing now than I did when I first started writing. In some ways I like that better. I think that there's a certain kind of consciousness always necessary when you're writing. Perhaps that's even more true now.

TATE: Does it bother you that writing by black women has not received so much serious critical attention as that by black males? And when I say serious critical attention I'm talking about stuff that fills academic journals.

JONES: It bothers me that works by women writers haven't been treated as significant.

TATE: Do you want to have a reputation, a recognizable name?

JONES: Well, the writers whom I would most like to be like are those whose works have a certain kind of reputation, but the person, the writer, is more or less out of it. I would want to maintain some kind of anonymity. I think of J. D. Salinger and "The Woods and May." I guess that's the kind of reputation that I'd like. It's the kind where you can go on with what you're doing, but you have a sense that what you do is appreciated. You have a sense that there is quality to what you're doing.

TATE: What are you working on now?

JONES: I'm working on a new novel now. It's about a man and woman, and it takes place in Brazil.

TATE: Is it a story about slavery?

JONES: Yes, but not totally. It takes place in the seventeenth century.

TATE: Are you working on any short stories?

JONES: A few, but most of them still need a lot of work.

TATE: Do you write them, put them down, and then revise them?

JONES: Yes. There are some stories that I have had about four or five years now. I recently revised a couple of them. That's pretty much my method. I'll frequently keep the stories for a long time before they are publishable.

Notes

1. "Palmares" has not been published to date, though some of the content material appeared in the book-length poem *Song for Anninho*.
2. John O'Brien, ed., *Interviews with Black Writers* (New York: Liveright, 1973) 192.

APPENDIX II

An Interview with Gayl Jones, by Charles H. Rowell

The following interview was conducted by mail in May 1982.

ROWELL: In a seminal essay in *American Poetry Review* (Sept.-Oct., 1976), John Wideman argues that there is a "relationship between literate and oral traditions" in *Corregidora,* your first novel.[1] The same could be said of your second novel, *Eva's Man.* Do you see your work as part of a continuum in Afro-American and Euro-American literary traditions? I do not mean to imply that you always consciously build on or draw from those traditions when you are in the act of creating fiction.

JONES: I've read John Wideman's article and found it interesting because I'd been thinking about similar things and so was pleased that he had mentioned *Corregidora* in that context. I was also pleased that he saw that while with other critics "other things" got in the way of their seeing that; when in fact the "relationship between literate and oral traditions" was more significant to me as someone telling that story/those stories. I'd been thinking about those things mostly in terms of the creative writing process, but I'd been considering Zora Neale Hurston's *Their Eyes Were Watching God* in terms of what Wideman calls "linguistic heirarchy" as it relates to the use of dialect in Afro-American fiction.

Ursa in *Corregidora* tells her own story in her own language and so does Eva in *Eva's Man.* I was interested in having their language do everything that anybody's language used as a literary language can do. But once after I gave a talk on *Corregidora,* a professor (I should say white professor) expressed surprise that I didn't *talk* like Ursa. That my "vocabulary" wasn't like hers. The implication of course was that I was more "articulate," at least within an acceptable linguistic tradition. So, because of that and because of other things — other comments about my language in those books — I've been wondering about my own voice — my other voice(s) and how it (they) relate to the voices of those women. I trust those voices, but always with black writers there's the suspicion that they can't create language/voices as other writers can — that they can't invent a linguistic world in the same way that other writers can. For instance, I couldn't imagine that same professor having made such a comment to Joan Didion or Margaret Laurence regarding the possibilities of their linguistic imagination.

I'm currently working on a book entitled *Oral Tradition in Afro-American Literature* and among other things it attempts to speak about how Afro-American writers invent linguistic worlds and structural and dramatic procedures using elements of the Afro-American oral tradition. In the telling of it there are also problems of language that I have to work through — for instance, avoiding the "dissertation voice" and still making it a scholarly work.

As I mention in the introduction of that work (at least in this revised form I'm working on now), my own early connection with Afro-American oral tradition(s) was subconscious. I didn't think out the fact that my early stories were written in first person as if an audience were being *spoken to* and that this sense of speaking to people rather than writing to them was important to me. But such early stories as "The Welfare Check," "A Sense of Security" and "The Return: A Fantasy" were written just in this way — the characters were storytellers. It wasn't until *Corregidora* that this became a deliberate decision and conscious working out, the specific connections between Afro-American oral traditions and literary forms. Ursa is telling her story and there are stories within stories. Eva is also telling hers. But there's a somewhat different case for Eva. She doesn't want to tell her story in the same way that Ursa does, and so there are more fragments, more jumbling of time and memory and imagination (most readers-critics haven't noticed the latter — that she actually retells a story twice — applying it to two different characters: I wanted to suggest that though this story is written in the manner and language of social reality (social realism) it might not be — it might be more psychological realism. How much "truth" is she really telling, what fabrications are deliberate.)

Eva doesn't talk to the policemen. Ideally — and the kind of character I imagine her to be — she wouldn't have even talked to the psychiatrist either. But to tell the novel I had to have her do that.

You also ask about Euro-American literary traditions — there are of course connections there. The Euro-American writers that I most admire are those whose narratives are connected with spoken voice, with creating ideas of American language as opposed to European, and with Canadian writers like Margaret Laurence who do the same with Canadian modifications of the English. But I think I more deliberately try to find techniques from Afro-American (and African) traditions — oral and literary — though I admit all; though I feel many Euro-American writers — whether it's admitted or not (and particularly the most innovative ones) — have been influenced by Afro-American "oral literatures and traditions" (this includes the music) as well as their own.

ROWELL: How important are Afro-American folk narratives to your fiction?

JONES: Oral narratives, I'd say yes, because of the "motives of oral tradition," but not specific folk narratives. I'd like to study more specific ones in terms of the legends and imaginations in them. But right now my work more often contains them generally in the form of oral storytelling monologues — stories within stories — not specific folk narratives other than what the imaginary characters generate. There is one book — a new novel — however in which I have a woman named Jaboti — named after the Brazilian trickster turtle. She's an American woman though and she tells the children turtle stories — so she's called the Turtle Woman. I don't mention the origin of her name in the text or the connection with the Brazilian folk narrative(s) — because I don't generally like to come out and tell readers what I'm doing or to suggest that there might be more behind the story. I might do more things like that with folk narratives — Afro-American and other Third World. This not wanting to "suggest more" to the reader can be a problem. I would like them to know that there are more levels to the story; but it is not as easy as when European-American writers make such references to their Protean myths. But this Jaboti, like African and Afro-American trickster transformation tales, is also a protean figure and also functions thematically and metaphorically in the story.

I'm especially interested in Afro-American, African and other Third World folk narratives that contain magic and transformations/metamorphosis — myths that challenge or provide creative alternatives to European ones of that sort of imagination. Also I'm interested in studying how time and space are handled (and transformed) in them.

Some of the influences toward narrative and storytelling in my poetry are the medieval Spanish ballads. I did a Spanish paper (written in Spanish) once that dealt with the use of dialogue in the ballads — which were of course originally oral and then collected and written down. But there are different kinds of these ballads — historical and magical. Some are fragments of epics. Also the Afro-American ballads and toasts have influenced the structural procedures of some of those poems. Again, I'm interested particularly in the ways time, space, and transformations of reality are handled in them, and such specific technical things as the narrative viewpoint, abrupt transitions, conflicts, uses of irony and paradox, and certainly the characterizations in them.

I'm also interested in Chaucer for that reason — and I don't see him as an "alien" literary tradition. When I was at Brown, I took an independent study course on the "oral interpretation" of Chaucer and made a tape of the Wife of Bath's introduction — the prologue to the tale — because I was interested in the orality of the tale and the storytelling in his poetry, which was written to be recited. As I've said, all literary traditions that draw on speech, the spirit of speech, and speech motives interest me and I see more of the connectives than differences. (Curiously, the first name of the professor of Medieval English Literature with whom I studied was Geoffrey, and spelled the same way as Chaucer's! He also thought that I was a Medievalist, for why else would I be interested?) But Chaucer as a personality was of course different from those voices that he "invented," even the intrusive narrators — but critics used to think that Chaucer himself was intruding into the stories; however, they've recognized (acknowledged) that as "invention."

ROWELL: You say, in your interview with Michael Harper that Zora Neale Hurston's *Their Eyes Were Watching God* is one of your "favorite stories," but, you add, "there is a tension ... between the narrative and the dialogue...." You also say that "Ernest Gaines solved the problem of perspective and narrative/dialogue relationship...." Will you say more?[2]

JONES: When I first read Zora Neale Hurston's *Their Eyes Were Watching God* and when I first started teaching it I would talk about the tension between the narrative voice and the dialogue voices — the two traditions — what I mentioned John Wideman calls "linguistic hierarchy" where it's always assumed that characters such as Janie can't tell their own stories, that these stories and these dialogues in order to be admitted into literature must be framed within the accepted language (of course this was also needed to prove that the writers themselves could write in that language and that proof was necessary). Since then, however, I've noted places where Hurston attempts to break out of the "frame" into Janie's language and thought processes. Gaines, unlike Hurston, assumes that his Miss Jane can tell her whole story in her own language, that it is a valid literary language, as valid as Twain assumed Huckleberry's language was, and more valid of course for Gaines' own purposes and from his own perspective in the sense that Twain of course liberates Huckleberry's language, character, and personality but "frames" Jim's within Huckleberry's perspective and linguistic and imaginative vision. Gaines "breaks" his Afro-American character out, again to refer to Wideman's use of "breaking out of the frame"; this applies to personality and character as well as language — and the relationships between them.

One of the things I sometimes ask my classes is to imagine what *Their Eyes Were Watching God* would be if Gaines had written it. Of course Janie would have told the whole story, though there wouldn't have been the same focus or selection of details and "significant events."

American writers of oral tradition, with such writers as Twain, had broken out of their frames *vis a vis* European literary tradition long before Afro-American writers had *vis a vis* European-American.

That was the format when Hurston wrote, though she did a lot of important things with "the dialect," extending its emotional and experiential range from the works of Dunbar and Chesnutt, which were even more restrictive.

There is a lot to say about the problem of dialect in Afro-American literature, but it would take too long to say those things here. "Invention" still isn't as easily acknowledged in Afro-American modifications of American English as it has been in Euro-American modifications of European — in terms of the imaginative linguistic choices I spoke of earlier. But I don't really want to go too deeply into that here.

I think that Afro-American writers can write in whatever varieties of English they wish to, and that they should write in any. I think that Gaines' work, though it appears conservative from the viewpoint of such clearly linguistic and structural (etc.) innovative writers such as Ishmael Reed, Imamu Amiri Baraka, Leon Forrest, Steve Cannon and others, it was nevertheless an important transition in terms of the "whole voice" re the (Southern) black literary tradition. And from Gaines we have other breaking of the frame — of course Wideman's own creative work — and then there are interesting multiple linguistic things that such black women writers as Alexis Deveaux are doing, Ntozake Shange and Toni Cade Bambara. Toni Morrison too blends oral tradition and "literary" narrative voice in such a way that both seem to occupy the same time/space. Because there is not the same "linguistic hierarchy" there used to be and because "the language" is allowed to do more and more fictional things and certainly because the "transcription techniques" have changed, most of my students don't even recognize these modifications as forms of "dialect" because these modern writers don't misspell the words in the old way — they make the same assumptions about their modifications of Euro-American that Euro-American writers have made of their modifications of the "King's English" — Imagine these writers making "orthographic" changes and other indications of "distortion" whenever their speakers did not pronounce words or string words together the way a Britisher might.

ROWELL: Will you explain why — as you say in the same interview, "I just felt the first person narrative was the most authentic way of telling a story — the first person narrative is for you aesthetically important? Ernest Gaines says in an interview that the first person narrative is comfortable for him.[3] The first person as a narrative device is, I believe, a preferred form in the oral tradition.

JONES: Jahnheinz Jahn in his book on Afro-American literature talks about blues as being "subjective testimony" and of course the "I" is the witness. There is a relationship between the "I" storyteller and the blues singer, though as I said with the early "blues stories" this connection wasn't consciously made.

Also, I think my most authentic stories are in first person when I enter the characters and tell their stories as they would tell them. I like the sense of that — the inner landscape and not the sense of explaining motives.

Though now I've been moving into third person stories — to do it and to see what changes there are — the "voice" of them is different, sometimes less "natural" though I want to get more of a fluidity in them. Many of the stories in *The Straw Woman* — a new collection — are in third person, in fact, I think most of them are — the opposite of the *White Rat* collection just from that.

I would agree with Gaines that the first person is also comfortable for me. I like the way I "hear" it when I'm working in that person, and again it's the sense of being that character, for me, and telling it the way he/she would tell it even if their beliefs and responses are contradictory of my own — I like the act of becoming those characters even then.

ROWELL: Is there a Southern Black literature? If so, who are the practitioners? I'll ask the question another way. Do you see similar aesthetic, cultural and social imperatives in certain Black writers' works which form what one might call a Black South literature?

JONES: I think yes. It's strange, but this is a question I don't really want to analyze or try to codify an answer for. I'm trying to become a critic, and at the same time I still back away from certain ways of dealing with literature. If there is such a tradition, I probably write from inside of it. Probably. There are certain things I would like to think are there — certain recurring themes which I won't name, the connection with history, the sense of history as a force even in the present. Maybe. Sometimes I think that Southern writers — at least those I can speak of, such as Alice Walker or Ernest Gaines — admit into their characters and themes ambivalences and contradictions of behavior — public and private — without making easy judgments. (I'm not sure this explains it.) This of course isn't exclusive to Southern writers — but the writers I most admire admit these things — there aren't easy explainable categories of human behavior, there aren't easy "rightnesses." I think critic George Kent uses the phrase "contradictory self" but I can't place it — I can't remember where I read it — I'd like to think that Southern black writers accept characters as "contradictory selves." (I don't know if all of this that I'm saying here is true, or if it says more of how I imagine my own work to be.) But to go on. I think Southern writers write about things that are considered "embarrassing" by Northerners or considered "improper" for fictional uses. Maybe this is so. I pull away from wanting to get too far into it. Of course, "region" gets into what we see as "significant events" and "significant details." W. E. Abrahams in *The Mind of Africa* uses the words "significant events" when talking about how different peoples view historical "significant events" from their cultural perspectives. I also think that this can apply to fiction and often use these words when talking about how writers select events in fiction. The same holds I think in how the sexes pick up on significant events and details. That's one of the reasons why cross-cultural criticism and cross-sexual criticism I think can be difficult (problematic?), why whites are often telling blacks, and men telling women what's significant to write about and what is not. I taught a class once where I used mostly works by black and Third World writers and women—such classics as Jean Toomer's *Cane,* Kate Chopin's *The Awakening* and Carlos Fuentes' *Where the Air Is Clear*—but also such "recognized" European classics as James Joyce's *Portrait of the Artist* and Miguel de Cervantes' *Don Quixote*. But one of the students' responses on the "course evaluation" was that the works that I had selected were "trivial"—"mainly dealing with blacks and women" when there were more "significant" stories. So that's also one of the things one has to go up against that I also think applies to Southern black literature and the kinds of details that are "significant events" from that cultural perspective. (For instance, European-American writers—American and I've discovered Brazilian too—used to feel that in order to be "significant" they had to write about things that were "significant" to those on "the continent"—often things that had nothing to do or said nothing about the American landscape or imagination, or even their own selves.) I don't know if the student critic also found Joyce's *Portrait* or Cervantes' *Quixote* full of trivial moments—or the facts that they were Stephen Daedalus' or Don Quixote's rather than a black's or woman's that elevated them. Even before the student's comment I had wondered over that aspect of literature—how does one deal authentically and imaginatively with experiences that certain readers (not *listeners)* will dismiss as "trivial"? Mary Gordon has a good article on that as it relates to women's work in *The Writer on Her Work,* edited by Janet Sternburg. I'm always wary of that word "trivial," you know. And then of course there is the other question: How does the (anybody's) "trivial event" enter fiction, what place does it have along with (anybody's) "significant event"; how do you make the reader re-see the trivial moment as significant events when that's the question. This is digression, but I think it might be something to be considered in a discussion of the "events" and their selection in a Southern black literary tradition and in the works of specific writers within that tradition.

ROWELL: Your short poems as well as *Song for Anninho* are narratives. When you read at the University of Kentucky a few years ago, you said that your poems are "little fictions." It is as if in poetry you are trying to break aesthetic boundaries of literary forms and categories. You seem to do the same in fiction: we don't read your novels; we hear them.

JONES: I was trying to write a kind of poetry that would work for me. I've never really considered myself a poet. I've written what I call poetry but I've always thought of myself as primarily a fiction writer and so I write poetry from the viewpoint and interest of a storyteller — the concern with character and event. I think I even criticize poetry as if it were fiction and am drawn to those poems that share things with fiction. Now I'm writing some "poetic narratives" which I call "Fiction Studies" — trying to get at more of the fragmentation (of character and event) that distinguishes some poetry from prose and also more of the "questions" that poetry suggests. Sometimes I've adapted stories as poems and poems as stories. *Song for Anninho* is an adaptation of a novel I've written called *Palmares*. But I'm drawn to the things that are now the content of fiction, but of course which used to be the territory of poetry. Storytelling poems like those of Yvonne's I admire and also Ai's (Pelorhankhe Ogawa's) poems. But sometimes my novels and fictions I think are more poetry. In fact, one of my graduate students included one of my experimental fictions in her Bibliography under "selected poems" — something called "Spaces" which was published in *The Black Scholar* in 1975.[4] In fact, the first version of *Song* was a lyrical novel entitled *Almeyda*, excerpts of which were published in *Chant of Saints*, *Puerto del Sol* and translated into Dutch by Jos Knipscheer for *Mandala*. It was more poem than novel. It was rewritten as a straight dramatic novel *Palmares* then that was readapted and published as *Song for Anninho*. There's a story I tell in the interview with Michael Harper in *Chant of Saints* about similar transformations for *Eva's Man*.

ROWELL: In *Corregidora,* you introduce us to your interest in the Afro-Brazilian slave experience. *Song for Anninho,* your book length poem, uses that experience exclusively. Why do you turn to that experience? Are there dramatic possibilities in it, for example, that you do not find in the American experience?

JONES: Yes and no. I want to get back to the American experience but still bridge them as I do in *Corregidora* though better than I do in *Corregidora.* I'd like to be able to deal with the whole American continent in my fiction — the whole Americas — and to write imaginatively of blacks anywhere/everywhere. In one of my short stories I've even brought two contemporary Brazilians to Kentucky to visit a friend there, mingling place and historical moment. But going to the Brazilian history and landscape helped my imagination and writing. I also wanted to write about someone and a time distant from my own. It was also a way of getting away from things that some readers consider "autobiographical" or "private obsessions" rather than literary inventions — that they don't accept as imagination from a black woman writing about black female characters in a certain American world. I've done the necessary research of historical and social facts for *Palmares* and *Song* but the characters and the relationships are invention/imagination. Real historical people are sometimes *named*— King Zumbi, Ganga Zumba, the governor de Almeida (with an "i") — but these people I chose not to bring into the works as characters.

I think the experience with Brazil will also help my American stories in terms of landscape and descriptions. In addition, the Brazilian experience (purely literary and imaginative since I've never been there) helped to give a perspective on the American one — I can't really say what this means yet.

ROWELL: Although you set *Song for Anninho* during slavery in Brazil, you do not concentrate on slavery and protest against it, say, as Richard Wright does with twentieth century oppression in Mississippi in *Uncle Tom's Children* and in Chicago in *Native Son.* In fact, *Song for Anninho* is a love story. [He quotes from the poem].

Your fictional conflicts are inward, personalized, psychological. Racism and other forms of political oppression are merely backdrops (and yet they account for some of the conflict) for your characters' worlds. Will you talk about your aesthetic approach to our collective experience? Do you think Afro-American writers of the past were too preoccupied with oppression and the need to make direct political statements at the expense of a deep exploration of the dramatic possibilities of Afro-American life? Implied in my questions is the concept that Afro-American writers have certain aesthetic, political and social responsibilities.

JONES: The center of *Song for Anninho* is a love story and I also wanted to move beyond the "blues relationships" of most of my earlier published stories to perhaps the "spiritual mode." I wanted the conflict to be not between the man and the woman but something outside of them. Their love relationship is the foreground and significant relationship — the "significant event," not the interracial confrontations, though they are there and clearly there, I think. But I like the focus to be personality and what Sterling Brown in *The Negro Caravan* calls "the revelation of personality." This doesn't mean that the work has to ignore the social-historical landscape that may affect personality and circumstances; it just doesn't have to take up the whole space so that, as Alice Walker said finely in an interview in John O'Brien's *Interviews with Black Writers*, it makes invisible the people's own "dreams, imaginings, rituals and legends" or relegates them to the background as seemingly "insignificant."

Of course, some critics would probably want a greater directness of political statement. I don't like direct political statements. Maybe that's why I don't write the "poetry of statement." I do like character and dramatic circumstance. I don't fault the early writers for being "too preoccupied with oppression." In fact, in my classes I give those writers great attention and talk about their relationships to the contemporary black writers. I don't dismiss them or their preoccupations, though I do discuss how these preoccupations give problems (ironically) in terms of the works' ability to reveal the characters — oppressed people — their fictions' center on, the complexity and imagination of those characters. I think that because they have done that, that contemporary writers unless they can do it better or explore some dimension of oppression in the "contemporary environment" and "modern experience" or in the "past" that hasn't already entered the literature.... For instance, unless the writer can say something different or explore some new dimension of the Afro-American slave experience that hasn't already been done and done finely by Ernest Gaines in *The Autobiography of Miss Jane Pittman* and Margaret Walker in *Jubilee*.... It's a genre I think and a truth of the American experience; what are the truths about it that haven't already been told? What can the writer imagine using that time — things that haven't yet entered that Afro-American literary genre. For instance, Frederick Douglass, because of the abolitionist purposes of his narrative, wasn't free to do the things that Gaines and Walker do in theirs — Walker's focus on personal relationships and complexity of Afro-American character; Gaines' range of character and event. Gaines and Walker free new writers to do new things with it or to make choices that don't involve it if they feel that they can add more elsewhere in subject matter and/or possibilities for the literature.

My own preoccupation is with personality and in some of the work "psychological obsessions and oppressions." The conflict between aesthetic, political and social responsibilities interests me as it involves dilemmas in Afro-American literary tradition but I don't dwell on it when I'm telling a story. I've had characters dwell on it. I do this in another novel called *The Birdcatcher,* where the central character is a black woman artist — a sculptor — and the relationship between the three responsibilities is one of the themes. The conclusion it draws is not done through statement, however, but dramatically. It "explores the dramatic possibilities" of that question.

There are moments in my literature as in any literature that have aesthetic, social and political implications, but I don't think that I can be a "responsible" writer in the sense that those things are meant because I'm too interested in contradictory character and ambivalent character and I like to explore them even without judgments entering the work — without a *point of view* entering though the characters themselves have *points of view.* There are certain recurring styles and themes in my writing that make it certainly out of an Afro-American and as you speak of a Southern Black Literary Tradition. But *Song for Anninho* is a poetic fictional account whose focus is on "spirit" and interior landscape — the landscape of imagination and dream and memory. The characters are certainly living in an "oppressive time and space," the battles with the Dutch and then the Portuguese to maintain their freedom in Palmares, the state formed by fugitive Brazilian slaves in the 17th century. But even in my book *Palmares* that the poem is adapted from, I don't even focus on the final battle because it is the consequences to character and circumstance that is the "significant event." If Anninho rather than Almeyda had told the story, the focus would have been the battle, I think, and the raids and spying expeditions and the trading, etc. Perhaps it's a flaw that I don't focus on the battle. Perhaps I bend the idea of the "significant event." I take Almeyda from the scene at the moment the Portuguese climb over the wall — after they had built their stockade next to the Palmaristas' soldiers appear. But neither *Song for Anninho* nor *Palmares* — as I've written them — neither one is political or social documents of the time. On one page of the book, Almeyda describes what it is and what it's supposed to be when she says — "But it's not the actions I wish to capture but the spirit!" Of course, the fictional version has to capture more events — but the focus is "personalized, psychological."

ROWELL: Before we can understand *Song for Anninho*, we must deal with your concept of time in it. Will you discuss time in the poem? From the outset and later through technique, we get a clue to the importance of time (and place) from Almeyda's words to Zabatra. [Quoting the poem.]

Then, too, there is the question of chronology and time in the poem: the narrator's voice is at once past and present. And at some moments her voice speaks from the real world; then suddenly it speaks from a dreamlike world. Then again Almeyda's voice seems to speak in silence: we literally hear her mind. Your narrative technique and time in *Song for Anninho* remind me of T.S. Eliot's lines in *Four Quartets*. [Quoting Eliot.]

JONES: The book tries not to deal with any straight chronology in either time or space — it attempts to transform them in the way that any time/space can co-exist in memory and/or imagination. It's flexible that way. There are also places in the book where Almeyda anticipates future circumstances — so really all three times co-exist. I'm also writing now with that non-chronological, flexible, jazz-time in the fiction that I'm doing. I've always been interested in getting the greatest flexibility in the rendering of time/place/space in fiction — there is some of it in the way that memory and imagination re-organize the sequences in *Eva's Man*, but my (longer) fiction now does more of it — trying to maintain a kind of "coherence" at the same time there is a looseness and flexibility of dramatic structure — the coherence and flexibility of jazz improvisation.

ROWELL: In a lecture at the University of Kentucky, Guy Davenport said that the problem of the "long modern poem is to solve the problem between texture and length." "The longer the poem the looser the pattern," he said, "doesn't hold. The modernist poem wants a variety of texture...." How did you address the problem of texture in *Song for Anninho?* Not many Afro-American poets have written long poems. Melvin Tolson, Jay Wright and Gwendolyn Brooks (if you can call "In the Mecca" and "The Anniad long poems) immediately come to mind.

JONES: Sometimes I like loose patterns. Can something have a loose pattern and still have texture? What holds the long poem together for me is character and story (not always details of events). Even though I write what I am calling poems.... They have the "lines" of poetry — which I like. But there are ways of building language and image and metaphors and meaning that real poets do, that I don't do. Those "other things" are, of course, in the long poems of the poets you mention — Melvin Tolson, Jay Wright and Gwendolyn Brooks.

ROWELL: Trudier Harris calls *Song for Anninho* a spiritual journey — i.e., a spiritual journey for Almeyda.

JONES: Yes, that's what it's meant to be, and also because Almeyda says that about wanting to capture the "spirit." It is a "spiritual journey." Another poet I know felt the poem was too abstract, preferred the "visibility" of my novels. But I wanted to get the "spirit" that Almeyda speaks of rather than the detailed and concrete events of the novels.

ROWELL: It is important that we remember Ursa in *Corregidora* as a blues singer?

JONES: Yes. Again, Jahn's comment re the blues as "subjective testimony" — the "I" voice of the blues. Jahn also says something else about the blues — that it "continues the techniques of African praise and mocking songs.... The Blues always has its reference to the social background...." I think all that applies. Although in my first person characters — maybe more some of those I'm writing about now — there's a hint of self-mockery, the "praise" directed away from the "I" character to perhaps other characters or another character in the stories who act(s) more as a moral center.

ROWELL: Will you talk about the importance of the past (again, T. S. Eliot's lines from *Four Quartets*—and the meaning of time in William Faulkner's *Absalom, Absalom!*) in *Corregidora*?

JONES: History and personality are interests there—the relationship between history and personality—personal and collective history—history as a motivating force in personality. As I've mentioned in another interview, while I was working on the book, Michael Harper—my advisor and teacher at Brown—asked me a question: What is the relationship between autobiography and history? So, much of the answer for it became a part of the creative process of writing that book. History affects Ursa's personality—the history of the women before her—their conflicts, frustrations, etc. She wants to make sense of that history in terms of her own life. She doesn't want to be "bound" by that history, but she recognizes it as important; and she accepts it as an aspect of her own character, identity and present history. However, she doesn't want to be told by those women and their Corregidora stories how she must feel about that past. Her story is connected to theirs but she also wants her own choices and acts of imagination and will—most of which come through singing her own songs.

ROWELL: Not a few of your readers have reacted negatively to your use of sex in *Corregidora* and *Eva's Man*. And in doing so, they missed, it seems to me, the important questions your novels raise. I read sex as metaphor in your novels. On a very primary level, I keep thinking about the effect of collective and private sexual histories on the lives of people. How they influence people's behavior. How such histories shape our world.

JONES: Sex is a metaphor, yes. I can understand the negative reactions to the use of sex in the books. It's something I'm interested in as a dilemma of subject matter in Afro-American literature. There's a lot that can be said about it. I'm working on an article on the erotic imagination in Jean Toomer's *Cane*. That subject is problematic for Afro-American writers—even more so women (and why many of our early writers scrupulously avoided it)—because when you write about anything dealing with sexuality it appears as if you're supporting the sexual stereotypes about blacks. So do you scrupulously avoid the subject as the so-called uplift writers did or do you go ahead with it? A white woman novelist of the early part of the century, Kate Chopin, felt compelled to give up her writing career because of the hostile criticism received by her novel *The Awakening* in 1899 — because she dared to explore the erotic imagination. But with those women — there was a recent T.V. movie on Mae West who's of interest re all that — still their assertion of eroticism can be an act of self-assertion and an act of "controlling" — whereas for a black woman it seems merely to assert, confirm and affirm what *they've* thought all along; and more unfortunately it refers collectively rather than simply personally — as Kate Chopin's and Mae West's (of course both are celebrated now), but their dilemmas then were merely personal ones. So it's very difficult for me to write now graphically about sex in the way that I did then. I had assumed that when one wrote modern/contemporary literature that a black woman could write about eroticism the same way as any other writer not in Chopin's time without its being particularly noticed, and that therefore the readers could see beyond those details of erotic consciousness to other meanings. In fact, I thought that modern readers no longer found anything unusual about such explorations. However and but. That problem of appearing to support stereotypes complicates the issue, as it complicates the issue of the early novels having the black man — at least the early *published* novels and I keep insisting on this because that's what has been *seen* and assessments made on the basis of — at least from the viewpoint of the women storytellers, as the antagonist.

Now I am extremely "double-conscious" when writing anything dealing with sexuality. I had to force myself to go ahead with such scenes in *The Stone Dragon* because they belonged there, but they're not as graphic and they don't use the same kind of vocabulary (that was true of the characters) of *Eva's Man* and *Corregidora*. Most of the other fictions neglect sexual scenes altogether or they enter in "spaces" (not seen), though I persist in my interest in relationships between people, particularly between men and women. Also, in a few of the stories when I need an antagonist to make the dramatic conflict, to complicate the action — some of the stories in *The Straw Woman*— I choose the woman rather than the man mainly because of the criticisms which suggest that the fictional invention must imply something about the personal relationships or the way I think "black men are."

There are a lot of dilemmas of subject matter that when I told my early stories I hadn't thought of in the same way. For instance, in *The Birdcatcher* I needed a character to do a certain kind of violence — so I decided to make the character a white woman — because of what I consider the too easy dismissal of any black characters who act in certain ways as stereotypes or supporting stereotypes. Black or white the woman I think would have the same degree of complexity — but if black the dimensions would be overlooked or negated because of the "horror" done by the woman. Of course, black characters stay the central and significant characters in the work, and they're not all "plaster saints." But that white woman is also there to do that thing that I needed done in the story — which I won't describe here. But the book itself deals with the problem I'm discussing here, because the white woman like the black woman central character is also an artist — but the paintings that she does are very erotic and violent, and the black woman sculptor envies her for being able to do that and not be condemned for it. In fact, the critics of the white woman artist's work see beyond the eroticism to the so-called "deeper themes" (or higher ones?). The black woman sculptor is resentful of this. She is working on a piece called "The Birdcatcher" — a sculpture made of scavenger objects, but a sculpture she leaves unfinished.... The irony though is that at the same time she envies the white woman artist's so-called "artistic freedom" she has a black woman writer friend who is doing similar things in prose — but she herself feels contempt for and embarrassment at that woman's writings. She never recognizes the irony of this or that even the situation might be more complex than she imagines it to be; that she herself considers the white woman artist, who has been described by critics as avant-garde, the best of her generation, and even the voice of her time — as "daring" and "innovative" and "risk taker." Even in her ambivalence, she considers the white woman artist all these things too, while her black woman writer friend's are the same in prose — she considers her vulgar, evil and embarrassing. Her friendship with both women continues ambivalent.

There's another Afro-American woman writer who's just completed a novel which is being reviewed by publishers. It's more, it's freer than any of my own early work re its insistence on the erotic imagination and the integrity of that imagination in literature. It's fine writing, though the subject matter will be controversial and I'm sure will get in front of many people's view of the work itself. And there will be all those questions. Certain men critics won't like it, not because it's negative re men — but I don't think they'll like the kinds of risks with the erotic imagination that women — especially black women — aren't supposed to take. It really does much more than I've done re that, the erotic imagination. Her book raises some important questions, but I think the readers will see the "sex" (a dangerous subject) and won't acknowledge the other significance in the way they would acknowledge it if it came from elsewhere (even the suppressed erotic writings of Edith Wharton are coming out now and being discussed intelligently!). She also does some good/interesting things technically that I like, things that I think are competitive with things that other modern writers are doing, but which I think will be overlooked because of "the other."

ROWELL: Why do you call *Eva's Man* "a horror story"? You also say that *Corregidora* is "a blues novel," but you say that the relationship of the men and women in *Eva's Man* "isn't a blues ritual."[5] What do you mean?

JONES: Because it is. I think what Eva does to the man in the book is a "horror." *Corregidora* is a blues. Eva carries out what Ursa might have done, but didn't. But the relationships between the men and women are blues relationships. I don't really want to continue that, the blues on the same level as in those books.

One critic of the book who disapproved of *Eva's Man* said that it went beyond the blues. I forgot where the critic said it went to. But most blues transcends, doesn't it? In *Eva's Man* there's no transcendence as there is in *Corregidora* — as there's supposed to be there. Maybe that's what I meant when I said that that situation wasn't a "blues ritual" and that it was a horror story. A dilemma like the other one — the sexual one.

ROWELL: Do the stories in *White Rat* form together a thematic pattern? Why is the title story the first in the collection? Does it have implications for the other stories?

JONES: Not an intentional thematic pattern. They were a collection of stories I'd written. There are some similarities. Most are written in first person and most deal with tensions in relationships, dynamics of psychology — psychic landscape — and what you called the "inward." My editor named the collection from the first story. There might be more thematic patterns. I hesitate to want to delve further into what they are. No patterns were intended. With subsequent short story collections there will probably be more deliberate thematic connections.

ROWELL: Will you comment on the title and the issue of talking/conversation in "Your Poems Have Very Little Color in Them" — i.e., on your artist-narrator's isolation and her concern for communication? I say *artist*, but I mean specifically potential poet and fictionist.

JONES: Actually this is derived from a journal I used to keep in college and is the only story of my stories that comes close to autobiography — my own trouble communicating (talking) and writing as a means of doing that. Even now, I talk in the classroom where I have to and with students in the office — but in social situations I'm usually taciturn. I usually avoid social gatherings. I don't even travel about and give readings like most other writers. The University of Kentucky reading was an exception and ones I've given here because I'm here. Often themes of communication and taciturnity enter my work. But I often like to have talkative people in my stories.

ROWELL: One of my favorite stories in *White Rat* is "The Return: A Fantasy." Of course, another version of the story is given from the point of view of Joseph Corey in "Version 2," the final story in the collection. Will you talk about both stories? First, why do you use the subtitle, "A Fantasy"? What are the ideational concerns of the two stories? Why do you give us two different representations of the same events — in two different forms and styles — in two different stories? Ernest Gaines in "Just Like a Tree" and William Faulkner in *Absalom, Absalom!* give us different versions of the same stories in the same narratives.

JONES: I gave "The Return" the subtitle "A Fantasy" because when I first wrote the story I was in college in my late teens — actually I was 19 when I completed revision on the story and when it was accepted for publication. But when I was a seventeen or eighteen I entered the first version of the story in a school contest. The reason they decided against it, I was told, was that they didn't think someone my age could write about people in their twenties without its being a fantasy. So, when I revised the story — I actually only added scenes rather than any verbal revision as I mostly do — I called it "A Fantasy" because of that criticism.

Anyway, two patterns that story has set. I generally find myself writing about people a decade or so older than myself — rarely younger, rarely my own age. My creative interest is usually with the older. Mostly the characters in stories now are in their forties. The other pattern is that my work often contains creative responses to criticism incorporated into the work — not as statements but dramatically and thematically. For instance, as I was discussing the sexual, criticism finds its way into one of the dilemmas of a novel and the controversies of subject matter.

"Version 2" — I was working on experimental stories — only a couple of pieces have been published in post-modernist journals — which dealt with how psychological states influenced speech and language patterns and the making of stories, the kinds of fragmentations that would occur in such storytelling. I do it somewhat in *Eva's Man* but not as extensively. "Version 2" represents one effort to do that. I think perhaps it works better when read aloud though.

ROWELL: In addition to addressing other subjects, "The Return: A Fantasy" and "Version 2" deal with the father-son relationship, a very important subject which, I think, needs further exploration in Afro-American literature. James Baldwin does a little with the subject in *Go Tell It on the Mountain*. And, of course, Ernest Gaines examines the subject at length in *In My Father's House*. Will you talk about that relationship?

JONES: I can't really. It's something I would like to write about more. Just that I'd like to deal more with it. Also, I'd like to work more with the men characters — the integrity of those characters. I'd like to write a novel from the point of view of a man. Of course, I want to continue the interest in women's stories and bring men in from their perspectives. A novel I'm writing idea notes on now is about two women and a man, and I'm considering having the man tell the story. I'm also considering having a young boy in the story. I haven't dealt a whole lot with that.

ROWELL: Will you talk about Dora's belief in "The Return: A Fantasy" that "Love can save"?

JONES: I don't really want to talk about it. She felt it was so, and it was so for the story.

ROWELL: The women characters in "Jevata" and "The Women" remind me of some of the women in your two novels. Will you talk about them? Of course, Mr. Floyd in "Jevata," like Anninho in *Song for Anninho*, is compassionate. Unlike most of the men in your novels, he seems to be free, to a great extent, of the macho socialization which many of your male characters internalize.

JONES: I find myself wanting to back away from some questions. I don't know why. Maybe there's still that feeling that I don't want to analyze things too closely. I should mention that the male characters in those early novels are unfortunate, like the sexual theme — in this society that looks for things to support stereotypes. I'd like to be free of that. I used to think one could be.

Actually, when I wrote those stories I didn't do much thinking about the stories, I just wrote them. Now I do more thinking about the stories and make extensive notes so that I can talk about them better. I mean I can talk about them better because they were thought out in a way the others weren't. But it also means that I could write many kinds of stories then that I can't write now, and I guess it works the other way too. There are stories that I'm able to tell now that I could not have told in those days.

I remember when I wrote the Jevata story of having this image/scene in my head of an older woman chasing a young man from her house, chasing him out the gate — so that the story began with a question — Why did she do it? And the story was an attempt to answer this question, Mr. Floyd's attempt to answer it. "The Women," I guess, is what is called an initiation story — into womanhood — and something that complicates that, ideas of womanhood and what it means. But I don't want to say more about those.

ROWELL: In your interview with Roseann Bell, you say that your "Knowledge of Ursa's past, going back to 1948, was extracted from conversations that my parents engaged in."[6] Will you say more — specifically how you use facts or stories you've heard of people and transform them into fiction?

JONES: Not deliberately or consciously extracted. It's just that I didn't have to research 1948 because I knew it as well as my own time. Nothing in the

Corregidora story really happened. By listening, I could write a story that takes place in that time. I knew the time as if I'd been there. The only time I had to "research for facts was the Brazilian history, and then I only had to know when slavery was abolished, what kinds of plantations there were, and luckily I came across the story of Palmares, which has become the basis for later work. But there aren't any facts or stories that one could say really happened. I like to tell stories *as if* they really happened. That's another reason I wanted to do the Palmares book, because there couldn't be those same questions there. But it's told, I think, as if it were a real story.

ROWELL: Please talk about your Lexington, Kentucky, background as far as its probable impact on you as a writer is concerned. I assume that it is important to you as a writer. For example, the interview you conducted with your mother, Ms. Lucille Jones who is also a writer, and the interview Michael Harper conducted with you suggest that your Kentucky background is invaluable to you. In the Harper interview, you also said that you "went to an all-black school until the tenth grade when there was integration. I say that because I think it's important."

JONES: I like to have some stories take place there and I agree it is important. It's important to me. I don't think, however, that it's unusual, since most people feel "connections" to home territory — connections that go into one's ideas of language, personality, landscape. The all-black school is important because there are certain things that I took for granted that when I came to the North people didn't take for granted. For instance, there were kids at Connecticut College who had never had a black teacher before. For instance, Zora Neale Hurston could take more things for granted than I could by being born in the first-incorporated all-black town and blacks doing *everything*. Does that make sense — without explaining?

ROWELL: Many creative writers often study certain literary traditions or they often read over and over certain writers. It is as if they unconsciously absorb the aesthetic energy of other writer/artists. I don't mean that they imitate them. They just read them over and over from time to time. You can tell that I'm avoiding the word "influence." Are there writers and aesthetic traditions — Afro-American and non–Afro-American — that you return to from time to time for private reading?

JONES: Chaucer, Carlos Fuentes, Jean Toomer, T. S. Eliot, Cervantes, James Joyce, Ernest Hemingway. I don't always reread them though to "return to them." Margaret Laurence. Alice Walker. Anton Chekhov, others.

ROWELL: Some writers encourage developing writers not to enroll in creative writing programs. Was the creative writing program at Brown University as important to your development as a writer as your mother's writing and reading to you when you were growing up in Lexington?

JONES: The Brown University program was important to my development as a writer because of Michael Harper. I preferred independent studies instead of workshops. Time to write was important and there was plenty. I wouldn't tell a young writer not to enroll in a writing program. A lot depends on who's there, and a lot depends on whether the young writer feels it's the right thing, though I think he/she should go there, then decide. I think I needed that time and place. Having the time to write and having a teacher I admired and trusted as my "first reader" was important. So I mostly don't think of Brown in the abstract, aside from that and for that I can't generalize on writing programs.

But I have to say though that if my mother hadn't written and read to me when I was growing up I probably wouldn't have even thought about it at all. I don't think it was something I would have thought about.

Notes

1. 5.5 (September-October 1976) 34–37.
2. Michael S. Harper, "Gayl Jones: An Interview," *Chant of Saints: A Gathering of Afro-American Literature, Art, and Scholarship*, eds. Michael S. Harper and Robert B. Stepto. (Urbana: University of Illinois Press, 1979) 352–375.
3. Charles H. Rowell, "'This Louisiana Thing That Drives Me': An Interview with Ernest J. Gaines," *Callaloo* 3.1 (May 1978) 39–51.
4. "Spaces." *The Black Scholar* 6 (June 1975): 53–55.
5. Michael S. Harper, "Gayl Jones: An Interview," *Massachusetts Review* 18.4 (Winter 1977) 692–715.
6. Roseann P. Bell, "Gayl Jones Takes a Look at *Corregidora*—An Interview," *Sturdy Black Bridges: Visions of Black Women in Literature*, eds. Bell et al (Garden City: Doubleday, 1979) 282–287.

Annotated Bibliography and List of General Works Cited

This bibliography consists of (1) identifications and descriptions (where applicable and necessary) of Gayl Jones–related primary and secondary sources; and (2) a non-annotated list of works cited, consisting of academic documents not specifically concerned with the work of Jones. I am indebted to Joe Weixlmann's bibliography of Jones's early work which appeared in the 1984 winter issue of *Callaloo*.

Works by Jones

Books

Chile Woman. Schubert Playbook Series. 2.5. 1974. Paper. Performed initially at Brown University in November 1973, the play would go on to win the New Play Award at the 1974 New England regional competition for the National American College Theatre Festival. In addition, "the play has been directed by George Bass, with musical direction by Brother Ahh (Robert Northern), and produced under a Shubert Foundation grant for the New Scripts Workshop." The Shubert Foundation also helped fund the play's publication.

Corregidora. New York: Random House, 1975. Cloth. Back of dust jacket contains notable blurb by James Baldwin: "*Corregidora* is the most brutally honest and painful revelation of what has occurred, and is occurring, in the souls of Black men and women ... it dares to confront the absolute terror which lives at the heart of love."

Corregidora. New York: Bantam, 1976. Paper.

Corregidora. Utrecht (Netherlands): Bruna, 1976. Cloth. Translated into Dutch by Frans Kellendonk.

Corregidora. Vienna: Europaverlags, 1979. Cloth. Translated into German by Liesl Nürenberger.

Corregidora. New York: Beacon Press, 1986. Paper. Back of book includes blurbs from Maya Angelou and John Updike.
Corregidora. London: Camden, 1988. Paper. First British Edition.
Corregidora. London: Serpent's Tail, 2000. Paper. Second British Edition.
Dunkle Melodie: Corregidora und Eva's Man. Vienna: Europaverlags, 1984. Cloth. Dual German publication of *Corregidora* and *Eva's Man*. Title translates as *Dark Melody*.
Eva's Man. New York: Random House, 1976. Cloth. Back of dust jacket includes photograph of Jones and four assessments of *Corregidora* from Maya Angelou, Christopher Lehmann-Haupt, John Updike, and *The New York Times*.
Eva's Man. Paris: Editions des femmes, 1977. French translation by Sylvis Durastanti. Cloth.
Eva's Man. New York: Bantam, 1978. Paper.
Eva's Man. Edizioni delle Donne, 1978. Cloth. Translated into Italian by A. Forcella.
Eva's Man. Vienna: Europaverlags, 1980. Cloth. Translated into German by Liesl Nürenberger.
Eva's Man. New York: Beacon Press, 1987. Paper. Cover contains quote from *Mademoiselle*: "Gayl Jones ... accomplishes the almost impossible: a second novel that's every bit as intense, brutally honest and haunting as her first."
The Healing. Boston: Beacon, 1998. Cloth.
The Healing. Boston: Beacon, 1998. Paper.
The Healing. Waterville (Maine): Thorndike, 1998. Cloth. Large print edition.
The Healing. London: Serpent's Tail, 2000. Paper. British Edition.
The Healing, Corregidora, Eva's Man. New York: Griot, 1998. Paper. Collection of three Jones novels also includes a previously uncollected 1977 interview with Jones conducted by her former Brown University professor, the poet Michael S. Harper.
The Hermit-Woman. Detroit: Lotus, 1983. Paper. Poems in this collection include "The Hermit-Woman," "Ensinança," "Fiction Study," "Wild Figs and Secret Places," "The Machete Woman," and "Stranger." Synopsis on back maintains, "Jones has woven together in this fascinating volume memorable narratives which, while separate, are nevertheless unified, providing a definition of Woman at her most intuitive depths and possibilities. That this is sheer poetry is evident in this collection's provocative implicitness and its wealth of quotable passages which the reader will wish to jot down and memorize. There is no doubt that Jones is as effective a poet as she is a fiction writer; the fusing of both genres offers an exciting reading experience."
Liberating Voices: Oral Tradition in African American Literature. Cambridge: Harvard University Press, 1991. Cloth. Includes an introduction; separate multiple-chapter sections considering poetry, short fiction and the novel; and a conclusion, glossary, notes, and index.
Liberating Voices: Oral Tradition in African American Literature. New York: Penguin, 1992. Paper.

Mosquito. Boston: Beacon, 1999. Cloth.
Mosquito. Boston: Beacon, 1999. Paper.
Song for Anninho. Detroit: Lotus, 1981. Paper. Consists of one long poem.
Song for Anninho. Boston: Beacon, 1999. Cloth. Back of dust jacket contains general blurbs on Jones's achievement from Valerie Boyd, Margo Jefferson, Raymond Sokolov, and John Updike.
Song for Anninho. Boston: Beacon, 2000. Paper. Cover includes blurb from Gloria Wade-Gayles: "Before there was Toni Morrison or Alice Walker, there was Gayl Jones. She is brilliant!"
Two Novels: Corregidora and Eva's Man. New York: Random House, 1976. Paper.
Die Vogelfängerin. Hamburg: Rowohlt, 1986. Cloth. Obscure novel published in Germany. Title translates as *The Birdcatcher*. The book has not been translated into English.
Der Weisse Nigger. Vienna: Europaverlags, 1980. Cloth. German edition of *White Rat*. Translated by Liesl Nürenberger-Körbler and Andreas C. Körbler.
White Rat: Short Stories by Gayl Jones. New York: Random House, 1977. Cloth. Jones's only published collection of short stories includes "White Rat," "Your Poems Have Very Little Color in Them," "The Women," "Jevata," "Asylum," "Persona," "The Coke Factory," "The Return: A Fantasy," "The Roundhouse," "Legend," "A Quiet Place for the Summer," "Version 2."
White Rat: Short Stories by Gayl Jones. Boston: Northeastern University Press, 1991. Paper. Contains foreword by Mae G. Henderson.
White Rat: Short Stories by Gayl Jones. New York: Harlem Moon, 2005. Paper. Includes introduction by Natasha Tarpley and a Reader's Companion consisting of seven questions.
Xarque and Other Poems. Detroit: Lotus, 1985. Paper. Last of Jones's three poetry collections published over a five year period by Detroit's Lotus Press. Consists of "Xarque," "Composition with Guitar and Apples," "Waiting for the Miracle," and "Marla." Summary on back concludes, "Ever the engaging story-teller, Gayl Jones has once again succeeded in making black history live. The African presence, which still permeates and influences Brazilian culture, is never more excitingly depicted than in the narrative poems of this literary giant."

Other Publications: Poems, Stories, Plays, Essays, and Reviews

"About My Work." *Black Women Writers (1950–1980): A Critical Evaluation.* Ed. Mari Evans. Garden City: Anchor P/Doubleday, 1984. 233–235.
"Almeyda." *The Massachusetts Review* 18 (Winter 1977): 689–691. Rpt. in *Chant of Saints: A Gathering of Afro-American Literature, Art, and Scholarship.* Ed. Michael S. Harper and Robert B. Stepto. Urbana: University of Illinois Press, 1979. 349–351.

"Alternative." *Callaloo* 5 (February 1979): 111.
"The Ancestor: A Street Play." *BOP* 1 (1974): 46–55. Rpt. in *The Greenfield Review* 4 (Fall 1975): 89–96. Also rpt. in *Yardbird Reader, Vol. 5*. Ed. Ishmael Reed. Berkeley: Yardbird, 1976. 246–252.
"Asylum." *White Rat*. Rpt. in *Midnight Birds: Stories of Contemporary Black Women Writers*. Ed. Mary Helen Washington. Garden City: Anchor, 1980. 128–131.
"The Beguine." *Center* 7 (April 1975): 9.
"Beyond Yourself (The Midnight Confession) for Brother Ahh." *B.O.P (Blacks on Paper)*. Chapter 3. Providence: Brown University, 1975. 79–92. Play is "based upon the concept and musical score "Beyond Yourself" by Brother Ahh (Robert Northern).
"Chance." *Callaloo* 5 (February 1979): 112.
"Choice." *Center* 9 (December 1976): 17.
"The Coke Factory." *White Rat*.
"Community and Voice: Gwendolyn Brooks's '*In the Mecca*.'" *A Life Distilled: Gwendolyn Brooks, Her Poetry and Fiction*. Ed. Maria K. Mootry and Gary Smith. Chicago: University of Illinois Press, 1987. 193–204. Investigates the connection between orality, autonomy, and culture in the context of Brooks's poem.
"Composition with Guitar and Apples." *Callaloo* 16 (October 1982): 85–88. Rpt. in *Xarque*.
"The Cup." *Panache* 15 (1975): 48.
"The Day of the God." *Callaloo* 16.3 (October 1982): 73–79.
"Deep Song." *The Iowa Review* 6 (Spring 1975): 11.
"Don't Nobody Mess with Me." *Ms.* 3 (May 1975): 70–72, 76–77.
"Ensinaça." *Confirmation: An Anthology of African American Women*. Ed. Amiri Baraka and Amina Baraka. New York: Quill, 1983. 174–176. Rpt. in *The Hermit-Woman*.
"The Father." *Iowa Review* 6.2 (Spring 1975): 4.
"Fiction Study." *The Hermit-Woman*.
"From Almeyda." *Puerto del Sol* 14 (Fall 1975): 32–34. Rpt. in *Mandala* 3 (December 1975): 23–29.
"From PROSS." *Center* 6 (July 1974): 69–70.
"From *Stop Dat Moda*: A Canvas of Colors or Elevating the Culture." *Callaloo* 26.3 (2003): 720–728.
"From *The Machete Woman*: A Novel." *Callaloo* 17.2 (Spring 1994): 399–404.
"From *The Quest for Wholeness*: Re-Imagining the African-American Novel: An Essay on Third World Aesthetics." *Callaloo* 17.2 (Spring 1994): 507–518.
"From 'The Storyteller's Art': A Literary Conversation (Lucille Jones on Storytelling)." *Callaloo* 26.3 (Summer 2003): 709–720. Jones's interview with her mother in which the latter discusses her views on poetry and fiction.
"The Fur Station." *First World: An International Journal of Black Thought* 2.4 (1980): 23.
"The Gathering." *Panache* 16–17 (1976): 54–55.

"Goosens." *Callaloo* 16.3 (October 1982): 54–58.
"The Hermit-Woman." *The Hermit-Woman.*
"Interview with Lucille Jones." *Obsidian* 3.3 (Winter 1977): 26–35. Jones's early interview with her mother in which they discuss family history and cultural conditions during Lucille's life.
"Jasper Notes." *Panache* 14 (1975): 27–33.
"Jevata." *Essence* 4 (November 1973): 66–67, 76, 78–79, 82, 86. Rpt. in *White Rat.* Also rpt. in *Midnight Birds: Stories of Contemporary Black Women Writers.* Ed. Mary Helen Washington. Garden City: Anchor, 1980. 132–149.
"Journal." *Center* 7 (April 1975): 9.
"Journal." *Obsidian* 2.3 (Winter 1976): 72–82. Rpt. in *Black Sister: Poetry by Black American Women, 1746–1980.* Ed. Erlene Stetson. Bloomington: Indiana University Press, 1981. 205–209.
"Legend." *White Rat.*
"Love, Another Story." *BOP* 1 (1974): 25–26.
"The Lovers." *Essence* 5 (May 1974): 89.
"The Machete Woman." *The Hermit-Woman.*
"Many Die Here." *Soulscript: Afro-American* Poetry. Ed. June Jordan. Garden City: Doubleday, 1970. 14–15. Rpt. in *Black Sister: Poetry by Black American Women, 1746–1980.* Ed. Erlene Stetson. Bloomington: Indiana University Press, 1981. 210–211.
"Marla." *Xarque.*
"Más Allá." *For Neruda, for Chile: An International Anthology.* Ed. Walter Lowenfels. Boston: Beacon, 1975.
"The Men." *Center* 7 (April 1975): 9.
"The Night of the Leopard: Theatre Poems." *Silo* 16 (Winter 1969): 15–38.
"Part IV of *Journal.*" *Black Sister: Poetry by Black American Women, 1746–1980.* Ed. Erlene Stetson. Bloomington: Indiana University Press, 1981. 205–208.
"Party." *Panache* 16–17 (1976): 55–56.
"Persona." *White Rat.*
"Prophet Powers." *Callaloo* 16.3 (October 1982): 80–84.
"A Quiet Place for the Summer." *White Rat.*
"Repetitions." *Center* 9 (December 1976): 23.
"The Return: A Fantasy." *Amistad 2.* Ed. John A. Williams and Charles F. Harris. New York: Random House, 1971. 136–167. Rpt. in *White Rat.*
"A Review of the Collected Poems of Sterling Brown." *Xavier Review* 3.1 (1983): 43–44. Favorably considers Brown's poetry in terms of "the variety and quality of characterizations, the interplay of voices, dramatic forms, histories, scenes, portraits, the range and integrity of voice."
"The Roundhouse." *Panache* 7 (1971): 7–12. Rpt. in *White Rat.* Also rpt. in *The Third Woman: Minority Women Writers in the United States.* Ed. Dexter Fisher. Boston Houghton Mifflin, 1980. 230–236.
"Salvation." *Essence* 1 (September 1970): 12. Rpt. in *Keeping the Faith: Writings by*

Contemporary Black American Women. Ed. Pat Crutchfield Exum. Greenwich: Fawcett, 1974. 94.
"Satori." *Soulscript: Afro-American* Poetry. Ed. June Jordan. Garden City: Doubleday, 1970. 15. Rpt. in *Black Sister: Poetry by Black American Women, 1746–1980.* Ed. Erlene Stetson. Bloomington: Indiana University Press, 1981. 210.
"The Seige." *Callaloo* 16.3 (October 1982): 89–94.
"A Sense of Security." *Essence* 4 (August 1973): 63, 87–88.
"Sentences." *Panache* 15 (1975): 45–48.
"The Shoemaker and the Sadism of the Senhora." *Ploughshares* 8 (December 1982): 42–52.
"Spaces." *The Black Scholar* 6 (June 1975): 53–55.
"Sticks and Witches Brooms." *Michigan Quarterly Review* 17 (Spring 1978): 205–208.
"Stranger." *The Hermit-Woman.*
"Those Rock People." *Callaloo* 16.3 (October 1982): 59–65.
"Toward an All-Inclusive Structure." Diss. Brown University, 1973.
"Tripart." *Soulscript: Afro-American* Poetry. Ed. June Jordan. Garden City: Doubleday, 1970. 13. *Black Sister: Poetry by Black American Women, 1746–1980.* Ed. Erlene Stetson. Bloomington: Indiana University Press, 1981. 209.
"Version 2 of a Fantasy." *BOP* 1 (1974): 106–109. Rpt. in *White Rat.*
"Waiting." *Center* 7 (April 1975): 9.
"Waiting for the Miracle." *Callaloo* 16 (October 1982): 66–72. Rpt. in *Xarque.*
"The Welfare Check." *Essence* 1 (October 1970): 67, 71, 74.
"White Rat." *Giant Talk: An Anthology of Third World Writings.* Ed. Quincy Troupe and Rainer Schulte. New York: Random House, 1975. 287–293. Rpt. in *White Rat.* Also rpt. in *The Norton Anthology of Short Fiction.* Ed. R.V. Cassill. New York: Norton, 1978. 656–663.
"Wild Figs and Secret Places." *The Hermit-Woman.*
"The Women." *White Rat.*
"Work in Progress." *Nimrod* 21.1 (1977): 124–126.
_____. *Obsidian* 2.2 (Summer 1976): 38–46.
"Your Poems Have Very Little Color in Them." *White Rat.*
"Xarque." *First World* 2.3 (1979): 13. Rpt. in *Xarque.*

Works about Jones

Essays and Book Chapters

Agusti, Clara Escada. "Strategies of Subversion: The Deconstruction of Madness in *Eva's Man, Corregidora,* and *Beloved.*" *Atlantis* 27.1 (June 2005): 29–39. The female protagonists in these books experience madness as a means of defining, resisting, and rejecting racist, patriarchal society.

Allen, Donia Elizabeth. "The Role of the Blues in Gayl Jones's *Corregidora*." *Callaloo* 25.1 (Winter 2002): 257–273. Traces various elements of American blues music as they appear in Jones's writing style for this novel.

Basu, Biman. "Public and Private Discourses and the Black Female Subject: Gayl Jones' *Eva's Man*." *Callaloo* 19.1 (1996): 193–208. Maintains that "attention to the language of the text, analysis of language and representation, far from being apolitical, unmasks the politics of language and the ideology of representation which are some of the most powerful instruments for the construction of the subject."

Bell, Bernard W. "The Liberating Literary and African American Vernacular Voices of Gayl Jones." *Comparative Literature Studies* 36.3 (Summer 1999): 247–257. Bundles *Liberating Voice* and *The Healing* against Jones's early fiction in pointing out a move toward formal experimentation and cross-culturalism.

Boutry, Katherine. "Black and Blue: The Female Body of Blues Writing in Jean Toomer, Toni Morrison, and Gayl Jones." *Black Orpheus: Music in African American Fiction From the Harlem Renaissance to Toni Morrison*. Ed. Saadi A. Simawe. New York: Garland, 2000. 91–118. Discusses blues as a means of liberation and healing against the backdrop of violence against women.

Bramen, Carrie Tirado. "Speaking in Typeface: Characterizing Stereotypes in Gayl Jones's *Mosquito*." *Modern Fiction Studies* 49.1 (Spring 2003): 124–154. Investigates the book's strategic use of stereotypes and other culturally-ascribed racial variables.

Byerman, Keith. "Afterword: Voicing Gayl Jones." *After the Pain: Critical Essays on Gayl Jones*. Ed. Fiona Mills and Keith B. Mitchell. New York, Peter Lang, 2006. 259–262. Contemplates Jones's place in African American literature while also revisiting the essays from *After the Pain*.

_____. "Black Vortex: The Gothic Structure of *Eva's Man*." *Melus* 7.4 (1980): 93–101. Asserts that "the degree to which Eva's ideology is taken seriously is a measure of Jones's accomplishment as a storyteller and not a measure of her polemical intent."

_____. "Intense Behaviors: The Use of the Grotesque in *The Bluest Eye* and *Eva's Man*," *CLA Journal* 25.4 (June 1982): 447–457. Concludes that "the incest of Morrison's book is outdone by the necrophilia and castration of Jones's."

Chandra, Sarika. "Interruptions: Tradition, Borders, and Narrative in Gayl Jones's *Mosquito*." *After the Pain: Critical Essays on Gayl Jones*. Ed. Fiona Mills and Keith B. Mitchell. New York, Peter Lang, 2006. 137–154. Interprets the book as a contemporary slave narrative that moves across different cultures as it constructs identity for its characters.

Coser, Stelamaris. "The Dry Wombs of Black Women: Memories of Brazilian Slavery in *Corregidora* and *Song for Anninho*." *Bridging the Americas: The Literature of Toni Morrison, Paule Marshall, and Gayl Jones*. Philadelphia: Temple University Press, 1994. 120–163. Examines the specters of slavery, memory, and history with regard to Jones's Brazilian material.

Davison, Carol Margaret. "'Love 'em and Lynch 'em': The Castration Motif in

Gayl Jones's *Eva's Man*." *African American Review* 29.3 (Autumn 1995): 393–410. Maintains the novel achieves a kind of liberation through lesbianism: in an "ecstatic moment of female pleasure, [Eva] simultaneously escapes patriarchal time and place, and undermines the Freudian theory of *penisneid*."

Dixon, Melvin. "Singing a Deep Song: Language as Evidence in the Novels of Gayl Jones." *Black Women Writers (1950–1980): A Critical Evaluation*. Ed. Mari Evans. Garden City: Anchor P/Doubleday, 1984. 235–248. Concentrates on Jones's linguistic invention and art of telling as means of testifying past abuses.

Epes, Heather E. "Identity and Conceptual Limitation in Gayl Jones's *The Healing*: From Turtle to Human Being." *After the Pain: Critical Essays on Gayl Jones*. Ed. Fiona Mills and Keith B. Mitchell. New York, Peter Lang, 2006. 11–20. Considers the novel in terms of identity politics and the limitations of language in delineating it.

Fahy, Thomas. "Unsilencing Lesbianism in the Early Fiction of Gayl Jones." *After the Pain: Critical Essays on Gayl Jones*. Ed. Fiona Mills and Keith B. Mitchell. New York, Peter Lang, 2006. 203–220. Offers readings of Jones's early lesbian fiction that generally was attacked or ignored when it first appeared.

Goldberg, Elizabeth Swanson. "Living the Legacy: Pain, Desire, and Narrative Time in Gayl Jones's *Corregidora*." *Callaloo* 26.2 (2003): 446–472. Argues that "rather than providing narrative closure in its call-response blues structure, the novel is left suspended in the troubled narrative time of historical legacy."

Gordon, Nickesia S. "On the Couch with Dr. Fraud: Insidious Trauma and distorted Female Community in Gayl Jones's *Eva's Man*." *Obsidian III* 6.1 (Spring-Summer 2005): 66–88. Examines how patriarchal communities, and namely the male-dominated psychological field, inflict upon trauma upon the female body and psyche in the novel.

Gottfried, Amy S. "Angry Arts: Silence, Speech, and Song in Gayl Jones's *Corregidora*." *African American Review* 28.4 (Winter 1994): 559–570. Considers how Jones asks "unpopular questions about how the political commodification of women's bodies forecloses the real simultaneity of 'correct' and 'incorrect' desires."

Graham, Maryemma. "Living the Legacy: Pain, Desire, and Narrative Time in Gayl Jones's *Corregidora*." *Callaloo* 26.2 (Spring 2003): 446–473. Deals with the largely problematic overlap between joy and trauma in the context of the novel's temporality.

Griffiths, Jennifer. "Uncanny Spaces: Trauma, Cultural Memory, and the Female Body in Gayl Jones's *Corregidora* and Maxine Kingston's *The Woman Warrior*." *Studies in the Novel* 38.3 (Fall 2006): 353–371. Body and voice are linked to recovery in these books as the protagonists seek to purge their traumas through the act of narrative repetition.

Harris, Trudier. Foreword. *After the Pain: Critical Essays on Gayl Jones*. Ed. Fiona Mills and Keith B. Mitchell. New York, Peter Lang, 2006. ix–xiv. Contextualizes Jones's alienated place in African American literature while considering her biography and critical reactions to her work.

_____. "A Spiritual Journey: Gayl Jones's *Song For Anninho*." *Callaloo* 16 (October 1982): 105–111. Concludes that Jones offers "a tale which is intense, historical, and at times exotic, always pleasantly and painfully engaging."

Hochberg, Gil Zehava. "Mother, Memory, History: Maternal Genealogies in Gayl Jones's *Corregidora* and Simone Schwarz-Bart's *Miracle*." *Research in African Literatures* 34.2 (Summer 2003): 1–13. Considers women's familial histories and how they may be recalled and constructed within the fictional worlds of these two novels.

Horvitz, Deborah. "'Sadism Demands a Story': Oedipus, feminism, and sexuality in Gayl Jones's *Corregidora* and Dorothy Allison's *Bastard Out of Carolina*." *Contemporary Literature* 39.2 (Summer 1998): 238–262. Compares Jones's novel with Allison's in terms of the way they provide avenues by which women may come to terms with and move beyond past sexual traumas.

Jackson, Richard. "Remembering the 'Disremembered': Modern Black Writers and Slavery in Latin America." *Callaloo* 13.1 (Winter 1990): 131–144. Characterizes *Song for Anninho* as "a spiritual journey through memory over time, a remembering beyond Palmares that establishes a place for blacks in the world."

Johnson, Patrick. "Wild Women Don't Get the Blues: A Blues Analysis of Gayl Jones' *Eva's Man*." *Obsidian II* 9.1 (Spring/Summer 1994): 26–46. Observes that the novel, "when read through the blues filter, provides a new way for listening to the 'other,' for through the creation of the blues text itself, the performer recreates her experience."

Karrer, Wolfgang. "Gayl Jones: Asylum." *The African American Short Story, 1970 to 1990: A Collection of Critical Essays*. Ed. Karrer and Barbara Puschman-Nalenz. Trier: Wissenschaftlicher Verlag Trier, 1993. 89–103. Asserts that Jones's "repeated negations" "stake a claim for her writing that makes her contribution a radical reconstruction of black myths, imposed or self-imposed alike."

King, Lovalerie. "Resistance, Reappropriation, and Reconciliation: The Blues and Flying Africans in Gayl Jones's *Song for Anninho*." *Callaloo* 27.3 (Summer 2004): 755–767. Rpt. in *After the Pain*. Mingles American Blues with elements of magic realism and variables from Brazilian culture in articulating Jones's attempt to give voice to history.

Li, Stephanie. "Love and the Trauma of Resistance in Gayl Jones's *Corregidora*." *Callaloo* 29.1 (Winter 2006): 131–151. Abuse and desire are coupled together in a reading of the novel that demonstrates the linked qualities of violence and utterance.

Lionnet, Francois. "Geographies of Pain: Captive Bodies and Violent Acts in the Fictions of Myriam Warner-Vieyra, Gayl Jones, and Bessie Head." *Callaloo* 16.1 (Winter 1993): 132–152. Articulates the cultural and artistic crisis that exists "so long as women's silences and body languages continue to be ignored or recuperated by the symbolic order, thus becoming "black holes" (so to speak) within and against which all interpretive discourses can only come to a halting stop."

Marr, Vanessa. "Slavery, Silence, and Song: Compulsory Heterosexuality in Gayl

Jones's *Corregidora.*" *Michigan Academician* 34.1 (Spring 2002): 107. Uses Adrienne Rich's theories of sexuality to read the book as a narrative of male-dominated, heterosexual dominion over victimized women.

Mills, Fiona. "Telling the Untold Tale: Afro-Latino/a Identifications in the Work of Gayl Jones." *After the Pain: Critical Essays on Gayl Jones.* Ed. Fiona Mills and Keith B. Mitchell. New York, Peter Lang, 2006. 91–116. Considers Jones in terms of the cultural intersections she explores between African American and Latino culture.

_____, **and Keith B. Mitchell.** "After the Pain: An Introduction." *After the Pain: Critical Essays on Gayl Jones.* Ed. Fiona Mills and Keith B. Mitchell. New York, Peter Lang, 2006. 1–10. An overview of Jones's critical reputation and a summary of the essays included in *After the Pain.*

Mitchell, Keith B. "Trouble in Mind": (Re)visioning Myth, Sexuality and Race in Gayl Jones's *Corregidora.*" *After the Pain: Critical Essays on Gayl Jones.* Ed. Fiona Mills and Keith B. Mitchell. New York, Peter Lang, 2006. 155–172. Couples mythology and psychoanalysis in interpreting the intersections of race and gender in the novel.

Nwanko, Ifeoma C.K. "The Promises and Perils of U.S. African-American Hemispherism: Latin America in Martin Delany's *Blake* and Gayl Jones's *Mosquito.*" *American Literary History* 18.3 (Fall 2006): 579–599. Argues that Africa American fiction typically is not parochial in its concerns and, instead, often conceptualizes a sense of community anchored around the idea of hemisphere rather than nation-state.

Ramsby, Howard, II. "Things Deserving Echoes: Gayl Jones's Liberating Poetry." *After the Pain: Critical Essays on Gayl Jones.* Ed. Fiona Mills and Keith B. Mitchell. New York, Peter Lang, 2006. 221–240. Traces elements of the historical, the unlikely, and the fantastic as they appear in Jones's poetry.

Robinson, Sally. "'We're All Consequences of Something': Cultural Mythologies of Gender and Race in the Novels of Gayl Jones." *Engendering the Subject: Gender and Self-Representation in Contemporary Women's Fiction.* Albany: State University of New York Press, 1991. 135–187. Offers that some of Jones's protagonists are all to "write in the margins of hegemonic discourse": "to push the hegemonic representations of black womanhood to their limits, and to empower black female subjects as agents capable of resisting those representations."

Rushdy, Ashraf H.A. "'Relate Sexual to Historical': Race, Resistance, and Desire in Gayl Jones's *Corregidora.*" *African American Review* 34.2 (Summer 2000): 273–296. Explores connection between Jones's characters and narrative, arguing that some characters "assume an intersubjective communion with their narrators."

Stallings, L.H. "From Mules to Turtle and Unicorn Women: The Gender-Folk Revolution and the Legacy of Obeah in Gayl Jones's *The Healing.*" *After the Pain: Critical Essays on Gayl Jones.* Ed. Fiona Mills and Keith B. Mitchell. New York, Peter Lang, 2006. 65–90. Focuses on female identity in the novel by articulating the manner in which folklore and mythology help to stabilize and articulate the self.

Streeter, Caroline A. "Was Your Mamma Mulatto? Notes towards a Theory of Racialized Sexuality in Gayl Jones's *Corregidora* and Julie Dash's *Daughters of the Dust.*" *Callaloo* 27.3 (Summer 2004): 768–787. Mulatto characters prove indispensable in these two works both in helping to reconcile questions of gender and identity, and in memorializing cultural history.

Sweeney, Megan. "Prison Narratives, Narrative Prisons: Incarcerated Women Reading Gayl Jones's *Eva's Man.*" *Feminist Studies* 30.2 (Summer 2004): 456–483. Rpt. in *After the Pain.* Seeks reactions to the novel by real "lawbreaking women" who are imprisoned in offering a reading that hopes to sensitize and enrich the manner in which we respond to violence and incarceration.

Tate, Claudia C. "*Corregidora*: Ursa's Blues Medley." 13.4 (Winter 1979): 139–141. Conceptualizes novel's triumph as its ability to combine "the highly sophisticated craft of fiction with the improvisational act of storytelling without making the process of relating the story seem contrived or abandoning subtle narrative techniques."

Terry, Jill. "'reads kinda like jazz in they rhythm': Gayl Jones's Recent Jazz Conversations." *After the Pain: Critical Essays on Gayl Jones.* Ed. Fiona Mills and Keith B. Mitchell. New York, Peter Lang, 2006. 117–136. Analyzes Jones's portrayals of African American culture through music, linking literary, cultural, and musical expression.

Venugopal, Shubha. "Textual Transfigurations and Female Metamorphosis: Reading Gayl Jones's *The Healing.*" *After the Pain: Critical Essays on Gayl Jones.* Ed. Fiona Mills and Keith B. Mitchell. New York, Peter Lang, 2006. 31–64. Examines the novel by tracing violence as a healing force for women, enabling them to move beyond stereotypes and other forms of oppression.

Ward, Jerry W., Jr. "Escape from Trublem: The Fiction of Gayl Jones." *Callaloo* 16.3 (October 1982): 95–104. Holds that Jones's first three books demonstrate "unpredictable structures ... [that] provoke questions about how we construct meaning from allowing our minds to play through the texts."

Wilcox, Janelle. "Resistant Silence, Resistant Subject: (Re)Reading Gayl Jones's *Eva's Man.*" *Genders* 23 (Spring 1996): 72–96. Concludes "that Jones's work and, to some extent, the writer herself, were silenced by the disciplinary function of the interpretive communities of the 1970s."

Young, Hershini Bhana. "Inheriting the Criminalized Black Body: Race, Gender, and Slavery in *Eva's Man.*" *African American Review* 39.3 (Fall 2005): 377–394. Approaches the novel as a prison narrative that partakes of aspects of the African American literary tradition while specifically problematizing the American judicial system.

Yukins, Elizabeth. "Bastard Daughters and the Possession of History in *Corregidora* and *Paradise.*" *Signs* 28.1 (Autumn 2002): 221–249. Investigates these novels by Jones and Morrison in terms of trauma as property that cannot be transmitted fully.

Reviews

Angelou, Maya. "The Long, Sweet Contemplation of Revenge." *Los Angeles Times Book Review* (1 June 1975): 1, 10. Articulates *Corregidora* in terms of its gender-informed focus on deferred vengeance.

Avant, John Alfred. "Review of *Corregidora*." *New Republic* 172 (28 June 1975): 27–28. Characterizes novel "of great power" as "so emotionally raw that some readers may find it embarrassing."

Bader, Eleanor J. "Review of *Mosquito*." *Library Journal* 124.1 (January 1999): 152. Concludes: "By turns exhausting and exhilarating, *Mosquito* is a stunning glimpse into one woman's search for her place in the cosmos."

Bannon, Barbara. "Review of *Corregidora*." 207 (24 March 1975): 40. Forecasts, accurately enough, that "this strong, somber novel by a major talent will be counted among the important additions to contemporary literature."

———. "Review of *White Rat*." *Publishers Weekly* 212.6 (8 August 1977): 63. Summarizes: "With the plots connected by one theme, the failure of blacks of any status to deal with life, the subjects are various horrors."

Birkerts, Sven. "Prior Use." *Transition* 55 (1992): 168–172. Concludes that "for all its local acumen — and Jones is a skillful close reader with a sure sense for the symptomatic textual turn — *Liberating Voices* is neither particularly liberating nor revelatory."

Champion, Laurie. "Review of *Mosquito*." *African American Review* 34.2 (Summer 2000): 366–368. Views novel positively as a result of its utilization of oral narrative: "a tradition that depends upon repetition to shape history from perspectives that allow a voice to those traditionally denied opportunities to inscribe their histories."

Cherry, Kelly. "Sins of the Fathers." *Chicago Tribune Book World* (18 May 1975): 4. Addresses *Corregidora* in terms of gender tension and patriarchal abuses.

Cooke, Michael G. "Recent Novels: Women Bearing Violence." *Yale Review* 66.1 (Autumn 1976): 146–155. Unsympathetic assessment of *Eva's Man* as a collection "of Southern ghetto misadventures, female variety."

Dixon, Melvin. "Review of *Corregidora*." *Obsidian* 3 (Spring 1977): 72–74. Concludes that "few writers since Ellison have been as articulate about the dimensions of the blues character and condition."

Dubey, Madhu. "Review of *Liberating Voices*." *Studies in the Novel* 21.1 (Spring 1993): 120–122. Finds that the study is "most incisive and engaging in … speculations upon the cultural distinctions between oral and literary forms."

Edmondson, Belinda. "Review of *Liberating Voices*." *Ariel* 23.2 (July 1992): 126–129. Criticizes Jones's choice of literary comparisons, her "rather effusive prose," and the decision to include a glossary before, concluding that Jones must have anticipated "a remarkably ill-informed audience for this work — or a very young one."

Edwards, Tamala M. "Review of *Mosquito*." *Time* 153.5 (8 February 1999): 72.

Presents book as overly dense and tangled: "In rare moments, Jones's virtuosity grins up at us, leaving hope that this is just a frustrating detour on the road to better storytelling."

Fabi, M. Giulia. "Review of *Liberating Voices*." *American Literature* 65.2 (June 1993): 391. A short, positive description of the study's organization and attempt "to recover and reinterpret the less-known works of pre–Harlem Renaissance writers."

Garrett, George. "Coming Out of Left Field: The Short Story Today." *Sewanee Review* 86 (Summer 1978): 461–473. Observes that the stories "are linked not only by their concentration on race and racism and their lean, spare mannerisms, but also by the fact that they are all intended to be echoes of and variations on the ways of oral history and telling."

Gates, Henry Louis, Jr. "Sanctuary." *New York Times Book Review* 104.46 (14 November 1999): 14. Laments, "Would that an editor like Morrison had helped Jones locate where she wanted her narrator to be, and to bridle in this sprawling, formless, maddening tale."

Gayle, Addison. "Black Women and Black Men: The Literature of Catharsis." *Black Books Bulletin* 4 (Winter 1976): 48–52. Considers *Eva's Man* through the lens of meaning and identity gained through suffering and travail.

Golden, Bernette. "Review of *Corregidora*." *Black World* 25 (February 1976): 82. Maintains that "Jones has opened the emotional baggage, locked and sealed, that Black women carry."

Goode, Ann. "Review of *Corregidora*." *Black Books Bulletin* 3 (Fall 1975): 46–47. Asserts that in *Corregidora*, "The past is prologue — and our ability to understand and move from its reality is a measure of our movement to more positive directions."

Grossman, Judith. "Love's Reward." *The Women's Review of Books* 15.6 (March 1998): 15–16. Maintains that in *The Healing* Jones "is telling us here an ultimately benign tale of love guiding a progress into humanity."

Hairston, Loyle. "No Feminist Tract." *Freedomways* 15 (1975): 290–292. Examines *Corregidora* in terms of the way that "the cultural sensibilities of the women's rights movement haven't yet been liberated from a white middle-class outlook."

_____. "Repelling World of Sex and Violence." *Freedomways* 16 (1976): 133–135. Characterizes *Eva's Man* as an "awful little book" that makes a "squalid appraisal of the souls of Black folks."

Harris, Jessica. "Review of *Eva's Man*." *Essence* 7.2 (June 1976): 87. Conceptualizes the novel as "a story that is as terrifying and as riveting as a basketful of squirming snakes."

_____. "Review of *White Rat*." *Essence* 8.6 (October 1977): 55. Concludes, "Reading these stories is like reading case histories, each one opening the door to a new malaise."

Hershman, Marcie. "On the Road to Healing." *Boston Globe* (15 February 1998): E1. Marvels at *The Healing*'s narrative risks, summarizing, "Taking aim differently, Gayl Jones still hits on-center."

Jefferson, Margot. "Making Generations." *Newsweek* 85 (19 May 1975): 84–85. Observes that *Corregidora* "is filled with sexual and spiritual pain: hatred, love and desire wear the same face, and humor is blues-bitter."

———. "A Woman Alone." *Newsweek* 87 (12 April 1976): 102–106. Describes *Eva's Man* as "a taut, compelling excursion into the lower depths of sexuality, where lust is inseparable from the need to control and dominate."

Jenkins, Candice M. "Review of *The Healing*." *African American Review* 34.2 (Summer 2000): 365–366. Conceptualizes Harlan Jane Eagleton as a representative African American woman in her "ability to transcend loss and to heal old wounds, in the self and others."

Jordan, June. "All About Eva: *Eva's Man*." *New York Times Book Review* (16 May 1976): 36–37. Worries over the African American cultural identity implications of Eva's characterization, lamenting she "is nobody I have ever known."

Keizer, Arlene R. "Gayl Jones and the Postmodern Moment." *Michigan Quarterly Review* 40.2 (Spring 2001): 431–436. Celebrates *Mosquito*'s "focus upon the multiple subjectivities of three working-class women of color."

Kulli, Elon. "Review of *Liberating Voices*." *Journal of American Folklore* 106 (Winter 1993): 106–107. Praises the study as "a welcome addition to the works on oral tradition for folklorists, students of literature, writers, and critics."

Kuskin, Karla. "Cycle of Sex and Slavery." *Village Voice* 20.21 (26 May 1975): 42. Articulates *Corregidora* in terms of "sex and slavery, the inseparable tyrannizers of black women."

Larson, Charles R. "Master and Slave Became Fused; Past Lives in the Present." *National Observer* (9 August 1975) 17. Remarks *Corregidora*'s "obsessive quality": "Reading *Corregidora* one feels that this is not a novel at all, but oral history finally got down on paper."

———. "Uneven Collection of Afro-American Tales." *Washington Post* (21 October 1977): D9. Compares collection to Jones's first two novels: "If the stories in *White Rat* are less successful, it is largely because of their unfinished quality."

———. "The Violent and Poetic Puzzle of *Eva's Man*." *National Observer* (17 April 1976): 19. Concludes that the book "lives up to the promise of Gayl Jones's earlier novel."

Lasker, Eben. "Review of *Mosquito*." *Africana.com* 1998 <http://www.africana.com/Reviews/books_4.htm> Describes Mosquito's story as "a one-woman conspiracy to spark a small but powerful revolution in the mind of its reader."

Lehmann-Haupt. "Women in Pain ... or Giggling." *New York Times* (21 April 1975): 27. Characterizes *Corregidora* as a paradoxical narrative that both "hurts you and makes you still want to listen."

Leonard, John. "Violence Born of a Woman's Hate." *New York Times* (30 April 1976): C17. Argues that in *Eva's Man* "the style and the psychic weather of a black Joan Didion."

Major, Clarence. "Review of *Eva's Man*." *Library Journal* 101.6 (15 March 1976): 834–835. Describes book as "a sad, dark chant ridden with sex and blood."

Marcus, Greil. "Review of *Eva's Man*." *Rolling Stone* (17 June 1976): 73. References the novel briefly, describing it as "beautifully written and utterly bleak."

McDowell, Deborah. "The Whole Story." *The Women's Review of Books* 16.6 (March 1999): 9–10. Laments, "*Mosquito*, unlike Jones' taut and economical early work, is sprawling and unruly, spilling over into territory too broad and meandering to map or summarize easily."

McMurtry, Larry. "A Bold, Strong First Novel from Gayl Jones." *Washington Post* (28 April 1975): B6. Describes *Corregidora* as "written in an admirably direct prose whose power, nevertheless, resides in the ultimately unresolvable ambiguities of its story."

_____. "The Second Novel as Virtual Twin to a First." *Washington Post* (12 April 1976): C5. Argues that in the wake of *Eva's Man* Jones's material "has managed to become monotonous."

Miller, Alicia Metcalf. "How an Abused Woman Turned." *The Plain Dealer* (25 April 1976): 27. Offers that negative socio-psychological and visceral forces systematically create the mad protagonist of *Eva's Man*.

Miller, James A. "A Talker, a Tale-teller, a Sojourner." *Boston Globe* (17 January 1999): E3. Ambivalent assessment of *Mosquito*: For some the book "will yield some rewards. For others, this work, like a mosquito, will buzz along — nagging, irritating, provoking, exasperating."

Moeller, Dianna. "Review of *The Healing*." *Library Journal* 122.20 (December 1997): 152–154. Cites Jones's "trademark blend of narrative and lyricism" in recommending the book to general readers.

Morrison, Toni. "Toni Morrison on a Book She Loves: Gayl Jones' *Corregidora*." *Mademoiselle* 81 (May 1975): 14. Characterizes novel as a "story that thought the unthinkable; that thought about the female requirement to 'make generations' as an active, even violent political act."

Nelson, Jill. "Review of *The Healing*." *The Nation* 266.19 (25 May 1998):30–31. Maintains that "Jones's ability to create bizarre yet believable characters is magical, requiring a subtle act of faith between writer and reader."

Pearl, Nancy. "Review of *The Healing*." *Booklist* 94.11 (1 February 1998): 899. Concludes that "the style of presentation — almost entirely dialogue and jumping forward and back with a carefully planned but seemingly reckless disregard for any linear narrative — takes some getting used to, but readers who persevere will find it is worth it."

Pearson, Carol. "Review of *White Rat*." *Library Journal* 102.14 (August 1977): 1678. Asserts that the collection is too dark and suggests "no alternative to solipsism and despair."

Pinckney, Darryl. "*Eva's Man*." *New Republic* 174 (19 June 1976): 27–28. Summarizes book as "a tale of madness, one exacerbated if not caused by frustration, accumulated grievances."

Pochoda, Elizabeth. "Shades of a Black Female Faulkner." *Glamour* 73.9 (September 1975): 97. Asserts that Jones "manages to retell Faulkner's *Go Down, Moses* from a black perspective."

Prothro, Laurie. "Review of *White Rat.*" *National Review* 30 (14 April 1978): 485. Concludes ambiguously, "The sounds outside fit with the sounds in your head; love wins out over rejection and poverty and life's other crises, and that is, after all, enough."

Pryse, Marjorie. "For 5 Days He Was Her Man — Then She Done Him Wrong." *Los Angeles Times Book Review* (9 May 1976): 1, 15. Implicit consideration of *Eva's Man*'s blues themes.

"Review of *Corregidora.*" *Kirkus Reviews* 43 (15 February 1975): 195. Compares novel to the work of Toni Morrison in its concern with "hurt and need." Sums it up as "raw, harsh, hypnotic."

———. *Booklist* 71.18 (15 May 1975): 941. Personifies the novel as "uncompromising in its stark portrayal of sexual demands and needs."

———. *Playboy* 22 (June 1975): 33–34. Summarizes the book as "an extended blues lyric about sexual fear and rage in the American black woman."

"Review of *Eva's Man.*" *Booklist* 72.16 (1976): 1164. Sees books as "a harsh portrayal of the repression of black women seen purely as sexual beings."

———. *Choice* 13.7 (September 1976): 823. Argues that the book "does not have the larger canvas and social perspective of ... *Corregidora*."

———. *Kirkus Reviews* 44 (15 January 1976): 90. Maintains that Jones "is one furious, lacerating writer. You don't read her easily, and you can't forget her at all."

———. *Virginia Quarterly Review* 52.3 (Summer 1976): 97. Offers that the "book is convincing neither as art nor as polemic."

"Review of *Mosquito.*" *Publishers Weekly* 245.47 (23 November 1998): 571. Qualifies the novel: "Though it is not for those easily distracted, this wonderfully inventive book begs to be read aloud."

"Review of *The Healing.*" *Publishers Weekly* 245.3 (19 January 1998): 372. Concludes: "It is through her flawed but gravely human voice that Jones's flinty work is quietly redeemed."

"Review of *White Rat.*" *Booklist* 74.2 (15 September 1977): 140. Jones achieves "a wide range of voices that give her a stunning gamut of points of view in each story tension is sustained throughout, rather than reaching a climactic level."

———. *Choice* 14.12 (February 1978): 1644. Links Jones's achievement in short fiction to her work in the novel form.

———. *Kirkus Reviews* 45 (15 August 1977): 872. Summarizes collection as follows: "Sacrificing intensity but gaining scope, novelist Jones adds some grace notes — mostly dissonant — to the familiar dominant chord: the American black woman, her sexuality skewed by a confused heritage of rape by white men and power over black men."

———. *Library Journal* 102.14 (August 1977): 1678. Maintains that "the stories themselves suggest no alternative to solipsism and despair."

Sayers, Valerie. "Faith Healer." *New York Times* (10 May 1998): E4. Celebrates the affirming direction of *The Healing* against the darkness of Jones's biography and earlier work: "Violence and paranoia are banished by the faith Eagleton now embraces."

Sokolov, Raymond. "A Woman Who Sings Blues: *Corregidora*." *New York Times Book Review* (25 May 1975): 21–22. Highlights Jones's autonomous, even eccentric nature as a writer: "If you think Jones has only a simple, political message in mind, look again."

Stookey, Richard. "Violence and Rage Aimed in a New Direction." *Chicago Tribune Book World* (28 March 1976): 3. Considers *Eva's Man*'s psychological angst and visceral action as thematic anomaly.

Tate, Greg. "Going Underground." *Village Voice Literary Supplement* February 1999 <www.villagevoice.com/vls/160/tate.shtml>. Mixed consideration of *Mosquito*: book demonstrates Jones's "storehouses of language, craft, and storytelling," but is also "long-winded, diasassociative, plotless, cutesy, full of hairsplitting deconstructive debates."

Updike, John. "Eva and Eleanor and Everywoman." *New Yorker* 52 (9 August 1976): 74–77. Asserts that the characters are dehumanized as much by [Jones's] artistic vision as by their circumstances."

_____. "Selda, Lilia, Ursa, Great Gram, and Other Ladies in Distress." *New Yorker* 51 (18 August 1975): 79–83. Describes *Corregidora* as "a living history of the slavery that otherwise will be forgotten."

Villanueva, Alma Luz. "Review of *Mosquito*." *Ms.* 9.3 (April 1999): 107. Ambiguous, albeit ultimately positive, concludes with the imperative, "Start at the end or the beginning of this American novel, written in the 'nonnegotiable' spirit of a warrior class woman (who don't take no shit)."

Wall, Cheryl A. "A Sure Attention to Voice." *Novel* 26.2 (Winter 1993): 223–224. Determines that *Liberating Voices* is a positive catalyst for suggesting reading "in a broad comparative context."

Watkins, Mel. "Books: Accent Put on Negative in Short Stories by Gayl Jones." *New York Times* (28 December 1977): C17. Laments, "It is the lack of character development that finally makes this assemblage of misfits and neurotics unbelievable or, worse, uninteresting."

Webster, Ivan. "Really the Blues." *Time* 105 (16 June 1975): 47. Praises *Corregidora*, asserting "No black American novel since Richard Wright's *Native Son* (1940) has so skillfully traced psychic wounds to a sexual source."

Wilentz, Gay. "Review of *White Rat* and *Liberating Voices: Oral Tradition in African American Literature*." *African American Review* 28.1 (Spring 1994): 141–146. Praises the enduring relevance of *White Rat* but laments that *Liberating Voices* "would have been much more useful and appropriate had it been published when it was first written."

Woodson, Jacqueline. "Review of *The Healing*." *Artforum International* 36.7 (March 1998): S24-S25. Observes, "Driven by a narrative rather than dialogue, this contemplative and muted novel concerns itself with the authentic confronting the imagined."

Interviews

Bell, Roseann P. "Gayl Jones Takes a Look at *Corregidora*— An Interview." *Sturdy Black Bridges: Visions of Black Women in Literature*. Ed. Bell et al. Garden City: Doubleday, 1979. 282–287. Discusses aspects of the novel, Jones's literary influences, the blues, oral storytelling, and African American culture and tradition.

Harper, Michael S. "Gayl Jones: An Interview." *Massachusetts Review* 18.4 (Winter 1977): 692–715. Rpt. in *Chant of Saints: A Gathering of Afro-American Literature, Art, and Scholarship*. Ed. Michael S. Harper and Robert B. Stepto. Urbana: University of Illinois Press, 1979. 352–375. Main subjects broached are artistic theory and method, literary influences, orality, and discussion of specific works by Jones.

Rowell, Charles H. "An Interview with Gayl Jones." *Callaloo* 16.3 (October 1982): 32–53. Discussion includes the nature of literary tradition, African American history and culture, influences, aesthetics, sex, and questions concerning various works by Jones.

Tate, Claudia. "An Interview with Gayl Jones." *Black American Literature Forum* 13.4 (Winter 1979): 142–148. Topics include the nature of specific works by Jones, storytelling, aesthetics, gender, psychology, and violence.

Miscellaneous Items (Biographical Material, Career Summaries, Etc.)

Chambers, Veronica. "*The Healing*." *Newsweek* 131.7 (16 February 1998): 68. Offers biographical background on Jones in the wake of her literary reemergence following the publication of *The Healing*. It was this article that would lead Lexington, Kentucky officials to discover the identity Jones's companion, Bob Higgins.

Eckhoff, Sally. "The Terrible Mystery of Gayl Jones." *Salon* February 1998 <http://www.salon.com/media/1998/02/26media.html>. Offers and overview of Jones's work and recounts her biography, focusing primarily on the tragic events involving Bob Higgins.

Harvey, Dennis. "Heal Thyself." *Guardian* (25 March 1998). Former student of Jones at the University of Michigan relates her teaching style in discussing her biography and *The Healing*.

Manso, Peter. "Chronicle of a Tragedy Foretold." *New York Times Magazine* (19 July 1998): 32–37. Most detailed account of the circumstances surrounding the death of Bob Higgins.

Plummer, William. "Beyond Healing: A Novelist's Triumphal Return Ends in a Day of Violence and Horror." *People Weekly* 49.10 (16 March 1998): 81–82. Focuses on events surrounding Bob Higgins and concern for Jones among former colleagues at the University of Michigan.

Sherman, Steve. "Yes, It's Beacon Press's First Novel: The 143-Year-Old House

Acquires Work from Reclusive African American Writer Gayl Jones." *Publishers Weekly* 244.50 (8 December 1997): 18. Description of Jones's relationship with Beacon Press; includes quotes from Jones's editor and an email interview with Jones.

Washington, Mary Helen. "Gayl Jones." *Midnight Birds: Stories by Contemporary Black Women.* Ed. Washington. Garden City: Anchor, 1980. 125–127. Summary of Jones and her work up through 1980.

Other Works Cited

Abel, Elizabeth. "Black Writing, White Reading: Race and the Politics of Feminist Interpretation." *Critical Inquiry* 19.3 (Spring 1993): 470–498.

Asante, Molefi Kete. 2003 <http://www.asante.net/articles/articles.html>.

Baker, Houston A., Jr. "There is No More Beautiful Way: Theory and the Poetics of Afro-American Women's Writing." *Afro-American Literary Study in the 1990s.* Ed. Houston A. Baker, Jr. and Patricia Redmond. Chicago: University of Chicago Press, 1989. 135–155.

Bakhtin, Mikhail. *Rabelais and His World.* Trans. Helen Iswolsky. Cambridge: MIT Press, 1965.

Baldwin, Joseph A. "The Role of Black Psychologists in Black Liberation." *African American Psychology: Theory, Research, and Practice.* Ed. A. Kathleen Hoard Burlew et al. London: Sage Publications, 1992. 48–57.

Bell, Bernard W. *The Afro-American Novel and Its Tradition.* Amherst: University of Massachusetts Press, 1987.

_____. *The Contemporary African American Novel.* Amherst: University of Massachusetts Press, 2004.

Benjamin, Walter. "The Storyteller." *Illuminations.* Ed. Hannah Arendt. New York: Shocken, 1977. 83–109.

Bernal, Martin. *Black Athena Writes Back: Martin Bernal Responds to His Critics.* Ed. David Chioni Moore. Durham: Duke University Press, 2001.

Bruce, Dickson D., Jr. *The Origins of African American Literature, 1680–1865.* Charlottesville: University Press of Virginia, 2001.

Burlew, A. Katherine Hoard, et al. *African American Psychology: Theory, Research, and Practice.* Newbury Park: Sage, 1992.

Cartwright, Keith. *Reading Africa into American Literature: Epics, Fables, and Gothic Tales.* Lexington: University Press of Kentucky, 2001.

Coleman, James. *Faithful Vision: Treatments of the Sacred, Spiritual, and Supernatural in Twentieth-Century African American Fiction.* Baton Rouge: Louisiana State University Press, 2006.

Dandridge, Rita B. "Male Critics/Black Women's Novels." *CLA Journal* 23.1 (September 1979): 1–11.

DuCille, Ann. "Phallus(ies) of Interpretation: Toward Engendering the Black Critical 'I.'" *Callaloo* 16.3 (Summer 1993): 559–573.

Etter-Lewis, Gwendolyn. "From the Inside Out: Survival and Continuity in African American Women's Oral Narratives." *Unrelated Kin: Race and Gender in Women's Personal Narratives*. Ed. Etter-Lewis and Michèle Foster. New York: Routledge, 1996. 169–179.

Everett, Percival. "Foreword." *Making Callaloo: 25 Years of Black Literature*. Ed. Charles Rowell. New York: St. Martin's, 2002. Xv–vii.

Fisher, Jerilyn. "From Under the Yoke of Race and Sex: Black and Chicano Women's Fiction of the Seventies." *Minority Voices* 2.2 (September 1980): 1–12.

Freud, Sigmund. *Standard Edition: Complete Psychological Works Sigmund Freud, Vol. III*. Ed. and trans. J. Strachey. London: Hogarth, 1953.

Fröschels, Emil, et al. *Psychological Elements in Speech*. Boston: Expression Company, 1932.

Gates, Henry Louis, Jr. *The Signifying Monkey: A Theory of African-American Literary Criticism*. New York: Oxford University Press, 1988.

Gilroy, Paul. *The Black Atlantic: Modernity and Double Consciousness*. Cambridge: Harvard University Press, 1992.

Goddard, Henry Herbert. *Feeblemindedness: Its Causes and Consequences*. New York: Macmillan, 1914.

Goldstein, Kurt. *Language and Langauge Disturbances: Aphasiac Symptom Complexes and their Significance for Medicine and Theory of Language*. New York: Grune & Stratton,1948.

Green, J. Lee. *Blacks in Eden: The African American Novel's First Century*. Charlottesville: University Press of Virginia, 1996.

Gruesser, John. *Confluences: Postcolonialism, African American Literary Studies, and the Black Atlantic*. Athens: University of Georgia Press, 2005.

Gubar, Susan. *Critical Conditions: Feminism at the Turn of the Century*. New York: Columbia University Press, 2000.

Guthrie, Robert V. *Even the Rat Was White: A Historical View of Psychology*. New York: Harper & Row, 1976.

Handley, George B. *Postslavery Literatures in the Americas*. Charlottesville: University Press of Virginia, 2000.

Iser, Wolfgang. "Context Sensitivity and Its Feedback: The Two-Sidedness of Humanistic Discourse." *Partial Answers: Journal of Literature and the History of Ideas* 1.1 (January 2003): 1–33.

Kayser, Wolfgang. *The Grotesque in Art and Literature*. Trans. Ulrich Weisstein. Bloomington: Indiana University Press, 1963.

Kent, George. "The 1975 Literary Scene." *Phylon* 37 (March 1976): 100–115.

Lee, Valerie. "The Use of Folktalk in Novels by Black Women Writers." *CLA Journal* 23.3 (March 1980): 266–272.

Lively, Adam. *Masks: Blackness, Race, and the Imagination*. New York: Oxford University Press, 2002.

Marable, Manning, ed. *Dispatches from the Ebony Tower: Intellectuals Confront the African American Experience*. New York: Columbia University Press, 2000.

Martin, Reginald. "An Interview with Ishmael Reed." *African American Literature Book Club*. 1–7 June 1983. 26 October 2002 <http:aalbc.com/authors/ishmael.htm>.

Meindl, Dieter. *American Fiction and the Metaphysics of the Grotesque*. Columbia: University of Missouri Press, 1996.

Meléndez, Theresa. "The Oral Tradition and the Study of American Literature." *Redefining American Literary History*. Ed. A. LaVonne Brown Ruoff and Jerry W. Ward, Jr. New York: MLA, 1990. 75–82.

Morokoff, Patricia J. "A Cultural Context for Sexual Assertiveness in Women." *Sexuality, Society, and Feminism*. Eds. Cheryl Brown Travis and Jacquelyn W. White. Washington: American Psychological Association, 2000. 299–319.

Nfah-Abbenyi, Juliana Makuchi. *Gender in African Women's Writing: Identity, Sexuality, and Difference*. Bloomington: Indiana University Press, 1997.

Nicholls, David G. *Conjuring the Folk: Forms of Modernity in African America*. Ann Arbor: University of Michigan Press, 2000.

O'Brien, John, ed. "Alice Walker." *Interviews with Black Writers*. New York: Liveright, 1973. 186–211.

Patton, Venetria. *Women in Chains: The Legacy of Slavery in Black Women's Fiction*. Albany: State University of New York Press, 2000.

Pullin, Faith. "Landscapes of Reality: The Fiction of Contemporary Afro-American Women." *Black Fiction: New Studies in the Afro-American Novel Since 1945*. Ed. A. Robert Lee. New York: Barnes & Noble, 1980. 173–203.

Rose, Tricia. *Black Noise: Rap Music and Black Culture in Contemporary America*. Hanover: Wesleyan University Press, 1994.

Rowell, Charles H. "'Down Don't Worry Me': An Interview with Michael S. Harper." *Callaloo* 13.4 (Autumn 1990): 780–800.

Sellers, Susan. *Myth and Fairy Tale in Contemporary Women's Fiction*. New York: Palgrave, 2001.

Smitherman, Geneva. *Talkin and Testifyin*. Detroit: Wayne State University Press, 1977.

Smythe, Mary-Jeanette. "Strategic Storytelling: Constructing Self through Narrative and Nautilus." *Untying the Tongue: Gender, Power, and the Word*. Ed. Linda Longmire and Lisa Merrill. Westport: Greenwood Press, 1998. 267–280.

Tate, Claudia. *Psychoanalysis and Black Novels: Desire and the Protocols of Race*. New York: Oxford University Press, 1998.

Thomas, Lorenzo. *Extraordinary Measures: Afrocentric Modernism and Twentieth-Century American Poetry*. Tuscaloosa: University of Alabama Press, 2000.

Wade-Gayles, Gloria. *No Crystal Stair: Visions of Race and Gender in Black Women's Fiction*. Rev. ed. Cleveland: Pilgrim, 1997 (1984).

Walker, Clarence E. *We Can't Go Home Again: An Argument About Afrocentrism*. New York: Oxford University Press, 2001.

Washington, Robert E. *The Ideologies of African American Literature: From the Harlem Renaissance to the Black Nationalist Revolt.* New York: Rowman & Littlefield, 2001.

Wideman, John. "Frame and Dialect: The Evolution of the Black Voice in American Literature." *The American Poetry Review* 5 (September/October 1976): 34–37.

Index

Abel, Elizabeth 10
"About My Work" 126–127
African Diaspora 10, 11, 14, 116, 136
Africanism 2, 14
Asante, Molefi Kete 12, 97–99, 102, 131
"Asylum" 57
The Autobiography of an Ex-Colored Man 63

Bader, Eleanor 109
Baker, Houston 8–9, 125
Bakhtin, Mikhail 49, 56
Bambara, Toni Cade 42
Bannon, Barbara 48
Baraka, Amiri 8, 51, 52
Basu, Biman 36
Bell, Bernard 101, 133
Benjamin, Walter 50
"Beyond Yourself (The Midnight Confession) for Brother Ahh" 12, 26, 29, 35, 77, 97
The Birdcatcher 27, 70
Birkerts, Sven 124–125
Black Arts Movement 27, 94
The Black Atlantic 11
blues 41–43, 75–79, 94, 128
The Bluest Eye 37
Bosch, Juan 25
Boutry, Katherine 42
Bramen, Carrie 110
Brooks, Gwendolyn 7, 98, 129
Brown, Sterling 74, 127–128, 151, 167
Brown University 3, 15, 17, 53, 76, 160
Bruce, Dickson D., Jr. 23
Bryatt, A.S. 75
Byerman, Keith E. 40, 48

Callaloo 129, 130
Carter, Angela 75
Chamoiseau, Patrick 25
"Chance" 78–79
Chaucer, Geoffrey 104, 146, 160
Chile Woman 22–24, 26, 32–33, 43, 77, 94

"The Coke Factory" 56–57
Coleman, James 133
Conjuring the Folk: Forms of Modernity in African America 12
Connecticut College 79
The Contemporary African American Novel 133
Corregidora 4, 9, 12, 15, 16, 23, 25–27, 29, 31, 33–36, 40, 42, 47, 70, 77–78, 94–95
Coser, Stelamaris 75, 82
Critical Conditions: Feminism at the Turn of the Century 9
"The Cup" 78

Davison, Carol Margaret 15
"The Day of the God" 69
"Deep Song" 76
Dixon, Melvin 36
Douglas, Kirk 65

Eden trope 10
Edmondson, Belinda 124–125
Edwards, Tamala 110
Eliot, T.S. 68, 169, 171, 179
eroticism 12, 17, 27–28, 44, 94
Etter-Lewis, Gwendolyn 6–7
eurocentrism 131
Eva's Man 4, 12, 15–18, 22, 25, 27, 29, 31, 35–36, 38–39, 41, 47–48, 70, 77–78, 94, 103, 127
Even the Rat Was White 52
Everett, Percival 134
existentialism 57

fantasy 13, 40–41
"The Father" 83
Faulkner, William 32–33, 171, 175
Feeblemindedness: Its Causes and Consequences 21, 22
feminism 9, 10, 105, 106, 112, 135
"Fiction Study" 86–87

203

Index

"Four Part Poem" 33
freedom 8, 11, 13, 53–54, 58–59, 65–66, 89–69, 86, 89, 103, 112, 117, 127
Freud, Sigmund 25, 30, 98–99, 130, 131, 132
Fröschels, Emil 18, 20–21, 53
"The Fur Station" 81

Gaines, Ernest 51, 144, 146, 151, 160–163, 168, 175–176
Garrett, George 50
Gates, Henry Louis, Jr. 110, 125
"The Gathering" 80, 81
Gaugin, Paul 69, 70
gender 25, 27, 29, 32, 36, 41, 51, 75, 105, 112, 115, 119
Gilroy, Paul 11, 136
Giovanni, Nikki 81
Glissant, Edouard 25
globalization 11, 136
Goddard, H. H. 18–19, 21, 53
Goldstein, Kurt 18–19, 2, 32, 53
"Goosens" 59–60
Gothic 40, 47–48
Gottfried, Amy 26
Grass, Günter 91
Greene, J. Lee 10
grotesque 48–50, 52, 54–64, 66–67, 69–71, 78, 134
The Grotesque in Art and Literature 48
Gruesser, John 136
Gubar, Susan 9
"The Guitar" 66
Guthrie, Robert V. 52

Hairston, Loyle 27, 47
Handley, George 23
Harper, Michael 76
Harris, Jessica 52
Harris, Trudier 83–84
Hayden, Robert 79
The Healing 14, 74, 90, 95, 98–99, 101–103, 106, 108–109, 111, 114, 116–117
Hendrix, Jimi 90, 107
The Hermit-Woman 86–87, 89, 95
Hershman, Marcie 101
Higgins, Bob 4
Holiday, Billie 76–77
horror 13, 40, 49, 59, 84, 86
Hurston, Zora Neale 50, 160

"In the Mecca" 98, 129
Iser, Wolfgang 33

Jackson, Richard 82
James, Henry 104

"Jasper Notes" 77–78
jazz 8, 17, 51, 117, 128
Jenkins, Candice 102
"Jevata" 55–56, 66, 68
Johnson, James Weldon 63
Johnson, Patrick 42
Jordan, June 27, 39
Joyce, James 122, 147, 164, 179
"The Judgement" 38

Karrer, Wolfgang 57–59
Kayser, Wolfgang 48
Kulii, Elon 126

Larson, Charles R. 16, 64
"Legend" 59
Lehmann-Haupt, Christopher 16
Liberating Voices: Oral Tradition in African American Literature 3, 5, 8–9, 12, 50–51, 73, 123, 125–129, 131–132
liberation 49–50, 52–53, 55, 127, 130, 132, 133, 135, 137
The Life and Loves of a She Devil 41
Lionnet, Francois 36
Lively, Adam 93–94
"Locating an African American Text" 97
love 14, 26, 31–32, 43–44, 56, 62, 64, 67, 75–79, 83, 86, 90, 112
"The Lovers" 77, 78

"The Machete Woman" 88, 100
"*The Machete Woman*: A Novel" 99, 100
Major, Clarence 47
Making Callaloo 134
Malcolm X 116
"Many Die Here" 80
Marable, Manning 10
"Más Allá" 80
McDowell, Deborah 110
Meindl, Dieter 49
Meléndez, Theresa 5
memory 34–37, 39, 54, 128
Meridian 25
metaphor 35–36, 40, 44, 122, 133, 135
Miller, James 109–110
modernism 124
Morokoff, Patricia J. 41
Morrison, Toni 9, 15, 37
Mosquito 14, 74, 95–99, 108–110, 115, 117–119, 131
music 12, 17, 43, 51, 94, 105, 125
"My Man Bovanne" 42
Myth and Fairy Tale in Contemporary Women's Fiction 75
mythopoesis 76, 84, 89, 91, 109

Naylor, Gloria 70
Nicholls, David 12
Nights at the Circus 41

objective history 76
O'Brien, John 9
oppression 7, 24, 33, 50, 60, 75, 80, 83, 90, 108, 115–116, 134
oral tradition 4–5, 42, 50, 110, 121, 124, 126, 128–129, 132
orality 5–8, 16, 132
The Origins of African American Literature 23

"Part IV of Journal" 79
"Party" 78
Patton, Venetria 135
Pearson, Carol 47–48, 64
"Persona" 67, 68
Petry, Ann 8
"Philosophy of Composition" 123
Pinckney, Darryl 27
Poe, Edgar Allan 123
Portrait of a Lady 104
post colonialism 14, 84, 99, 110, 124
"Prophet Powers" 70–71
"Pross" 31
Prothro, Laurie 57
psychoanalysis 17–19
Psychoanalysis and Black Novels: Desire and the Protocols of Race 18
psychology 12–13, 17–22, 24–26, 29–37, 41, 44, 47, 52–53, 55, 59–60, 63, 65, 78–79, 87, 94, 103, 122, 137
Pudd'nhead Wilson 63

The Quest for Wholeness: Re-Imagining the African-American Novel: An Essay on Third World Aesthetics" 96
"A Quiet Place for the Summer" 64–66

Rabelais and His World 49, 56
race 63–64, 74–75, 93, 107, 111–115, 118, 125, 135–136
racism 4, 7, 11, 14, 22, 24, 33, 48, 50, 52, 59–60, 107, 114, 134
rap 105, 106, 125
rape 59, 65, 84
Reagan, Ronald 4
Reed, Ishmael 23, 27
Renaissance 48
"The Return: A Fantasy" 53, 61, 66
"A Review of the Collected Poems of Sterling Brown" 74
Robinson, Sally 39
Romado, Jorge 25

Romanticism 108, 112
"The Roundhouse" 66–67
Rowell, Charles H. 129
Rushdy, Ashraf 42

"Salvation" 80
Sanctuary Movement 111, 115–116, 118
Santana, Carlos 107
"Satori" 79–80
Sayers, Valerie 101
"The Seige" 61–62, 66
Sellers, Susan 41, 75, 76
"A Sense of Security" 63
Sewanee Review 129
sex 15–16, 25, 27, 29–35, 40–41, 47–49, 55–56, 67–68, 70, 75, 78–79, 87, 106, 112
Shakespeare, William 104
Shepperson, George 10
"The Shoemaker and the Sadism of the Senhora" 85
slave narrative 121
slavery 11, 13–14, 17, 22–25, 45, 59–60, 75–76, 79–84, 86, 90, 100–101, 134–135
Smitherman, Geneva 6
Smythe, Mary-Jeanette 8
Sokolov, Raymond 15
"Someone Sweet Angel Chile" 74
Song for Anninho 75, 81–84, 86, 90, 95
Stein, Gertrude 122
"The Storyteller" 50
storytelling 13, 37, 41–42, 50–51, 74, 81, 91, 98–99, 110, 117–118, 121, 127, 128
The Straw Woman 60

"Take Refuge in Madness" 22, 37–38
Tate, Claudia 18–19, 131
Tate, Greg 109–110
Tennant, Emma 75
Their Eyes Were Watching God 50, 160, 161
Thomas, Lorenzo 74
"Those Rock People" 68, 117
"Toward an All-Inclusive Structure" 122
"The Trial of a Man and a Woman" 35
"Tripart" 65
Truth, Sojourner 33
Twain, Mark 63

"Uncle Joe" 127
University of Michigan 4
Updike, John 16, 27, 39

Velho, Domingos Jorge 81
"Version 2" 31, 33, 55
Villanueva, Alma Luz 111
Die Vogelfängerin 27–28, 70–71, 134

Wade-Gayles, Gloria 40
"Waiting for the Miracle" 91
Walker, Alice 9
Walker, Clarence E. 11
Wall, Cheryl A. 125
Ward, Jerry W., Jr. 63
Washington, Mary Helen 57
Washington, Robert E. 93–94
Watkins, Mel 52
We Can't Go Home Again: An Argument About Afrocentrism 11
Weldon, Fay 41, 75
"The Welfare Check" 63
West African music 8
White Rat 13, 47–48, 50, 59–60, 63, 68, 94

Wideman, John 16
Wilcox, Janelle 36
"Wild Figs and Secret Places" 89–88
Wilentz, Gay 50, 125
Williams, Sherley Anne 74, 90
"The Women" 67–68
Women in Chains 135
"Work in Progress" 90

"Xarque" 89
Xarque and Other Poems 89–91, 95

"Your Poems Have Very Little Color in Them" 64–65

www.ingramcontent.com/pod-product-compliance
Ingram Content Group UK Ltd.
Pitfield, Milton Keynes, MK11 3LW, UK
UKHW042001140426
5217IPUK00015B/911